Rebel
with a Conscience

To Bill and Iva Futrell,
 With admiration
and thanks for all you
are doing to save the earth;
 your friend,

 Russ Peterson
 4/27/99

Rebel
with a Conscience

Russell W. Peterson

With a Foreword by Peter Matthiessen

DELAWARE

Newark: University of Delaware Press
London and Toronto: Associated University Presses

Associated University Presses
440 Forsgate Drive
Cranbury, NJ 08512

Associated University Presses
16 Barter Street
London WC1A 2AH, England

Associated University Presses
P.O. Box 338, Port Credit
Mississauga, Ontario
Canada L5G 4L8

This book is printed on recycled paper.
The paper used in this publication meets the requirements
of the American National Standard for Permanence of Paper
for Printed Library Materials Z39.48-1984.

Library of Congress Cataloging-in-Publication Data

Peterson, Russell W. (Russell Wilbur), 1916–
    Rebel with a conscience / Russell W. Peterson : with a foreword by
Peter Matthiessen.
        p.   cm.
    Includes index.
    ISBN 0-87413-681-4 (alk. paper)
    1. Peterson, Russell W. (Russell Wilbur). 1916–   . 2. Governors—
Delaware—Biography. 3. Political activists—Delaware—Biography.
4. Delaware—Politics and government—1951– 5. Environmentalists—
Delaware—Biography. 6. Businessmen—Delaware—Biography.
7. Delaware—Biography. I. Title.
F170.4.P48   1999
975.1'04'092—dc21
[b]   99-10337
                                                                            CIP

PRINTED IN THE UNITED STATES OF AMERICA

To
Lillian and June
and Our Families

Contents

Part VIII. Confronting the Main Causes of Environmental Degradation

IX. A Call to Action

List of Illustrations

Foreword

How peculiar it seems that Russell Peterson, a near-lifelong Republican well-connected to the Establishment, should turn to a near-lifelong critic of Establishment values in this country for the foreword to this inspiring account of an exceptionally valuable life of public service. But in fact, the choice is characteristic of an open, generous, and optimistic mind that cannot be easily contained within restrictive labels such as "Republican" or "Establishment." Russell Peterson is something rarer and more interesting, an independent citizen who holds fervently to the democratic principles at the heart of our Constitution and applies them to that broader vision of man's place on Earth which must deal with "the global predicament" if our beleaguered world is to survive.

Dr. Peterson spent the first twenty-six years of his career in the research, marketing, and sales operations of the DuPont Company in Wilmington, Delaware, which he describes as "a giant operator of pollution-prone chemical, oil, coal, and pharmaceutical industries." In those Cold War years after World War II, most great corporations were unrestrained by environmental considerations, enlightened labor practices, or any real sense of responsibility toward the public that had filled their ample coffers for decades—by much of anything, in fact, which might interfere with rapid profits, regardless of the health and welfare of the commonwealth. Not surprisingly, Dr. Peterson became disillusioned by the company's racial policies—a dismay which he credits with turning his interest and energies toward civic activism and politics. In 1968, he left DuPont and ran for governor as a "Rockefeller Republican;" he was elected in 1969. "Concern yourself with what kind of state we want to pass on to our children and grandchildren," the new governor told his state planning council a few weeks after taking office. Almost immediately he set about eliminating the whipping post and debtors prison and reforming a primitive judicial system to provide those without wealth or influence with the hope of justice. Instead of encouraging the con-

struction of more prisons—a remedy of proven uselessness that
is still popular among conservatives, especially when prisons can
be made a business and run "efficiently" for private profit—he
introduced such enlightened concepts as out-of-prison punishments for "victimless" crimes and work-release programs for prisoners judged harmless to others. He also took personal part in
the resolution of a serious prison revolt at Smyrna in 1971, when
the guards taken hostage were rescued without an organized assault upon the inmates, in complete contrast to the bloody botch
at Attica, New York, which took place only a week later.

In this same period, "Delaware's greatest natural and economic
asset, its glorious coastline," had come under serious threat from
imminent construction of a Shell Oil refinery, and the governor
issued a moratorium on shore development, pending a report
from his new task force on coastal affairs. That report would
culminate in his promotion and support of the Coastal Zone Act,
an inspired piece of environmental legislation designed to protect
the bay from a consortium of huge oil corporations and their
dependent companies, including a bulk shipping and storage outfit called Zapata Norness, led by a Texas congressman named
George Bush. What was envisioned for Delaware Bay was a deep-
water port for gargantuan oil tankers and cargo vessels to comple-
ment the vast oil refinery complex which had already ruined the
Delaware in New Jersey and Pennsylvania, all the way upriver to
Philadelphia. The Zapata plan was to construct (and then double
in size) a brand-new 300-acre island in Delaware Bay as a storage
terminal for coal and iron ore. (Bush's coal mountain would have
risen higher in the sooty sky than any natural promontory in
the entire state, most of which would have been visible from its
black peak.)

By fighting off billions of dollars worth of rapid industrial development despite the new taxes and jobs it would provide, Governor Peterson had startled the industrial establishment, yet he
managed to do this without making many enemies, at first because
the industries assumed that as a former DuPont man, he would
be on their side when the smoke cleared, and later because his
plan had the public's support. Not until January 1971, when they
realized that the governor's bill forbade all new development of
heavy industry in coastal zones of the Atlantic coast and Delaware
Bay about two miles wide and 115 miles long, did the commercial
interests rush forth to do battle. Peterson was charged with "ex-

treme discrimination" by his own State Chamber of Commerce, which voted unanimous opposition, and was branded by various loud voices as a traitor to DuPont, to American industry, to the Republican Party, and to President Nixon, whose support had been enlisted by Congressman Bush through the Commerce and Treasury Departments. Commerce Secretary Maurice Stans actually summoned Peterson to Washington to straighten out his thinking. When he saw that the Governor meant business, this Nixon crony (later indicted by his government) said patriotically, "We think you are being disloyal to our country."

* * *

In 1973, Governor Peterson lost his bid for a second term, a defeat he attributes to a budgetary mix-up. Subsequently he forsook elective office for a third career in a series of high appointive positions on boards and committees in state and federal administrations, nonprofit organizations, and the United Nations, in which he continued the dedicated commitment to environmental matters which began with the farsighted Coastal Zone Act. He was already convinced that the stabilization of human populations was "the single most important thing to protect the global environment and reduce poverty," and as president of the National Audubon Society from 1979–85, he enlisted the Society in that great cause. Far better than most conservationists, Dr. Peterson understood that environmental problems are not separable from social problems—poverty, world populations, the growing and dangerous inequities between rich and poor—all problems to which the Grand Old Party under Reagan-Bush was increasingly indifferent.

In Peterson's view, the business world was finally coming to realize that economic growth "has been a principal cause of environmental degradation, including urban smog, acid rain, oil spills, greenhouse gases like carbon dioxide, and radioactive waste" and that mankind must move more rapidly to "environmentally benign and abundant solar energy and wind energy." That Republican administrations in the 1980s had abandoned federal programs to stimulate alternative energy development he rightly calls "a major disservice to America." Despite his relentlessly positive outlook, Russell Peterson spcaks firmly about these habitual lapses of vision, and also about such ill-advised excesses as the wasteful Star Wars program against the Evil Empire. Peterson quotes a remark made by an aide to Gorbachev when Ronald Reagan's boosters credited Reagan with "winning" the Cold War: "'That's like the rooster taking credit for the dawn,'" said this wry man.

In the positive sense of making things happen, the former governor has remained a consummate "motivator" and "problem solver" (to use terms that he himself prefers), favoring optimism and persuasion over anger and denunciation in winning others to his views—though not, of course, the chronically recalcitrant Republican Party, which has considered him a renegade and pest ever since the days of the Coastal Zone Act. In the twelve long years of Reagan-Bush, Peterson was regularly denied a hearing on overconsumption of resources, environmental degradation, and uncontrolled population growth—the "global predicament," as he refers to it, a bit mildly. However, it was the programs and performance of the new Gingrich Republicans of 1994 and 1996 that finally persuaded the best of their more moderate former governors to give up on the GOP for good: "It was obvious that the party was moving farther and farther to the right. I concluded I could do little in my remaining lifetime to help turn that around. I also knew time was running out on our facing up to the global predicament. . . . On October 8, 1996, I became a Democrat."

*   *   *

"What could be better than working to provide humanity, including one's own descendants, with a sustainable livelihood?" Dr. Peterson asks. "What better vocation is there than striving to save life on Earth? The opportunity for job satisfaction is high, as millions of people have already discovered. And the risk is minor: being belittled by those who do not believe the predicament exists . . . those who champion the status quo."

Peterson grants that "the task is huge and the problems are still growing," yet in his belief, these problems can be solved. It is simply a matter of paying for it, and the money is there, in both public and private accounts—so much money, indeed, that "many multinational corporations have more resources and power than most nation-states." Thus the capital and technology for avoiding world disaster are already at hand; whether or not they will be made accessible in good time will depend on a crucial evolution in our leadership.

Since Russell Peterson for many years was closely associated with large industry, his book is an invaluable resource for all those in the business world who seek to support the fight for environmental and social progress at whatever level. Among the most notable of these in recent years has been Edgar S. Woolard of DuPont, who in 1989, his first year as CEO, "told a meeting of the International Chamber of Commerce in London that industry had a duty and responsibility to be a leader in environmental protection." A few years later, he went further, observing that if society were to achieve its goal of sustainable development, only industry had the required resources to make it happen. Meanwhile he had turned DuPont toward the formerly unthinkable goals of zero pollution and zero waste. According to Peterson, his former employers have been making excellent progress in these and other aims in DuPont plants across the world.

"Because business is responsible for much of the past and present damage to the environment, it must now be the locus for correcting many of the problems," the author says, in what seems to me to the most critical point made by this book. "Business has the necessary capital, technical competence, and management know-how to develop the environmentally benign products and processes that will be required. Enlightened corporate leaders are beginning to see business as a positive force in integrating economic growth with many environmental objectives."

This is encouraging indeed, and the world will be glad of all the real help it can get. But we must never fool ourselves about the source and motivations. As this book teaches all too well, the environment and human welfare cannot be entrusted to industry and its emissaries in public office. As citizens (as opposed to mere consumers), we are responsible for those we put in office, to make sure the public good takes precedence over the interests of the professionally self-serving. It is up to us.

PETER MATTHIESSEN

Acknowledgments

As I contemplate whom to thank for helping with this book, I see a long, long line of family, teachers, professors, authors, employers, colleagues, friends, financial supporters, heroes, public servants, and voters who helped to shape my lifetime of experiences about which I have written. I thank them for their important roles in our joint efforts and for helping to make my life so exciting and rewarding.

I especially express my gratitude to my wife, Lillian, who as my loving partner shared so constructively in my experiences for fifty-seven years. And to June, my wife of three years, who has encouraged and facilitated the writing of this memoir. Among other things, she has provided an isolated cabin high in the Rocky Mountains surrounded by wilderness for me to write and rewrite with pen and pad during three tranquil summers.

Every page of this book started out in my handwritten scrawl, but thanks to Rita McWhorter and her word processor, they were transformed into a neat manuscript. And her good humor persisted through draft after draft.

I am also indebted to my friends and former colleagues, Richard Beamish and Robert and Pat Cahn for their strong encouragement, helpful suggestions and editing of my drafts of some chapters. The title of this book resulted from a suggestion by Raymond Anderson, Professor Emeritus of Journalism, University of Wisconsin. I am particularly grateful to Peter Matthiessen for writing the Foreword.

I am especially appreciative of the work of Jerry Sapienza and Chris Perry in managing the affairs of the governor's office. Special thanks also to Mary Joy Breton who served as my stellar secretary while I was governor, while I worked in Washington, and when I was head of the National Audubon Society. For fourteen years she established extensive files specifically for my use on the day I decided to write my memoirs. Now she too is an author;

21

her book, *Women in the Environmental Movement,* was published in September 1998.

It was a good day when the University of Delaware Press decided to publish *Rebel with a Conscience.* Thanks to Professor Carol Hoffecker who read my manuscript and then convinced the editorial board under Chairman Donald Mell to publish it, and to Karen Druliner who has served well as my copyeditor.

Thanks also to Andrew Jenkins, Kim Adams, and TEAM Marketing Group for their major support in designing and producing the CD-ROM that accompanies this book.

Finally I express my gratitude to Julien Yoseloff, director of Associated University Presses, and his dedicated staff for converting my manuscript into an attractive, finished book.

Introduction

THIS BOOK IS ABOUT THE JOY, CHALLENGE, PERILS, AND JOB SATIS-faction that have resulted from a lifetime occupied with solving problems. Along the way, I have been called a do-gooder, a damn liberal, and a misty-eyed visionary. And I've reveled in it!

After fifty years of leading the charge (and on a few occasions having my horse shot out from under me) in industry, government, and the nonprofit field, I am convinced that the world needs more activists who can motivate others to work together in pursuit of well-defined and worthy goals—of which there are enough to keep us all well occupied for a hundred lifetimes.

My career of problem solving started, I think, in figuring out how to deal with our class bully in the sixth grade. From then on there was no shortage of problems that seemed calculated to test me and build character. One was the necessity of earning my way through college while helping my family survive the Great Depression. Later, I was handed the challenge of leading the Du-Pont team that developed Dacron and, in so doing, helped to revolutionize the fiber industry.

During my twenty-six-year career with DuPont, while launching new business ventures, my disillusionment with the company's racial policies (long since corrected) led me to become a dedicated citizen activist. This in turn led to my election as governor of Delaware, where I learned firsthand how the power of such a position can magically magnify one's ability to work with others to get things done. In four revolutionary years while I was in office, we managed to drag the state, sometimes kicking and screaming, into the twentieth century. We abolished the whipping post and the debtors prison, incredible anachronisms in the modern world. We converted Delaware's archaic commission form of government into a cabinet form and, in the process, insured that southern Delaware, then 30 percent of the state's population, could no longer control the entire state. We markedly increased opportunities for the disadvantaged. We won the hard-fought bat-

23

tle to protect Delaware's greatest natural and economic asset—its glorious coastline—from imminent industrialization by a formidable array of thirteen oil companies and several international shipping companies that seemed, in the beginning, almost impossible to stop. But stop them we did. In so doing, little Delaware showed the world how to preserve a splendid natural legacy. And not only preserve it, but use and enjoy it in a respectful, sustainable, even *profitable* way.

From there the course of my life seemed clear. Defeated in my bid for a second term as governor, partly for trying to accomplish too much in too little time, I moved on to the cutting edge of the burgeoning environmental movement. Seeing the mess we have made on our own planet, I set out to persuade at least a portion of my fellow human beings to live in harmony with nature and to recognize and stay within the carrying capacity of Earth's finite systems.

I was appointed to successive positions as chairman of the President's Council on Environmental Quality, director of the congressional Office of Technology Assessment, president of the National Audubon Society, and head of a number of international organizations dedicated to advancing the welfare of human beings, as well as that of the plants and animals with which we share the Earth.

Along the way I had the good fortune to work with and learn from many leaders including Nelson Rockefeller, Jimmy Carter, Carl Sagan, Al Gore, Margaret Mead, Jacques Cousteau, Mother Teresa, Henry B. duPont, Gerald Ford, and even Richard Nixon.

This book covers many of the conflicts we environmental activists have had with business leaders and conservative politicians. Throughout, it shows how we managed to mobilize others to overcome such obstacles and advance our cause. Thus the book offers a perspective on the history of the modern environmental movement.

Early on, I was fortunate to be able to provide for the basic needs of my wife and children while solving problems in DuPont. In time this freed me financially to apply my penchant for problem solving in the political, social and environmental arenas. Most satisfying has been the sense that my efforts were contributing to the welfare of others, including those not yet born—the "future generations" the environmental community is so fond of evoking.

I have been asked many times to identify the characteristics of training and temperament that helped me to become an effective advocate for difficult causes. As I look back on my experiences, I believe the following traits, either inherited or developed, were important factors.

• **A strong desire to make a significant contribution in my lifetime.** Among role models whose life achievements helped plant this seed were Charles Lindbergh, Lou Gehrig, and Thomas Edison.

• **A determination to do what I thought was right.** As a boy I was deeply concerned about inequities and injustice I saw in my home town. I remember the outrage I felt when my dad showed me a big oak tree where, years earlier, the only black in our home town had been hanged by an angry mob. My dad told me the man was clearly innocent of the rape he had been accused of committing.

• **An ability to motivate people.** While in elementary school, I organized other kids in a variety of activities, such as building from scratch all the facilities needed for a track meet. Someone has commented that I have a "contagious optimism and persuasiveness" that entices others to join and feel committed to a project or cause. Early on I learned that my ability to solve problems was markedly enhanced by going to those people in the best position to help, talking through the problems with them, and gaining their help.

• **Persevering until results are obtained.** Some might call it stubbornness. My first example of this was the sustained effort it took to overcome obstacles to getting a college education. As I look back on my careers, it appears that without stick-to-itiveness I would have accomplished very little.

When I was young, sports were my consuming interest. In high school, making the football and basketball teams was my most exciting and rewarding achievement. This accomplishment meant even more than the fact that I led the honor roll each year. Sports taught me to be competitive, to win well and lose well, to work with others, and to respect discipline.

But it was my high school teachers who opened my eyes to the larger world and inspired me to want a higher education. My chemistry teacher made chemistry and problem solving so exciting that I decided firmly as a junior to become a chemist. After earning a Ph.D. in chemistry and then working for DuPont, I became well versed in the scientific method of solving problems and was able to bring that training to bear later in governmental and environmental pursuits.

The extent to which I have succeeded in reaching my personal goals of defending the underdog, promoting justice, and advocating environmental sanity is for others to judge. But one thing is certain: getting there, and even just *trying* to get there, have given me tremendous satisfaction. The journey has been rewarding, full of learning, camaraderie, and hope. I recommend such a trip to anyone. And I hope that what I have experienced along the way, as set forth in the following pages, will help guide others to an equally satisfying life.

Toward this end I have produced the CD-ROM which accompanies this book. It provides students who are choosing a career, others who wish to change their careers, and career counsellors with easily accessible pathways through my book by describing my experiences and the lessons learned in each of my five careers: environmental activism, politics, science, technology, business, and criminal justice. Each offers great challenges and opportunities.

Rebel
with a Conscience

I
Gateway to the American Dream

1
Early Years

On March 29, 1998, a beautiful, unseasonably warm day, I placed a wreath at the Carl Milles monument at The Rocks on the Christina River in Wilmington, Delaware. Three hundred and sixty years earlier the Swedes had landed there to establish the first permanent colony of Europeans in the Delaware Valley. Because I was the first governor of Delaware of Swedish descent since colonial days, I had been selected to participate in the celebration of this anniversary. As the American and Swedish flags whipped in the breeze and a fife and drum corps played, the 1638 landing was reenacted. A contingent of Swedes disembarked from their landing craft and were greeted by a group of friendly Leni Lenapi Indians.

While I sat on the reviewing stand observing the ceremony, I could not keep my mind from wandering back to the time only 109 years ago when my grandparents and their seven children, including eleven-year-old John Anton Peterson, landed in New York City from Sweden. To the left of the reviewing stand was a log cabin reminiscent of the housing introduced into America by the early Swedes, bringing to mind a stone that lies on my desk at home. I collected it in 1971 from the foundation of the one-room log cabin in Verhult Parish, Småland, Sweden, where my grandparents and their children lived before emigrating to America. What a different world I now lived in!

My grandparents settled in Nebraska where they were hired to work on a farm. Eventually John Anton left his family and moved to Minnesota where he took a job driving horse-drawn grain wagons into Wisconsin. On one trip he met my mother, Emma Anthony, then seventeen years old. They were married the following year (1895) in my mother's hometown, Camp Douglas, Wisconsin, population 100. There they had four sons before moving to Portage, Wisconsin, population 5,000, where my father worked

31

for a time as a bartender. Four more sons were born in Portage; I was the seventh of their eight sons.

Neither of my parents had much formal education. My dad's education had ended with the fifth grade in Sweden. He worked very hard all his life to support our big family. While I was growing up, he was an assistant baker, working from 6 P.M. to 6 A.M. six days a week, coming home with flour on his clothes, and sleeping most of the day. He weighed about 180 pounds and was 5 feet 10 inches tall. He was almost bald, but he sported a well-trimmed mustache. My mother, who only went to fourth grade, was a warm, caring person who readily smiled, loved everyone and was highly protective of her sons. She, too, worked hard, running a home business on the side, baking and selling cakes, which we boys delivered around town. We were proud of the fact she made the best angel food cakes in Portage.

We never owned a home or a car. My parents rented a house from Hank Niemeyer, a bachelor who lived upstairs. He was the mayor of Portage. He liked to drill the Peterson boys in military arms in his living room. On Sunday mornings, his apartment was a popular place for reading the funnies.

Our quarters downstairs were quite sparse—two of us to a bed. On Saturdays we took our weekly bath in a tub placed on the kitchen floor. Donald, Gordon, and I—the three youngest sons—used the same bath water.

Our dad was a strict disciplinarian. When he walked to work in the evening and passed a neighborhood playground which we frequented, he would whistle and point in the direction from which he had come. At that we would beeline home. On occasion he disciplined one of us by taking the offender to the basement and whipping his rear end with a razor strop, a thick leather band about three inches wide and eighteen inches long that Dad used to put a fine edge on his straight razor.

He stropped me only once, when I was about ten. A neighbor, Bill Brown, had received a set of boxing gloves for his birthday, and I convinced him that we should form a boxing club. We built a pretty good boxing ring in Bill's yard and signed up about eight others. Then we decided to stage a public boxing match between the two of us. We put signs on telephone poles to advertise the match and charged an admission price of one cent. Dad saw one of those signs and ordered me not to box. "I don't want my kids to be fighters," he said. But how could I back out? I boxed. The

Russ Peterson's mother and father, Emma and Anton. 1933, Portage, Wisconsin. Courtesy of the author.

12-year-old referee called it a draw, though I thought Bill had won. (He went on to become a champion boxer in high school.) Our gate receipts were not all we had hoped—only three kids paid admission.

The next day, when my dad asked me if I had boxed, I replied, "Yes." He took me to the basement. Knowing beforehand that I was certain to be punished, I consulted with my older brother, Donald, who had been whipped many times. He told me to yell as loud as I could, because then Dad would not hit very hard. Instead, I chose to remain silent. The stropping didn't hurt my backside very much, but it did diminish my respect for my dad. I thought he had been unfair in ordering me not to box. Certainly I had disobeyed him. In retrospect, I think this incident caused me to make a fateful (if not entirely conscious) decision that in the future, when I was committed to something I believed in, I would go through with it and take the consequences.

Throughout my childhood, starring in the Big Leagues was my only ambition. I wanted to hit home runs for the Yankees like Lou Gehrig, play fullback for the University of Wisconsin like my hometown hero Harold Rebholz, and pole-vault for the U.S. Olympic team. Sports were the life blood of all the Peterson boys. We knew the career records of most of the Big Leaguers and followed their batting averages daily. From elementary school age on, we organized neighborhood baseball and basketball teams and competed with others in our small community.

My brothers and I knew little else about the world beyond Portage. We had only one book in our house, a Bible used for recording births, weddings, and deaths. I don't recall ever discussing literature or the arts or politics at home. There was, however, some reluctant exposure to music when my mother signed me up for piano lessons. Since we had no piano, the teacher gave me a cardboard keyboard to practice on. Have you ever tried to get music out of a piece of cardboard? After my third lesson, when the teacher told me we would be having a recital in a few weeks, I quit. My mother was quite disappointed.

In sixth grade I faced a special challenge. Big Bob Clement made life difficult for his classmates. He had failed to pass twice and thus was two years older than the rest of us, and he was big for his age. He seemed to enjoy beating up smaller kids. I decided to do something about that and convinced four pals to help. One day we five deliberately walked a few yards ahead of Big Bob on our way home from school. As we expected, he grabbed one of our group and threw him to the ground. As planned, I tore in and tackled the bully around his ankles while the others piled on and beat him unmercifully. Then we got up and walked away slowly, although we were scared. He did not follow. When I saw him the next morning, he gave me a friendly smile. As far as I know, he never beat up smaller kids again.

I spent the following summer getting the boys in my neighborhood involved with track-and-field events. I marked off the 100-yard dash, the 220 and 440 on the sidewalk around our block. A shed a neighbor was tearing down provided the lumber for building hurdles and for the uprights for our high jumping and pole vaulting stations. I even talked a carpet-store manager into giving us a bamboo pole to use as a vaulting pole, and the high school coach gave us an old battered discus and a javelin.

Making the shot put was a special challenge. Mr. Samuels, the junkyard owner, helped me out. I had been working with him for some time, collecting junk along the alleys around town and selling it to him, my earliest experience in recycling. Old storage batteries were particularly valuable. Not yet a chemist or an environmentalist, I dumped the battery acid on the ground, then broke up the batteries and sold the lead to him.

Now I asked Mr. Samuels to show me how I could convert ten pounds of that lead into a shot put. He could do anything. He spent a long time actually making the shot put for me. He melted the lead in an old metal ladle over an open fire, then poured it into a spherical container he had buried in some sand. The shot put wasn't perfectly spherical, but it weighed ten pounds and served the purpose.

I participated in all of our track-and-field events but was not good in any of them. On the other hand, my friend Bill Malisch excelled in all. When he later became captain of the University of Wisconsin track team, I claimed credit for having trained him well.

During my elementary school years I also held a number of jobs. For several years I delivered two newspapers after school. I did three routes on Sunday, which I found was a legitimate way to avoid Sunday School. One year I worked in my oldest brother Clarence's restaurant, peeling raw potatoes before school and boiled potatoes after school. He paid me fifty cents a week. I gave half to my mother and took my younger brother Gordon to a

Russ Peterson (back center), and his seven brothers. January 1937. Peterson Brothers: (back row from left) Donald, Harold, Russell, Gordon, Edwin, (front) Earl, Glen, Clarence. Courtesy of the author.

Saturday matinée with the remainder. Our favorite movies included *The Iron Horse* and serial cowboy movies starring Tom Mix and Hoot Gibson.

Only one of my six older brothers went to high school, and he for only two years, but my younger brother and I graduated from high school. For me, attending high school was a wonderful experience. Most important was that I could now participate in organized sports. Making the basketball and football teams in my last two years was by far my most satisfying accomplishment, even more than heading the honor roll. I guess that was because studies came easily, while making the first team—particularly in football—was a real challenge.

In those days, going to the county fair was a big event. Our schools even closed for one day so everyone could attend the fair. But, with our first game of the season only one week off, the high school football coach, Harold Rebholz, a former Big Ten star fullback, ordered our team out for practice that morning. Unhappy with our performance, he told us to come back again in the afternoon.

Instead, Bill Malisch, the 225-pound star end of our team, and I, a 129-pound second string tackle, decided to skip the afternoon practice and go to the fair. While sitting in the grandstand watching a baseball game, we were embarrassed when Rebholz, dressed in his coaching togs, appeared at the foot of the grandstand and loudly ordered us to come down from our seats.

"Get back to the practice field now or you are off the team," he threatened.

"Give us a ride," I suggested.

"No," he said. "Get back the way you got down here." And then he left.

Bill and I considered our options and then went back to watching the baseball game.

The next morning the Portage High School Superintendent, Mr. Henkel, called us to his office. He knew all about the previous day's events, but he still asked us to go out that afternoon for practice.

"Coach Rebholz will accept you," he said.

Bill Malisch stayed away for one day, but I went out.

The coach called us all together and said, "We're going to scrimmage. I want the first team to run all its plays over Peterson."

Now this was quite a surprise. Why did he do this, I wondered. Did he consider it a punishment? But there was not much time to mull it over.

Knowing that the ball carrier would be coming directly at my position, I decided to dive toward the feet of the charging opposition so they could not take me out of position. Then I was able to squirm through a tangle of legs and tackle or trip up the ball carrier who was coming right at me. I did this repeatedly. The coach put me on the first team that afternoon, and I stayed there for the whole season.

That was quite a reward for someone whose whole life revolved around sports. But the next year I received an even greater reward from Coach Rebholz. He invited me back from the University of Wisconsin to attend the usual pep rally in the high school auditorium before the homecoming game. I was seated in the front row with 500 students and teachers behind me. The football team, the band, the cheerleaders and Coach Rebholz were on the stage, whooping it up.

Then the coach called me up on the stage and asked the crowd, "How many feet of guts does the average person have?"

Someone cried out, "Twenty-nine."

Coach Rebholz put his arm around me and proclaimed loudly, "Yes, but this guy has twice as much."

Imagine that. In front of many of my former teammates, schoolmates, teachers and, although I didn't know it then, my wife-to-be, Lillian Turner, I had fifty-eight feet of guts. Clearly, going to the county fair against the coach's directions had been a risk worth taking.

But the most important thing that happened to me in high school was being inspired by my teachers to want to go to college. Charles Warren had the greatest impact. He made chemistry so exciting that I decided as a junior to become a chemist. Imagine learning about all the elements that make up the world and that chemists have the potential to combine these elements in unique ways to make great discoveries that will serve mankind. I remember best Mr. Warren's stories about the great chemists, Antoine Lavoisier, who discovered oxygen and was guillotined for his political beliefs, and Marie Curie, who discovered radium and later died from its radiation. Helen Rhyme, my American history and English teacher, not only made American heroes come to life, she appointed me business manager of our high school annual and taught me how to write a check.

In June 1934, as president of my class, I gave my first speech, calling on my classmates at our senior dinner to "never despair." This was the time of America's Great Depression. It was also the year after President Franklin D. Roosevelt, in his First Inaugural Address, declared, "the only thing we have to fear is fear itself." Whether or not his words influenced my speech, I do not recall. I was, however, well aware of the fear of my classmates. Few were going on to college. Most were about to start looking for jobs in a crippled economy with a national unemployment rate of 25 percent. I tried to encourage them to think positively.

Only one classmate congratulated me on my speech—a big disappointment. Several teachers did, however, including Helen Rhyme and Charles Warren.

And so we graduated in the midst of the Great Depression.

2

Rocky Path to a Career

THAT SAME YEAR MY FATHER DEVELOPED RECTAL CANCER AND could work only part-time. In spite of important help from one of my older brothers, Harold, who was a foreman in a hosiery factory, my proud family had to accept some relief from the county. My parents and my brother Earl tried to talk me out of going to college. I should stay home and help, they said.

But I was determined to go. With a college education I knew I could better help my family later, so I set out to make the money I would need for college.

It was tough going. My brother Edwin, who drove a truck delivering groceries to homes throughout Portage, hired me to help him on Saturdays. He gave me one of the $18 he earned per week. My brother Glen, who ran a small restaurant, hired me as a part-time short-order chef. I also fell back to my earlier profession of collecting junk and selling it to Mr. Samuels.

I visited two banks and the Wisconsin Power and Light company to try to convince them to hire me to deliver their monthly statements, pointing out that I could do it for less than the cost of mailing them. No sale. They apparently thought the post office was more reliable.

My biggest project, with the help of my younger brother Gordon and a retired relative, Will Peer, was to build a stand at the county fair to sell hamburgers, hot dogs, ice cream, and soft drinks. After paying the bills, I netted $25, a real bonanza at that time.

That summer I gave my mother over half my income, ending up with $37 to begin college. In September 1934, I hitchhiked to Madison and shared a small room in a rooming house with my friend from Portage, Doug Heberlein. We signed up in the chemistry course at the University of Wisconsin, paying a $12 fee, the only charge for in-state students. We bought secondhand books and shared them.

During the next two weeks, between classes, I visited every restaurant and retail store on the two main streets, over 100 establishments, trying in vain to find a job. Completely broke and hungry, I went to see Villiers Meloche, the chemistry professor assigned as my adviser. I told him I would have to leave the university. Fortunately his girl friend was head of the university's employment office. Before I left Professor Meloche's office, I had two jobs: as a bus boy in a downtown restaurant and as a laboratory dishwasher in the chemistry building. There I gained a special bonus. I met Al Pavlic who became my close friend and colleague for the next sixty-four years. Thus I became established as a university student. My persistence had paid off.

My student years were enjoyable indeed, though there was little time for outside activities, since I always worked two or more jobs.

In January 1937, my father died. I had visited him frequently when he was a welfare patient at the University of Wisconsin hospital, where he was used as a human guinea pig in painful, experimental treatments for his cancer. I still remember how his whole body shook in fear as they wheeled him off for his daily ordeals. It was then that I first seriously considered becoming a medical doctor who would conduct cancer research. I was convinced then, as I still am sixty years later, that chemistry would play a key role in eliminating this dreadful disease.

After Dad died, I persuaded my mother to move to Madison to run a rooming and boarding home. Our family friend, Will Peer, agreed to help. We rented a large house just off the campus, and I sold some of my friends on living with us. This turned out to be a blessing for Mother. She enjoyed having young people around to take care of. They seemed to enjoy her, too—especially her cooking. And Mother now had better financial security than during most of her earlier years. After several years she and Will Peer married and lived happily and comfortably together with some financial help from me until Mother died at age 80.

At the beginning of my junior year, a high-school acquaintance from home, Lillian Turner, entered the university as a freshman. Her first night there, I ran into her on the campus. We started dating, going Dutch, of course. And soon we fell madly in love. We eloped that June, much to her parents' consternation. She was eighteen and I was twenty. At first we lived in my mother's house, but shortly we rented our own small apartment for $25 per month.

One day before we were married, Lillian saw me as I was walking to the chemistry building. She waved and with a big smile called out, "Russ, Russ, today's *Daily Cardinal* reports that you have been elected to Phi Beta Kappa. Congratulations." When I asked what it was, she explained it was an honor society.

I didn't think much of it until I reached the chemistry building, where my major professor, James Walton, invited me into his office with two other professors. They shook my hand and patted me on the back, and then explained what it all meant. At that time, the University of Wisconsin elected sixty top students each year to Phi Beta Kappa—fifty seniors and ten juniors. I was one of the juniors chosen in 1937.

Shortly thereafter a letter arrived inviting me to a jacket-and-tie awards dinner. The letter also said I must pay $12 for a gold Phi Beta Kappa key. I declined the invitation; I had neither the $12 nor a jacket. However, my brother Harold had married a university graduate, Agnes More, who knew about Phi Beta Kappa. They gave me the $12 and bought me a suit. I went to the dinner in style and got my key, which dangled pretentiously from my watch chain for the next few years. Occasionally I still take it out of my bureau drawer and remember what it meant to me.

Nine months after Lillian and I were married, our son Glen, our future artist, was born. The delivery went smoothly enough— our new baby was healthy and, of course, beautiful—but the euphoria was short-lived. Lillian became stricken in the hospital with so-called childbed fever, a streptococcus infection. On two occasions her doctors told me she would not live through the night, but she did. In despair, we took her to her parents' farm near Portage to die. There our hometown doctor, James MacGregor, came to the rescue. Dr. MacGregor located an abscess behind her uterus, lanced it on three occasions, and saved Lillian's life. I thought that if I could do something like that just once in my lifetime, my life could be counted a success. To this day, I still have a picture of Dr. MacGregor on a shelf at home.

Lillian's living was a blessing in so many ways. Not only was she a loving wife and dedicated mother, but she opened my eyes and mind to the world beyond sports and science. She had majored in the Romance languages and read extensively. She taught me

Lillian and Russ Peterson on Lillian's 75th birthday with their four children, Peter, Glen, Kristin, and Elin. November, 1993. Courtesy of the author.

to enjoy classical music, ballet, and the visual arts, and she was responsible for polishing the homespun traits I brought to our marriage. Throughout my several careers she was always beside me, counselling and helping me at every turn. She deserves at least half of the credit for any successes I have had. After fifty-seven years together, our marriage and partnership ended with her death in 1994. Oh, how I loved her.

We raised four wonderful children—Glen and Peter, Kristin and Elin—all of whom, with their spouses, produced families of which we became very proud.

Glen started out to become a chemist, but after two summers living and studying with the Wyeth family in Maine, he decided to become an artist and art teacher.

Peter, a born naturalist, sparked my interest in birding when he was still a young boy. He went on to become a student of the world's religions, practicing today with admirable intensity his vision of Christianity.

Kristin was imbued early on with a love of nature. After venturing from her parents' Unitarianism to become a devout Roman Catholic, she now manages a nature center in Connecticut for disciples of her church.

Elin, who lived at home while I was governor, became deeply interested in public affairs. After serving as a vice president for Future Options on Wall Street, she obtained a law degree from New York University and now plans to become an environmental lawyer. She and Glen are still Unitarians.

When I received my Bachelor of Science degree, it was the conventional wisdom in my field that a chemist couldn't get very far without a Ph.D. I knew I needed to go to graduate school. But how could I do that? I had a wife and baby and owed two hospitals and three doctors a total of $5,000.

I told our five creditors I wanted to go to graduate school and asked if they would permit me to forego payments for four years. They all agreed. Each wrote on my note of indebtedness, "Zero percent interest."

I received a four-year assistantship teaching freshman chemistry and assisting Professor James H. Walton in his lectures to 500 students. During those lectures we carried out many large-scale and spectacular experiments.

Probably our most spectacular experiment, run at the end of a lecture, was the Thermit demonstration. Thermit, a mixture of aluminum powder and iron oxide, could be used as an incendiary bomb or as a source of molten iron to weld railway rails together. I placed some Thermit in a large crucible suspended several feet over the lecture desk. When the Thermit was triggered, a stream of white-hot molten iron was produced, falling through the air amidst a tremendous shower of sparks into a bed of sand, where it welded two iron bars together. This brought the students out of their seats, cheering the professor.

Professor Walton had received his Ph.D. from the strict and highly disciplined University of Heidelberg in Germany. He demanded perfection. Every experiment had to work. "Double check everything," he told me. "Drop a weight every morning to be sure gravity is still working."

Professor Walton also supervised my four-year research project, "The Inhibition of the Air Oxidation of Ascorbic Acid." He left me pretty much alone, but always came through with the chemicals and equipment I needed. During the nine months after Glen's birth, while Lillian remained ill, he loaned us money and excused me from teaching some classes so I could visit her in Portage.

My assistantship paid $62 per month. I supplemented this with a variety of jobs, including running lab tests for the state criminologist and tutoring many students.

My education was by no means confined to the university. One summer job stands out as especially educational for me in dealing with man's inhumanity to man and woman. I worked for the Wisconsin Highway Department, analyzing asphalts and tars. My boss was Mr. Zapata, who claimed to be a nephew of the famous Mexican bandit chieftain, Emiliano Zapata. He was a despot. My first day on the job he called me into his office to show me the enlarged knuckles on each hand, pointing out that they had been broken one at a time by Mexican rebels who had captured him many years earlier.

"And I didn't even wince," he said. I well remember his saying that he was the boss and that he was not afraid of anyone.

What a strange introduction. Later I learned that each new employee had the same experience.

A few weeks later, when I delivered some test results to his office, I heard him yelling at his secretary and saw him throw his inkwell at her, hitting her shoulder and splattering ink all over her and the floor. She started to leave, crying and holding her shoulder.

He shouted, "Get back here and clean up this mess"—which she did.

This, the latest of many outrageous acts triggered a meeting of about twenty of the full-time lab employees at one of their homes. I was invited to attend. They decided that someone had to visit the commissioner of highways, Zapata's boss, to ask him to get rid of Zapata. They asked me to do it. Since the full-time employees had much more to lose than I, a summer employee, I agreed.

With some trepidation I visited the commissioner in his office in Wisconsin's impressive state capitol, a miniature of our U.S. capitol. He said he was aware of Zapata's behavior but couldn't fire him. He agreed to talk to Zapata, however.

Three days later the lab supervisor gave me sixty asphalt samples to analyze, telling me confidentially that they were all from the same container. He also confided that Mr. Zapata was raving about my going to the commissioner and wanted to "get something on me."

I carried out the tests with the greatest care. Although the results from the sixty samples were quite close, there were definite differences from sample to sample, as one acquainted with such testing would expect from nonconformity in the test material and from variations in the precision of the test.

When Zapata received the results, he came tearing into the lab, accused me of cheating, and ordered me into his office. He told me all sixty samples were from the same batch, so my results should be identical. When he calmed down, I replied that I knew the samples were the same before I tested them, so now he had a good measure of the standard deviation one could expect from this test. I also told him I didn't like his trying to trap me and suggested he and I go to the commissioner together and tell him about it. He yelled, "Get the hell out of here!" Which I did.

During my remaining few weeks on the job, I never saw Mr. Zapata. My friends there thanked me for what I had done and, from time-to-time over the next year or so, they reported that Mr. Zapata had calmed down, and was no longer the tyrant he had been before.

It had been a risk worth taking.

During graduate school, I again considered pursuing a medical degree after I finished my Ph.D. in chemistry so I could become a research professor working on the causes of cancer. (I certainly had no interest in industrial research at that time.)

Then, in 1941, I received an unsolicited letter from E. I. duPont de Nemours, offering me a summer job at the Experimental Station in Wilmington, Delaware. This, graduate students agreed, was the prime location in the country for chemists who wanted to work in industry. The job would pay three times what I could make teaching that summer. Furthermore, I could see the East. Although Lillian, as a young daughter of a naval officer, had lived in several U.S. port cities, I had never been beyond Chicago. So Lillian, three-year-old Glen, and I packed up and boarded a train for Wilmington.

The Experimental Station was truly a great place to work. Its facilities far surpassed those at the University of Wisconsin. It was brimming with outstanding scientists working on exciting and rewarding projects, and I accomplished more that summer than

I had accomplished in three years of graduate school. That the work contributed to our national defense made it especially rewarding.

The Japanese had cut off our supply of silk which was essential for parachute shroud lines. No other known material could withstand the impact on the shroud lines when the parachute canopy opened suddenly, stopping the free fall of the parachutist. My job was to find out if nylon could replace silk. (Nylon had been successfully commercialized eighteen months earlier for use in women's full-fashioned hosiery in place of silk.)

Our first nylon shroud lines were far from adequate, with impact strengths only one-third that of silk. By changing the way the nylon filaments were spun and processed and the way the shroud lines were assembled, we gradually improved the test results until nylon was twice as good as silk. For the remainder of World War II, all the shroud lines manufactured for the Allied forces were made from nylon.

This was a very satisfying experience. It clearly influenced my subsequent decision to accept DuPont's offer to return to the Experimental Station nine months later, after receiving my Ph.D.

Despite the extremely hot, third-floor apartment in which we lived that summer, Lillian, too, enjoyed Wilmington. My colleagues and their spouses welcomed and entertained us.

After studying nearly every evening in the air-conditioned comfort of the Wilmington Public Library, I was ready for my doctoral exams when we returned to Madison in September.

That fall Dr. Preston Hoff, head of DuPont's Nylon Research Division, called me to offer me a job at the Experimental Station when I completed my Ph.D. He followed that with several letters over the winter, encouraging me to accept. I was still enamored with the idea of becoming a research professor and conducting cancer research. But after much discussion and soul-searching, Lillian and I decided that it was better, at least for the near term, to accept the DuPont offer. Among other things, we could pay off our $5,000 indebtedness sooner.

In June 1942, I received my Ph.D. in chemistry. A few days after that our second son, Peter, was born. On June 22, I reported to work for E. I. duPont de Nemours as a research chemist. It now seemed that Lillian and I had our passport to the American dream.

Graduation Day, June 1942, with four-year-old son Glen. Courtesy of the author.

II
Rewarding Years in Research and Development

3

Entering DuPont's Research World

A MONTH AFTER I MOVED TO DELAWARE, LILLIAN ARRIVED AT WIL-
mington's Baltimore & Ohio railroad station with Glen and Peter.
What an exciting and memorable day! We moved into a two-room
furnished apartment in downtown Wilmington with all our pos-
sessions—a crib, an end table, and a trunk filled with our clothes.
Four weeks later we moved to a furnished house in the small,
single-tax community of Arden. It had an attractive lawn and
room for a Victory garden. Shortly, Lillian and I were deeply
involved in the affairs of this lively, stimulating town.

From Arden I rode the bus to Wilmington, transferred to a
Wilmington bus, and walked the last-half mile to my job in the
Carothers Research Laboratory at DuPont's Experimental Sta-
tion. It would be five years before we owned a car.

Still we were riding high. We were all in good health, Lillian
and I were deeply in love, and I had a great job. My pay was $250
per month, up from the $62 per month I had been receiving as
a teaching assistant. Now I could begin to pay off my debts and
send my mother $25 per month.

Carothers Research Laboratory was named after Wallace H.
Carothers, the brilliant research chemist who discovered nylon.
Dr. Carothers had been enticed away from Harvard University in
1928 by Dr. Charles Stine, who headed DuPont's Central Research. Stine had convinced DuPont's Executive Committee to
fund a research unit that would focus on fundamental research,
the search for new knowledge. This appealed to Carothers. He
was provided with a team of six highly talented Ph.D. chemists
and all the resources they needed. In spite of the Great Depression that followed in the early 1930s, and which led other companies to retrench, The DuPont Company maintained its support
for fundamental research.

Carothers was interested in learning how to get small molecules

51

to join together end-to-end in long chains to produce linear condensation polymers. One day one of his assistants, Dr. Julian Hill, later a birdwatching friend of mine, pulled a stirring rod from a molten experimental polymer in a test tube and out came a long thread. A precursor to nylon was born.

Carothers was obsessed with his research, even to the point of sleeping in his laboratory. He also suffered from depression, and at the young age of 41 in 1937, he committed suicide by taking sodium cyanide in a Philadelphia hotel room. He never knew about the huge success of his inventions. Nylon became the single biggest moneymaker in the long history of The DuPont Company. Its management's trust in basic research and willingness to invest in the future during bleak financial times paid off handsomely.

I went to work at Carothers Lab seven months after the Japanese attacked Pearl Harbor and the United States had officially declared war. My assignment, working with others, primarily engineers, was to help develop nylon tire cord for heavy bomber tires. Existing tire yarn could not survive the landing impact of such planes. Our job was to develop a yarn that had the necessary impact strength, test it in experimental tires made by the tire companies, and then develop a process for its large-scale manufacture. This was a ten- to sixteen-hours per day, six days a week job. We got it done in time to supply the fleets of B-17 and B-24 bombers the United States used against the German, Italian, and Japanese war efforts.

In the midst of this, my draft board ordered me to report to Philadelphia for a medical exam. Lillian, the daughter of a naval officer, and I decided that I should not ask for a deferment. I passed the exam and was told to report the next week for duty in the army. Lillian was prepared to make the most of it with our two young boys.

Before I could report, the Quartermaster Corps asked my draft board to defer me for scientific work on military projects. Many DuPont scientists already had left the Experimental Station to work on the then mysterious Manhattan Project, to build the Hanford Works for producing plutonium for atomic bombs. There were other critical war assignments for those of us who remained. To this day I feel guilty that I never fought in World War II, in spite of my conviction that I probably did more for our war effort than if I had been drafted.

After the war (1946) I was promoted to research supervisor

and put in charge of an eight-person team, primarily engineers, to develop a process for continuously polymerizing nylon. It was then made in large batches, and it took over one hour to extrude a ribbon of the finished molten polymer from the vessel in which it was produced.

The ribbon was then water cooled and subsequently cut into chips that were blended. Since the nylon, while molten, underwent some side reactions, the end of a batch had a slightly different chemical composition than the first of the batch. When spun into filaments, woven into a fabric and dyed, the difference showed up as streaks. We needed to learn how to polymerize continuously, so that each increment of nylon produced had the same thermal history.

Working first in glass equipment at the lab bench, then in semi-works equipment, and finally in the large pilot plant, we demonstrated how to do this. Subsequently, all new nylon plants were so equipped and all existing plants were so converted.

4

Taking Dacron® Polyester
Fiber from Lab Bench
to Commercial Success

IN 1949, I RECEIVED A LETTER WHICH STATED, "YOU ARE HEREBY promoted to Research Manager in charge of the research and development on Fiber V." DuPont later named it Dacron® polyester fiber.

Wallace Carothers had given a speech in the 1930s in which he stated that the condensation polymer, polyethylene terephthalate, could not be made, since its building blocks would not fit together structurally. In the 1940s two chemists, J. R. Whinfield and J. T. Dickson, at the Calico Printers Association in Great Britain, proved Carothers wrong. They received a patent for polyethylene terephthalate and the fiber made therefrom.

DuPont's Pioneering Research Division in Buffalo, New York, confirmed the findings of Whinfield and Dickson, melt-spun small samples of polymer into filaments which they named "Fiber V," and found the fiber had very attractive properties. DuPont subsequently obtained a license from the British inventors to produce it.

The development was then transferred to Carothers Research Laboratory where I became manager. We received from Pioneering Research a one-pound sample of polyethylene terephthalate in the spherical glass flask in which it had been made. Dr. Ed Kane, later to become president of DuPont, spun it into yarn. Although this was the largest sample yet made, it was still a long way from the huge enterprise DuPont was to build. We quickly put dozens of chemists and engineers to work to determine if this new fiber merited commercialization.

We designed and built a semiworks of stainless steel equipment

54

so we could produce larger quantities of yarn, weave it into fabrics, evaluate its dying and tactile qualities and eventually provide the DuPont Sales Division with samples for test marketing. Analyses of the potential of this new fiber made it look more and more like a winner—a natural for what we later called wash-and-wear clothing. We demonstrated that it had great resistance to wrinkling, was excellent for sailcloth, and was also good for industrial products like ropes and tire cord. At this point, DuPont's top management decided to go ahead with the commercialization of Dacron.

I became chairman of the design committee for the 25-million-pound per year commercial plant and had the responsibility for specifying and approving every detail of the plant to be designed and constructed by DuPont's Engineering Department, a world-class organization. At the same time I was transferred to the Manufacturing Division and made technical superintendent of the yet-to-be built Dacron plant.

This was a traumatic experience. Nearly everyone, if not everyone, in Research had a low opinion of Manufacturing. After all, Research had been the source of all DuPont's successes. My immediate supervisor tried hard to talk me out of accepting the transfer. I thought I was being demoted. Years later I learned I had actually been promoted.

When I got to Manufacturing, I quickly learned its people were smart and competent too. Ironically, they did not think much of Research or Sales. Four years later when I was transferred to Sales, I found they, too, were pretty bright, and I joined them in criticizing inappropriate statements coming out of Research and Manufacturing. It was at this time I started my evolution from chemist to generalist. I became increasingly aware of our interdependence and our propensity for criticizing others of whom we know very little and are ill-equipped to judge.

My transfer to Manufacturing had another traumatic aspect. We had just moved into our dream house, a stone and glass house surrounded by huge trees at the top of a steep hill, looking down on a boulder-strewn creek whose waters raged after even a mild rain. This was Lillian's house. After four years of studying architecture on her own, she had produced the detailed drawings and specifications from which the builder constructed the house. Imagine her disappointment when, after only a few months, we had to abandon this gem and move to Seaford, Delaware. There we in the Dacron development group were building and evaluating a pilot plant and assembling and training the team for starting up the commercial plant near Kinston, North Carolina.

I travelled much during this period, from Seaford to our research labs and engineering offices in Wilmington, to the Kinston, North Carolina, plant site, and to university campuses where I was recruiting for the Kinston team. One of my early decisions was to move the completely staked-out plant site about 50 feet to save a red oak, *Quercus rubra*. It was a beautiful tree. For years it graced the front of our plant until a hurricane destroyed it.

Just before the Kinston plant start-up, I was promoted to assistant plant manager in charge of all technical, manufacturing, and engineering operations, reporting directly to Wilmington management on the start-up. This was an exciting, rewarding time. Under the fine leadership of our plant manager, Bill Gladding, we had put together an excellent, experienced management and technical team and hired hundreds of diligent and conscientious operators from the neighboring, primarily agricultural communities. We worked hard to make everyone an important member of our team. The foremen were taught that their primary responsibility was to present the interests of their operators to management. Each of us regularly wore a name tag to facilitate getting to know each other; the resulting morale was terrific. We worked long hours, encountering and overcoming a myriad of start-up problems, while still getting our whole plant in full operation ahead of schedule.

I remember well one environmental, public-relations problem we encountered. During the first few days of start-up we produced an abundance of waste that we piled on an adjoining field and burned. A huge cloud of black smoke rose and drifted across neighboring farmers' tobacco fields. The next day several irate farmers came to my office, threw tobacco leaves covered with black soot on my desk, and asked what I was going to do about it. I apologized, told them we had improperly burned our waste, would not do that again, and would pay them for any losses they might have incurred. I was not sure I had the authority to make that commitment, but they smiled, shook hands and left.

A subsequent rain washed off the soot and the farmers' yields were unusually high that year, as were the prices they received at the tobacco auctions. I jokingly suggested to the farmers that they should pay DuPont a bonus for their good harvests.

Dacron went on to become one of DuPont's most profitable ventures, earning many hundreds of millions of dollars. It continues to prosper today, 45 years later. In fact, the production of polyethylene terephthalate, the polymer that Wallace Carothers said could not be made, reached 35 billion pounds worldwide in 1995, according to the May 13, 1996, issue of *Chemical and Engineering News*. Of this, 71 percent was used for fibers. In that year, polyester fibers constituted 60 percent of all synthetic fibers produced globally.

In later years when Lillian and I drove to Florida, we occasionally visited our old neighborhood in Greenville, North Carolina, a bittersweet experience. The first thing we always did was to put a single rose on the grave of our two-day old son who died on Christmas Day, 1952.

Then we drove to the parking lot at the Kinston plant. I did not bother going in, because my old colleagues were no longer there. Some had died; some had moved on to top-level jobs in DuPont. (Quite a few now live in the Wilmington, Delaware, area and are still cherished friends.) But I did reminisce about my years with the Dacron venture and said out loud to Lillian, "That's my plant!" Such a statement may seem full of pride. But building that plant was glorious experience.

Today when I reflect on my years at the Kinston plant, I marvel at how a large team of over 2,000 people recruited from many walks of life and numerous geographic areas worked together so harmoniously and effectively to build a major new industrial enterprise. Our top management put up the tens of millions of dollars required and cheered us on. At the other end of our organizational structure, the men and women recruited from the cotton and tobacco fields of eastern North Carolina to operate our manufacturing equipment did a superb job. I do not recall any bickering among team members. We were all working on a clearly defined, common objective, and our efforts were adequately financed. No one was trying to tear us down or question our motivation, as happens so often in the political arena, making it difficult solve community problems.

In 1954 I received a three-step promotion back to Wilmington as a director of research. At the time, I was told by Assistant General Manager Bill Wood of the Textile Fibers Department, that I would be getting a large bonus for my work on Dacron. It never materialized. Later he reported that the DuPont Bonus Committee stated that since I would be moving up to the top echelon of the company, I needed no bonus. I had no complaint. My salary increases were frequent and, more important to me, my job satisfaction was terrific.

Not often in life can one see something concrete result from his work. But the Kinston plant was one. The harmony and success of those exhilarating days make me realize how important it is for us to search for ways to foster clearly focused, adequately financed team efforts in the civic arena.

5

Nylon Tire Yarn:
Conflict with Big Three Auto Companies

In 1955 I was transferred to sales as director of a new merchandizing Division as part of my training for more general management assignments. My most memorable experience there was helping to solve the problem of getting the auto manufacturers to adopt nylon tire cord for reinforcing their tires. Extensive testing had shown that tires reinforced with nylon had much greater resistance to impact than tires reinforced with the standard cord of the time, Cordura,® another DuPont product. Nylon cord led to fewer tire blowouts and thus fewer serious accidents.

We had been working with tire companies, especially Goodyear, to develop nylon-reinforced tires and had acquired our own facilities for building and testing tires. Through extensive advertising of the superior safety provided by nylon-reinforced tires, more and more consumers were buying them as replacements for their worn out tires.

Yet, the automobile companies refused to put them on new cars. They complained about flat spotting. When a car sat for some time on nylon-reinforced tires, a flat spot developed on the bottom of the tire which caused a minor vibration during the first two or three miles the car was driven. Most of us never felt the vibration, but the sensitive fannies of the auto company engineers did.

We were determined to change the minds of the auto companies and several reluctant tire companies. Armed with extensive data on the superior safety of the nylon-reinforced tires, I set out with Dr. Philip Walters, the merchandising manager for tire yarns, to tell the auto and tire companies that we were going all out to replace DuPont's Cordura tire yarn with nylon. Phil Walters was another Ph.D. chemist, a friend of mine from our days at the University of Wisconsin and at the Experimental Station.

We first visited the tire companies in Akron, Ohio. Confidentially, they agreed with our assessment of the safety superiority of the nylon-reinforced tires, but they were not going to pressure the auto companies, their biggest customers.

Next we went to Detroit to see the big three—General Motors, Ford and Chrysler. They were all opposed, but GM was most outspoken. They gave us a ride on their test track to demonstrate the flat spotting problem. I still could not feel it, as hard as I tried, but Phil did. Then we went to Charles Cole's office. He was head of the Chevrolet Division and reportedly the leader of the auto industry's opposition to our objective. Phil said Cole was "a tough customer," a powerful force in GM, who would probably throw us out.

He received us in a friendly way, but when I told him about our mission he became quite belligerent and said something like, "Who do you think you are? What do you know about tires and cars?" Then he picked up his phone and pretended he was calling the U.S. Department of Justice to tell them how DuPont was trying to force the auto industry to do an unsafe thing. I asked him to let me talk to the Department of Justice when he finished so I could relate the opposite—how the auto industry was refusing to provide customers with safer tires. At that, he slammed down the receiver on his faked call and stood up. We thanked him for seeing us, handed him a folder of data from our safety tests, and left. One of Cole's staff told Phil later that Cole had studied those data carefully and discussed them with others.

DuPont's program got a big boost from its advertising showing a man driving GM's top-of-the-line Cadillac, telling his wife and children why he had replaced the original tires on his new car with nylon-reinforced tires. Cadillac customers started asking for the safer tires and shortly thereafter Cadillac started installing them as original equipment. Over the next few years nylon-reinforced tires became standard throughout the industry. During this period the tire companies, with DuPont's help, got rid of the flat spotting problem.

We had solved our problem of getting auto companies to face up to the superior safety performance of nylon-reinforced tires. Accidents from tire blowouts almost disappeared. Years later, after

Charles Cole had retired as Chief Executive Officer of General Motors, I met him at a dinner meeting in Washington and asked if he remembered our encounter in his office. As I recall, he said, "I sure do. I tried to frighten you off, but you wouldn't budge. And you were right."

6

Revolutionizing the Carpet Business; Overcoming Institutional Barriers

AFTER MY ASSIGNMENT IN SALES, I WAS PROMOTED TO ESTABLISH and head a new research division, the Textile and Industrial Products Research Division, an attempt by General Manager Andy Buchanan to improve our effectiveness in developing new products. Up to this time our approach was to discover some material and then find out what it might be used for. My new assignment was to look to the future, decide what new products consumers might need or desire, and then develop products involving fibers to fill those needs.

Initially we concentrated on paper studies—analyzing markets, brainstorming to define what consumers might need, making detailed economic appraisals. My right arm in making these studies was F. J. H. Trepagnier, a creative Ph.D. chemist unencumbered by the established ways of the textile industry and gifted with broad vision.

Our end-use research labs at DuPont's Chestnut Run location now reported to me. We had nearly every kind of equipment that the textile industry used in processing fibers: equipment for carding, drafting, and spinning short fibers (staple) into yarns; looms, knitting machines, dyeing and finishing equipment; extensive testing facilities, technicians skilled in operating such equipment, and the financial resources to acquire or build what else we might need.

By far the most important contribution we made was to revolutionize the carpet industry and get DuPont into the carpet fiber business in a major way, earning hundreds of millions of dollars over the years. To do so we had to overcome the not-invented-here, we-have-already-proved-it-won't-work syndromes that so often plague new product development.

Wool carpets were the standard at the time. The short wool fibers (staple fibers) were spun into yarn and then woven on looms into carpets. Wool yarn took dye beautifully and was resilient, but wool was also highly expensive, hard to keep clean, and not durable. Attempts had been made to make wool carpets on the new, less-expensive carpet-tufting machines, but the wool yarns were too weak to withstand the tension frequently applied during tufting.

When nylon fiber is manufactured, strong continuous filaments are produced. If one desires a spun yarn, like cotton and wool yarns, then the continuous filaments must be cut into short lengths and, as is done with cotton and wool, "spun" into yarns. Obviously, if a continuous filament yarn can be used for an end product, it is more economical than using a spun yarn.

Nylon Sales was working with carpet companies on woven nylon carpets made from spun yarn, but with no significant results. Such carpets were even more expensive than wool. Although nylon continuous filament ran well on tufting machines, the resulting carpets were far from satisfactory. The filaments packed together so closely it took inordinate amounts of nylon to cover a floor. And the carpets had no resilience. Despite this, we decided nylon was an ideal carpet fiber and could revolutionize the carpet industry if we could learn how to put a permanent wave in nylon continuous filament yarns to make them bulky and then process such yarn on a tufting machine.

I asked Nylon Research to undertake the development of the bulked yarn. They refused. Sales had said they had tried continuous filament yarns and they were far from satisfactory.

The nylon business was then managed by a triumvirate—the heads of Sales, Manufacturing, and Research. Failing to convince this group, I decided that my independent research division would make the bulked continuous filament yarn. Earlier pioneering research had studied the properties of nylon yarns put through a steam jet. It appeared this might be a route to the yarn we needed, so I asked my group to explore it. Within four months Carl Hallden, a research engineer, had produced what appeared to be the bulked yarn we wanted.

I asked Sales to run a sample of this yarn on one of their customers' tufting machines. Again they refused, so we ordered our own tufting machine. Within one month it was delivered and operating. Now we could make carpet samples. We thought they were great! I even carpeted my office with a beautiful light blue sample and persuaded many from management to come have a look.

By this time, my experience had taught me that we humans have a superabundance of appreciation for that which we have created. Just as we each think our baby in the hospital nursery outshines all others, so it is with new products.

To gain a more objective appraisal of our new carpet, we prepared a number of samples, two feet by two feet, taped them around the edges so no one could see how they were made, purchased high- and moderate-quality wool carpets, taped them also, and took them to a hotel suite in Chicago where three carpet buyers for Sears Roebuck, whom we had hired, appraised them. Some of our samples were rated among the most expensive wool carpets.

I was convinced it was time for DuPont to start producing bulked continuous filament nylon carpet yarn. We installed facilities in our own laboratory for producing much larger quantities of yarn for test-marketing. Still the nylon management triumvirate would not budge. Our problem was that our division had been created by General Manager Andy Buchanan as a new approach and given the authority, the responsibility, and the resources to do things that traditionally were in the territory of Research, Manufacturing, and Sales. They did not like our intrusion into their territory.

About this time Andy Buchanan called me to his office on another matter. I took along a sample of our carpet. After we covered his business, I asked if he had a few more minutes. He said, "Go ahead."

I said something like, "Andy, you have been concerned about our department's failure to develop enough new products. Do you know what the problem is? It's the management."

I then told him my story. He was convinced. That same day he called a meeting of about a dozen members of top management from Research, Manufacturing, and Sales and asked me to tell them my story. What I had to say was not news to several of them.

When I finished, Andy said, "I'm not asking any of you for your opinion. I'm telling you that we are going ahead with this development. You get together with Peterson, learn what has to be done, and get going." He assigned his right arm, Bill McGowan, a former Manufacturing executive, to expedite the program.

The development took off like a rocket. We ran our modest production facilities around the clock to supply the initial test-marketing, while large-scale facilities were installed at the Seaford, Delaware, nylon plant. Bulked continuous filament carpet yarn (BCF) became one of the most profitable ventures DuPont ever experienced, earning many hundreds of millions of dollars. It is now extensively used all over the world, and it is projected that over two billion pounds will be produced in the United States in 1998.

While wool carpets were used primarily in living rooms, BCF carpeting now covers most rooms wall-to-wall in most homes, even running out onto patios. Many builders eliminate wood flooring and install the carpet directly on the subflooring. These carpets are highly durable, resistant to stain, and can be readily steam cleaned in place.

Years later, when Dr. Robert Hershey was a vice president and member of DuPont's Executive Committee in charge of all the company's research, he interviewed me about my views on launching new business ventures. Among other things, I told him about my experience with the nylon carpet yarn venture. He said, "They should have fired you." At first I thought he was kidding. But then he made it clear he meant it. He did not like my bucking the system.

I speculate that Bob Hershey's irritation with me stemmed from my early years when, as a 30-year-old research supervisor, I was selected by the Textile Fibers Department to be its spokesperson in a major confrontation with the Ammonia Department over the quality of the hexamethylene diamine, the nylon intermediate that Ammonia supplied Textile Fibers. Our nylon business was plagued by streaks in dyed fabrics. My group had established that streaks resulted from varying amounts of an impurity in hexamethylene diamine. After my presentation at a large meeting at Ammonia Department's Orange, Texas, plant, Bob Hershey, then Director of Research for that department, bitterly attacked me personally in front of several echelons of top management from both departments. He belittled my competence and my qualifications for judging the quality of their hexamethylene diamine. This was my first exposure to such public defamation. My sin was telling the head of research and development in the Ammonia Department that "the emperor had no clothes." He was so angry that if he had been a ruler in olden times, he would have had this messenger of bad tidings executed.

He did himself much harm that day. That very afternoon his superiors overruled him and agreed to invest many millions of dollars to install equipment to better purify hexamethylene diamine. After that our dyeing problem disappeared. But Bob Hershey did not. Years later he was still angry.

I believe that any objective analysis of the history of DuPont's BCF venture would judge positively our actions in overcoming the objections of the nylon management team. The record should show, however, that the key to making this highly successful development happen was General Manager Andy Buchanan's decision to establish a separate research division and give its leadership the authority and resources to launch new ventures on its own.

7

Making Waves with DuPont Management

IN THE 1950S IT WAS EXTREMELY DIFFICULT FOR YOUNG BLACKS TO obtain decent jobs. The pattern of subjugating the black populace in this country that began with slavery 400 years earlier had continued, in a modified form, since the Civil War. Even as we approached 1960, blacks were still the sharecroppers, house cleaners, rest room attendants and laborers, while many of us with white skin enjoyed an upward mobility that was the envy of the world.

Someone like me, for example, benefitted almost beyond belief from the educational and economic opportunities offered by such a fluid society. Though I was one of eight children in a poor family in Portage, Wisconsin, the son of a Swedish immigrant who worked as a baker's assistant, I managed to put myself through college, obtain a doctorate in chemistry, and land a job as a research chemist with DuPont in Delaware.

At that moment I was riding high in my chosen profession. Since arriving at DuPont fresh out of graduate school in 1942, I had been repeatedly praised by management and rewarded with frequent promotions and raises. I led the team that developed Dacron and helped to establish DuPont as a pioneer in the development of wash-and-wear clothing; I spearheaded the development of bulked continuous filament nylon, which put DuPont at the forefront of a revolution in the carpet industry; and I zealously promoted the use of nylon-reinforced tires, which made millions of dollars for the company and saved thousands of lives by nearly eliminating the dangerous blowouts of an earlier automotive era.

One day in 1958, General Manager Andy Buchanan called me into his office. This leader of the company's largest department greeted me with a big smile and asked me to sit down across from him. Then he pushed a large piece of paper, which he had been studying when I walked in, over to my side of his huge, mahogany desk.

It was the company's legendary skimmer chart, plotting the trajectory of its executives. Although I had heard much speculation about this chart before, I never expected to see it. Andy pointed to my dot on the plot and explained its significance. My present salary put me in front of everyone else near my age (forty-one) in the company.

"Keep it up and you will be running this company some day," he said. It was a heady moment.

Then, for the first time, he explained DuPont's strategy in having moved me through research, manufacturing, and sales. The idea was to give me a full understanding of the company's overall operation. I was being groomed, he told me, for top management.

That night I told Lillian about my meeting with Buchanan and my privileged place on the skimmer chart. We thought about how far we had come together since our marriage twenty years earlier, our four healthy, happy children, our lovely new home, and my rosy prospects with DuPont. Best of all, we were having a wonderful time. And though I devoted long hours to my work, I found it challenging, rewarding, and fun. For Lillian and me, the American Dream had come true.

Also in the American tradition, we had become active in community work. In addition to raising a family and creating a warm, loving haven for all of us, Lillian volunteered with Planned Parenthood, advising mothers in low-income neighborhoods who wanted to avoid unwanted pregnancies. Together we participated actively in the Unitarian Church whose philosophy of personal involvement and individual responsibility for helping others had impressed both of us. In fact, my passion for problem solving at DuPont earned me the job of chairman of the church's Social Action Committee.

Through this position I became aware of the problem building in black neighborhoods. As most of the country prospered, the plight of our inner cities seemed to worsen. There, when young people reached the age when they needed and wanted to take care of themselves, they could not find jobs. Or if they did, the jobs were menial and poorly paid. They would be stuck, regardless of initiative and ability, for the rest of their lives. This seemed especially unjust when the only reason for such a fate was the color of their skin.

One night our Social Action Committee met to discuss what we could do about the situation in the black neighborhoods of Wilmington, because resentment had begun to smolder. Everyone acknowledged that a root problem of the inner cities was the lack of employment opportunities. What, individually and as a church group, could we do to help? We discussed a number of possibilities but developed no plan of action. As I drove home that night, I wondered again what life might have been like for me had I been born an African American instead of Swedish American. Could I have worked my way through our state university, through four years of graduate school to a job at DuPont as a research chemist, and then moved up the corporate ladder with seemingly limitless opportunity for advancement? The answer was obvious.

Had I been born black instead of white, where would my energy and ambition have taken me? To inciting riots against an oppressive society that would not give me a chance to prove myself? To putting my organizational ability to work as a gang leader? To becoming a thief or drug dealer because I refused to spend my life pumping gas or sweeping floors? Or would I have moved in a more constructive direction, as an activist in the civil rights movement which was then beginning to make waves in the South? I guessed it would have depended on how impatient, angry, or desperate I had become.

Then I thought about my position at DuPont. At that time, I was head of the Textile and Industrial Products Research Division. DuPont's Chestnut Run plant—about 2,000 employees—reported to me. Perhaps I could do something here.

The next day I called Bike Barkley, the plant manager, and asked him to find out how many black employees we had. I also asked for a rundown on the jobs they performed. Bike seemed surprised by the request, but he came back a day or two later with the information. We had sixty blacks working in the plant—sixty out of 2,000 in an area of Delaware where about 20 percent of the population was black. All of the black employees were males, Bike reported, and all were laborers. One of them had three years of college, another had completed two years. Not one of the sixty workers had ever been promoted, nor was likely to be. They had begun as laborers and presumably would end their careers, thirty or forty years after being hired, in the same job.

It seemed time for a change—at least a slight one—to signal that a new day had arrived, but not enough to cause company management to panic and overrule me. I went to the plant and told Bike about my idea to promote a few of the blacks. He agreed immediately and enthusiastically. So now it was *our* idea. Then I personally talked to the supervisors and foremen who were enthusiastic about the prospect. Because they worked closely with plant employees, they were aware that talent was going to waste. They knew that some white workers in higher positions were much less competent than some of the black workers in the lower positions.

We agreed to provide five higher-level jobs for blacks by promoting four men and hiring one black woman. The promotions for the men were to truck driver, chemist's helper, machinist's assistant, and pipe fitter's assistant. The woman would be a typist. This was a long way from the affirmative action of the next decade, but it was a beginning.

The support from Bike Barkley and his staff at the plant also proved to me, once again, that when the boss exerts positive leadership in a potentially controversial matter, his subordinates will usually go along. Unfortunately this is also true when a boss wears his prejudices on his sleeve.

A few years earlier, I had seen an amusing example of this tendency to follow the leader at our nylon plant in Martinsville, Virginia. There the boss went to the Methodist Church, as did many of the people who worked for him. When he was transferred, and a new manager took his place, the new manager joined the local Presbyterian Church. In short order, many of the Methodists who worked for him also switched to the Presbyterian church.

Now, with my subordinates in agreement, I took up the matter with Thomas Hale, director of the Personnel and Industrial Relations Division. Since Tom was neither above nor below me in the corporate hierarchy, I did not go to him with the intention of seeking his approval. It was an informational meeting. I explained the situation at Chestnut Run, which I assumed he knew about, and described my plans for a modest upgrading of a few black employees.

Tom had a fit. He told me my proposal would establish a very dangerous precedent. He stressed that kind of meddling would get us in big trouble in our plant communities, especially in the South. His job was to keep things harmonious, and he feared what I had in mind would cause discord.

I told him that was ridiculous and that he was behind the times, reminding him that President Truman had integrated the armed forces a decade earlier, and that worked harmoniously. I clearly recall his replying that the DuPont Company was not the U.S. Army.

"Well," I replied, "when DuPont built its first Dacron plant in Kinston, North Carolina, and I chaired the design committee, we got rid of some of the customary dual facilities. We integrated the drinking fountains and waiting rooms without complaints from the white employees, despite some dire predictions."

"And we would have gotten by with one cafeteria, too," I added, "if it hadn't been for you."

When he told me we were not in business to solve social problems, I knew our discussion had run its course. I left, determined to proceed with the plan. I also left knowing that I really could not be too angry with Tom Hale for what seemed like narrow-mindedness. He was simply expressing the conventional wisdom of the time. As personnel and industrial relations manager, he wanted smooth sailing in the plants and with the local communities. As the company man whose job it was to promote harmony, he found it easier to stick with the status quo, which had worked well for the company so far (if not so well for its black laborers), than to risk jeopardizing that harmony.

A few days later, Andy Buchanan invited me to join him for dinner in the opulent Green Room at the Hotel DuPont. He did not tell me the purpose of the meeting, but I assumed it had to do with the reorganization plan I had prepared to streamline the research and technical work of the department. If he liked the plan, I thought he might ask me to implement it, which would mean another promotion and another advance on the skimmer chart. My relations with Andy had always been good. I admired him and respected his leadership. To dine with him alone was a special treat.

As we walked to the hotel, I told him of my plan to upgrade some blacks at Chestnut Run. He made no comment about it. But during dinner he did discuss my reorganization plan, and in flattering terms. For the rest of the meal we mostly reminisced. We recalled how Andy's backing had been critical in the launching of Dacron. Within the company, the competition had become intense between the developers of Dacron polyester fiber and the developers of Orlon® acrylic fiber, which was well suited for knitted fabrics such as sweaters and socks.

It seemed unlikely the company would approve commercialization of both new products, since each would require a huge investment. So the Dacron faction vied with the Orlon faction to get the nod from management. But we had underestimated Buchanan. As general manager of the Textile Fibers Department, he went before the company's executive committee to report on the tremendous potential of both products. He told them they should feel like parents who are blessed with twins. "You don't raise one and toss out the other," he said. "You raise them both. That's what we should do with these two fibers." The executive committee agreed, and their decision proved profitable. Within a few years, both Dacron and Orlon became household words.

We talked for about two hours. By that point the Green Room had emptied, except for a few waiters who were probably eager to finish up and go home. Then Andy suddenly shifted gears and told me he had invited me to dinner in order to discuss my plan for promoting black employees at Chestnut Run. I clearly remember his saying, "As you now know, I plan to reorganize all our research and technical work according to the plan you worked up. I intended to put you in charge of this, but now, frankly, some of us are worried about your stability."

This was one of the few times in my life that I found myself speechless. Andy went on about the need to avoid public relations problems for the company, and used a few of the words, such as "harmony" and "discord," that Tom Hale had used with me earlier. I listened, but said nothing. When we parted I thanked him for dinner, shook hands, and headed home in what must have been a state of shock.

Though Lillian immediately sensed that something was amiss, I decided not to discuss the matter with her yet, not until the issue had settled out more and I knew better where things stood. The settling-out process did not take long.

The next day Dr. Gerald Gordon, the DuPont Company psychiatrist, invited me to lunch. Jerry was an old friend—we were members of the same Great Books Club and served together on a Unitarian Church committee that was planning the dedication of a new building. Jerry generally wore a big, friendly smile on his face. This time he was not smiling at all. He seemed to be seething.

As soon as we were seated, he practically exploded, expressing his irritation about a request he had received that morning from Buchanan and Lester Sinness.

Dr. Sinness was number two in the Textile Fibers Department. He put great store in psychiatrists—years earlier I had irritated him by confiding that DuPont's first staff psychiatrist (Jerry's predecessor) seemed more in need of a psychiatrist than anyone I knew.

I will never forget how it felt when Jerry said, "They asked me to check out your stability. I told them you were probably the most stable person in DuPont."

I had trouble believing what Jerry was telling me. Where I came from, to be investigated by a psychiatrist was a serious matter. It was downright insulting to have one's bosses order such an investigation, especially when they had a seventeen-year record of my character. The disillusionment of the previous evening was now complete.

That day I went home from work sharply at 5 P.M. Lillian greeted me with a surprised and then a worried look. "What are you doing home at this hour?" she asked. Now she knew for sure that something bad had happened. "Tell me what's wrong, honey," she said.

I took her by the hand and walked into the living room of this second wonderful house she had designed for us. We sat down on the davenport where we frequently sat to admire our superb view of the rolling countryside. I had told her earlier about my plans for Chestnut Run, about the good reception to the idea from Barkley and his crew, and about the reaction from Tom Hale. Now I told her about the discussion with Andy Buchanan, the lunch with Jerry Gordon, and the concern about my stability. I told Lillian I probably could get back in the good graces of Buchanan and Sinness by apologizing for my behavior and catering to their prejudices.

"Don't you dare do that," she said, though we both knew that I never would. She kissed me and said, "They are the ones who need the psychiatric help, not you. Russ, we don't need them."

She was right. We did not need them. We were two strongly independent souls. Everything we had we had earned ourselves. And we knew what I had tried to do at Chestnut Run was the right thing. We also recognized that, short of putting my tail between my legs and begging forgiveness for my actions, the rapid rise of Russ Peterson at the DuPont Company had most likely reached its peak. And for the most deplorable of reasons.

Lillian and I knew that with a top-level job at DuPont we could become quite wealthy. In fact, we were well-off by conventional standards. But making a lot of money had never been our priority. Financial security, of course, was important, especially with four children to put through college. But we were confident that I could find another job readily, if it came to that, and would be able to take care of our financial needs.

Through our involvement in the Unitarian Church and Planned Parenthood we had become increasingly concerned about the failure of the community to solve critical social problems. Finding solutions to these problems was much more important, we both agreed, than developing another new product for DuPont. After all, it was 1959, not 1859, and it seemed to us that everyone in this country should have the opportunity—the same opportunity that I had—to pull themselves out of poverty. But the obstacles to doing so, especially if you were black, seemed monumental. I had just encountered one such obstacle at DuPont. And DuPont, compared to many other companies, was enlightened and progressive.

On the other hand, DuPont alone had thousands of talented people working on new products. They could easily hire many more. They did not need me, at least not all of me almost all of the time.

We agreed that I should stay with DuPont for the time being. I would continue to work as hard and creatively there as possible, but more evenings and weekends would now be devoted to solving problems in the social arena. Lillian reminded me of an aphorism we had recently discussed: you make a living by what you get, but you make a life by what you give.

With vacation coming up, we decided to celebrate our decision by spending five weeks in Europe. Leaving our younger children with friends, we set off alone. It was the first time we had ever done this.

We flew to London, then rented a car and drove all over England and Scotland, delving into British history, which was Lillian's hobby. Then on to Milan, where we heard Maria Callas at La Scala. Afterwards we drove to Venice, Florence, Rome, and Naples, visiting the famous museums, cathedrals, and palaces along the way. Then Paris, where we strolled around the city, savored great cooking, visited the Louvre and practiced our French. We also sailed down the Rhine, saw the Bolshoi Ballet in Brussels, and hiked in the Swiss Alps. What a glorious time! It seemed like the whole world embraced us. We felt completely free, forgetting about what had happened back home. Since we had never had a honeymoon, we called *this* our honeymoon.

When we returned to Delaware and I resumed work at DuPont, Dr. Howard Swank, another Ph.D. chemist, had been chosen to head the overall technical work of the Textile Fibers Department. It was he who would carry out the reorganization plan I had prepared for Buchanan. Twenty-nine years later Dr. Swank wrote in *Science and Corporate Strategy*, a history of DuPont's research and development efforts:

Responsibility for new product and process development (after the reorganization) was now crystal clear. As one observer said, "A miracle happened! Almost overnight, the climate changed, the bickering stopped, the committee system disappeared, people and facilities were made available, decisions came promptly, and markedly less time was spent on coordinating with other groups. What's most significant is that the program went from an unproductive, pessimistic status to a highly productive, optimistic status."

Dr. Swank was the person I had reported to several years earlier during the start-up of the first Dacron plant. He was my mentor at the time, but as I moved up the ladder to his level, our working relationship showed signs of strain. After his promotion to carry out the new technical reorganization, he called me into his office one day and told me that I was no longer the fair-haired boy in DuPont, that I had done some good things, but also some "damn fool things."

When I asked for some examples of the latter, he cited two. One was a memo I had written projecting what I saw as a major potential for producing yarns that would be made into nylon carpeting. Swank believed those projections were unrealistically high, and that they had pushed the company in the wrong direction. (As it turned out, the projections *were* off base—they grossly *under*estimated the potential of a product that was to revamp the carpet industry worldwide.) The other example of my foolishness was, of course, the proposal to upgrade four out of sixty black laborers at a company plant and to bring in a black woman typist.

Ironically, Howard Swank himself was forced to execute the

very same plan at Chestnut Run one year later. In 1960, President Eisenhower had asked the CEOs of every large corporation in America to come to the White House. He warned them that rioting would be occurring in black neighborhoods if businesses failed to provide more jobs for blacks. He asked for their help. Following that meeting, Crawford Greenewalt, DuPont's president, asked his key people to take immediate action.

Shortly after that, Bike Barkley called me from the Chestnut Run plant to tell me that he had been asked by Dr. Swank to implement our modest proposal. I heard nothing else from anyone in DuPont on the subject. I did, however, run into Swank several weeks later at a cocktail party and congratulated him on DuPont's action.

"Russ," he said, with no trace of sarcasm that I could detect, "You were just ahead of your time."

"No," I said. "DuPont was behind the time and missed a great chance to get out front, albeit in a very modest way, on a critical national issue."

At that he walked away.

Today, of course, the status of black employees at DuPont has markedly improved, as it has throughout much of the industrial world. In 1992 DuPont was one of twenty-five U.S. corporations cited by *Black Enterprise* magazine for providing more and better opportunities for black employees. There is still a very long way to go, however, before African Americans enjoy the same opportunities as the white community. Though I do not expect to be around to see that day, I like to believe that my grandchildren will.

8

Launching New Business Ventures

DURING MY LAST NINE YEARS WITH DUPONT I BECAME INCREAS-
ingly involved in managing the development of new businesses.
In spite of my earlier disillusionment with DuPont management,
I found this experience to be challenging, enjoyable, and rewarding. At the same time I used my evenings and weekends to
become ever more committed as a citizen activist to social and
political issues. Living these two roles was highly demanding of
time and energy. Fortunately, I could get along on five to six hours
of sleep and was endowed with high energy. Most important, Lillian strongly supported me, while masterfully managing our
home and family.

This period provided me with skills and experiences that
proved to be of great value in my subsequent careers. For example, my firsthand experience with all aspects of a wide variety of
businesses provided me with knowledge and credentials important later in negotiating with business leaders on environmental and social issues. When, as often happened, a business leader
asked me, "What do you know about the real world, Peterson?
Have you ever had to meet a payroll?" I could thoroughly deflate
such an intended put-down and gain a level playing field for
our discussion.

It is exciting to take an idea for a new product and carry it
through to a commercial success—through semi-works and pilot
plant production, laboratory and market testing, economic evaluation—and ultimately convince management who control the
purse strings that it is time to commercialize.

Big business, including DuPont, was not very good at this. Most
successful developments such as the telephone and the electric
lightbulb came from individual entrepreneurs who, enraptured
with an idea, worked day and night to make it happen. They
shared the responsibility for success or failure with no one and

were not encumbered, as are new-venture managers in big companies, by a long chain of decision makers, including many professional naysayers, some of whom are capable of vetoing the manager's plans. The lone entrepreneurs, however, had to struggle to find the necessary funding and competent assistants. Most failed.

Because I thought DuPont could combine the best of these two worlds, I promoted the idea of the Textile Fibers Department's establishing a venture manager system. One individual would be put in complete charge of a new development and given the authority and responsibility for its success, much like an entrepreneur in the broader community. He would have access to the company's large financial resources whose management was generally committed to funding promising new ventures; he could recruit needed talent from other parts of the company; and his success or failure would depend on his project's outcome.

When Textile Fibers created a New Products Division and made me director, I was able to establish the venture manager system.

Three of our largest new ventures were based on the conviction that if DuPont could learn how to produce desirable fibrous sheets from synthetic polymers in one continuous operation, spewing the filaments from a long bank of spinnerets onto a traveling belt, calendering and bonding the resulting sheets as they moved along the belt, and winding the finished product in large rolls, the cost of such spunbonded sheets (nonwoven fabrics) would be markedly lower than that of woven fabric.

Relying on much new polymer and fiber processing technology developed by the Textile Fibers Department's Pioneering Research Laboratory, we decided to develop three different spunbondeds simultaneously. Our management agreed to fund this risky, expensive approach. One spunbonded, made from Dacron filaments, was subsequently named Reemay,® one from polypropylene Typar,® and one from polyethylene Tyvek.® All three products were commercialized after spending over $100 million in the pre-commercialization phase. All three became profitable, but Tyvek® was the most successful.

In 1986 DuPont sold its Reemay and North American portion of the Typar business to an independent entrepreneur who subsequently sold them to DBA, a British conglomerate. In 1994, DBA's Reemay and Typar were still being produced at DuPont's Old Hickory, Tennessee, plant, using the same equipment and most of the personnel that DuPont had employed eight years earlier. That year DBA's spunbonded sales totalled $200 million and were growing profitably.

By 1994 DuPont's sales of spunbondeds totaled $700 million, having grown 40 percent between 1990 and 1994. DuPont is now the most profitable player in the huge nonwovens market, and Tyvek is the star. It is sold in more than fifty industrial markets, especially as express and priority mail envelopes and as a breathable, water-impervious house wrap.

Ironically, DuPont's restructuring in recent years reestablished the spunbonded business as a separate entity reporting directly to the chief executive officer, rather than through tier after tier of managers. The resulting increased profitability makes me think this may be an appropriate time for DuPont to reclaim the Reemay and Typar businesses.

Another major venture was an attempt to get into the home building products business. We even considered marketing *The DuPont House.* We built a house within our laboratory to depict what we might do with a myriad of DuPont products: roofing, siding, shutters, bathroom and kitchen basins and tubs, carpeting and finishes. Although some of these developments reached the market through other DuPont businesses, the grandiose plan for DuPont to enter the home building business never materialized. Our products, although of good quality, were too expensive at that time for the mainstream home building industry. However, subsequent DuPont research has produced many more materials for home construction. Recently *DuPont Magazine* highlighted DuPont's showcase home, *Signature Place,* in Chester, New Jersey. It employs more than three dozen DuPont products. Today the idea of integrating forward to market The DuPont House might be practical.

Not long after organizing the New Products Division in the Textile Fibers Department, I was transferred to the Development Department, where I reported to the head of that department, Dr. Ed Gee. My assignment was to organize and head a new Research and Development Division to help the company solve its problem of successfully launching entirely new business ventures. Embryonic new developments were brought to us from many research groups within the company, but especially from the Central Research Department, DuPont's prestigious research institution.

This type of work was different from my experiences with in

the Textile Fibers Department. There our primary objective was to extend the market for fibers such as our highly profitable bulked, continuous-filament carpet yarns. Here we subjected proposals for new businesses to a computerized venture analysis, turned them down if they did not look promising and, if they did, assigned them to venture managers.

At the time, both DuPont and big industry in general were interested in our approach to launching new ventures. *The Harvard Business Review* invited me to write an article for its May-June, 1967, issue. In it I described how new venture management in a large company can combine the advantages of size with the spirit that motivates the individual entrepreneur in launching his own new business. Despite all the interest, we were not as successful in our work as we had hoped. The DuPont Executive Committee became seriously frustrated by the company's lack of success in launching new businesses and began talking about limiting DuPont's research to extending markets for existing products. Several years later, after I had left to run for office, the Development Department's effort was terminated. I believe insufficient time had been allocated for evaluating our venture management approach to launching new businesses, universally recognized as long term projects that required ten years or more to come to fruition.

Today it is difficult to judge the merits of our approach. To be given the authority and resources to try to build a successful business from an embryonic development was stimulating and satisfying. And I personally believe the venture managers of that era did a good job moving their ventures along more expeditiously than was done by earlier, more diffuse, and shared management.

But how does one know for sure without running the impractical experiment of subjecting a new development to simultaneous exploitation by the two management schemes? A venture manager in a big corporation is not as free from other management impact as one might hope, as I learned back in the Textile Fibers Department when several venture managers and I presented a status report to General Manager Andy Buchanan and about twelve of his key people who were fully absorbed in current businesses. We projected where our ventures might be ten years in the future.

Afterward Andy came to my office. As I recall, he asked me to keep thinking long range, while only telling him about the next year or two. This was upsetting. The other venture managers and I knew most major new developments take at least ten years before they start making any profit. Our job was to bring our projects to the point where they provided a good return on investment as soon as possible. How could we justify the huge investments in our ventures without explaining quantitatively how and when they might become profitable? Our work was about the future.

Later in the Development Department I had a similar experience. I was asked to make a presentation about our new ventures to the Executive Committee, a group of six vice presidents and the president and CEO of the company. I adopted the format used by the Executive Committee in their reviews of current businesses. The seven men sat in leather-upholstered chairs in a chart room provided for this purpose, while large charts riding on an overhead rail were pulled directly in front of them.

My venture managers prepared similar charts for the future businesses we thought DuPont could build. We were proud of our work and excited about presenting it in "the chart room." Yet, our presentation failed. One member of the Executive Committee said, "Hell, we don't even know what's going to happen in the next quarter."

A different and much more serious management problem was encountered later. My job required that when we had completed the pilot plant and test marketing stages and felt confident that the venture would succeed, we were to transfer control for development to a general manager of one of the operating departments.

One day I tried to sell a general manager our Corian® development, which later became a substantial commercial success. Corian is an extraordinary surfacing material that combines the permanence and elegance of marble with the design flexibility of wood. It is widely used for sinks, bathtubs and countertops. The general manager said he thought we had a good development, but he did not want it. "I'm going to retire in two years," he said. "Your development will only add to my costs during that time. I'm already getting criticized for insufficient profits."

It was hard to believe those words.

A few months later, when I had almost exactly the same experience with another general manager, I was thoroughly disillusioned. He was going to retire in three years and did not want to add to his costs during that period. Yet he, too, praised our development. To put their personal interests ahead of the interests of the DuPont Company, which they were being handsomely paid to represent, was reprehensible enough, but even more disturbing was the open way they acknowledged such behavior as though it were of little significance.

After this experience I asked three members of the duPont family who were friends of mine, each from a different branch of the family, to meet with me. They were Irenée duPont, Chic duPont, and Reynolds duPont, all major shareholders. I told them about the priorities of two of DuPont's professional managers and suggested that the duPont family once again take over management of the company. They had an heritage to uphold and a huge financial stake in the future of the company that the professional managers did not have. None of these three men alone could do much to correct the management problem I cited, but I hoped they would discuss it with other family members who might make some progressive changes. They told me later that the family decided to leave the matter in the hands of the company's professional managers. All three continued to be friendly to me, and later each provided financial support for my two campaigns for the governorship of Delaware.

Let me cite one other management practice that made DuPont less progressive, as I saw it, than it might otherwise have been. This was the seven-member Executive Committee of predominantly Ph.D. chemists who ran the company. This committee made all major decisions by majority vote. That meant that their decisions were normally determined by the fourth, least progressive member of the committee.

When Crawford Greenewalt was the CEO and Chairman of the Executive Committee, he occasionally did not call for a vote and instead made the decision himself. No one challenged him. After all, he had married into Irenée duPont's big family and was popular with them. He was competent, articulate, and a progressive thinker—better qualified to make the big decisions than was the Executive Committee.

One time Andy Buchanan had a big item coming before the Executive Committee. He told me how he had lobbied the members of the Executive Committee and had the four votes he needed. Yet when he returned from presenting his request to the

Executive Committee, he was downcast. Greenewalt had decided, *no*. No opposition was raised by the other six members.

Now, in 1998, DuPont does not have an executive committee. The president and CEO rules by himself, a big step forward.

The most interesting new venture we worked on in the Development Department was chromium dioxide. It was a superb magnetic material, much superior to the ferric oxide conventionally used in magnetic tapes. Central Research had developed this product at the Experimental Station. Dr. Paul Salzberg, Director, and his deputy, Dr. Ted Cairns, claimed chromium dioxide was Central Research's biggest find since nylon and would bring DuPont more earnings than nylon. At this time Salzberg and Cairns were under great pressure from the Executive Committee for their failure in recent years to develop adequate new products. They asked for my division's help in launching the chromium dioxide venture.

After listening to their scientists describe their chromium dioxide work and observing demonstrations of the superb performance of this material in magnetic tapes, I, too, was impressed. Compared to conventional ferric oxide tapes, much more information could be packed on a given length of chromium dioxide tape, and the TV images and sound were of much higher quality. We envisioned DuPont's manufacturing not only video and audio tapes but also superior video and audio equipment, capitalizing on the special properties of chromium dioxide, which was well protected for DuPont use by a solid patent.

I appointed Dr. Maurice Ward as the venture manager. We set out immediately to build a pilot plant to produce substantial quantities of magnetic tape for thorough evaluation. At start-up, we experienced so many flaws in the tape we were able to produce only short lengths of high quality. This was far from what we needed for properly evaluating and demonstrating our product. After repeated changes in our process failed to reduce the flaws adequately, we approached tape manufacturers, including Control Data and 3M, to see if they were interested in a joint venture. They were not. Obviously they did not want to help put DuPont in the tape business. Possibly they concluded that DuPont would have a hard time developing the know-how for quality tape production and eventually would sell its chromium dioxide powder.

That is precisely what happened several years later. Today Du-

Pont sells chromium dioxide to tape manufacturers who produce and market a high-quality, still quite expensive product. DuPont's return is but a small part of what it might have been if the company had learned how to make a marketable chromium dioxide tape.

What might have happened if DuPont's top management had accepted Salzberg's and Cairns' vision of the chromium dioxide venture and enthusiastically supported it as earlier DuPont management had done with nylon? DuPont might have carved out an important role in the emerging telecommunications revolution.

In the middle of the Development Department's effort on the chromium dioxide venture, I retired from DuPont and went off on a new venture of my own—trying my problem-solving skills in the political arena.

III
Citizen Activist

9

The Three S Campaign:
Salvage People—Shrink the Crime Rate—
Save Dollars

DURING MY LAST NINE YEARS AT DUPONT, I CONTINUED TO WORK long hours, but I expended more and more effort as a volunteer on social problems. As chairman of the Social Action Committee of the Unitarian Church, I became deeply concerned about the plight of Delaware's prisoners. Therefore, I accepted membership on the board of the Prisoners Aid Society where I learned how little we board members knew about the status of ex-offenders. Every Tuesday night for six months, I went out to Delaware's decrepit Greenbank prison to interview the men who were about to be released to the community. During one such interview, I remember asking a man who had been imprisoned over eighty times for minor offenses what he was going to do when he got out. He said he would take the few dollars he was given on discharge, get drunk, and then throw a brick through a store window so he could get back in prison. "I'll have no home to go to, and it's too cold out there on the street in the winter time," he said. "No one ever tried to help me find a home or a job on the outside."

Our committee kept track of those who were released and found that 80 percent were back in prison within two years.

On another visit I noticed a new suitcase and a guitar case, as well as a new suit and overcoat, in the room where incoming prisoners' clothes were kept. I asked to whom they belonged and was told, "A young student who was arrested for hitchhiking through Delaware on his way to Ohio State University." He had been sent to prison for ten days by a notoriously incompetent magistrate. Now he had a prison record for life. I knew that such a record, when seen by an employment officer, would outweigh the college degree the young man was striving to obtain.

Other people were in prison because they could not pay a fine. Someone who ran a traffic light, for example, was fined $25. If he could not pay, he went to prison. To point up the absurdity of this situation, if you or I had been fined $25 for a similar infraction, we would have paid, thereby easily, and with finality, covering our debt to society. For those who could not pay, there was no happy ending. When released, they could not get jobs if they honestly answered the standard question on job application forms: "Do you have a prison record?" If they lied, were hired, and later discovered, they would be fired. Their lives would be ruined for lack of $25.

Moreover, it was impossible for a visitor to tell the difference between the correctional officers and the commingled juvenile and adult prisoners. The officers had no uniforms; the prisoners wore their own clothes.

Knowing all this, and convinced that the state was part of the problem, I started speaking around Delaware about our debtors prison and the need to provide jobs for ex-offenders. As a result, the owner of a window washing company came to see me in my DuPont office. He said he had been moved by my speeches and wanted to talk about his contract with the DuPont Company. It required that he not employ anyone to wash DuPont company windows who had a prison record. Several of his employees, he said, had such records, but for very minor offenses, such as their inability to pay a fine.

I talked to Henry B. duPont, DuPont Company finance chairman, about this. He was surprised and upset to learn about such a provision and shortly thereafter it was rescinded. Later the owner of the window washing company paid me another visit to thank me for my efforts on behalf of his men. How easy it seemed to do something so vital to those men and their families.

Because all these experiences added to my growing interest in solving community problems, I took a two-week vacation from my DuPont job in December 1960, and spent the full time at home reading and thinking about community problems. It was clear we were not solving them. I methodically listed what I thought we citizens of Delaware should do. Instead of going after all our problems at once, I thought we needed to take one problem and attack it statewide, get the citizens behind it, and persist in our efforts until we made the necessary change happen.

During this time I was also a member of the Wilmington Kiwanis Club. Each year Kiwanis International adopted a theme for the year. In 1961 it was "Build Responsible Citizenship." I wrote to the club president, Francis I. Ponsell, on January 1, 1961, calling his attention to the many problems in the community and suggesting that the Wilmington Kiwanis Club take seriously the 1961 international theme and show the community how to get action on one of these problems. He invited me to speak to the whole club on March 8, 1961.

My speech expressed my concern about our failure as residents of Delaware to practice "responsible citizenship" and illustrated the especially dire need for doing so. I emphasized that, "the key to the solution of problems of our state is sustained participation by thousands of us as individual citizens." Because of my belief that citizen action can lead a reluctant government to face up to critical problems, I called upon Wilmington Kiwanis to enlist the other seventeen Kiwanis clubs of Delaware in initiating a statewide citizen effort to tackle one serious state problem and stick with it until our objective was assured. I argued that, "We must think positively, for there is little if anything we can't do if we set our minds to it. As Shakespeare wrote, 'Our doubts are traitors, And make us lose the good we oft might win, By fearing to attempt.'"

This speech was well received, and I was assigned to the club's Business and Public Affairs Committee to develop a specific proposal. Four of us on that committee were also on the board of the Prisoners Aid Society. Together we convinced the others that the corrections and rehabilitation problem was the one to attack. I then travelled around the state to urge the other Kiwanis clubs to join the program. Together they formed the Delaware Kiwanis Committee for Citizen Action and made me president.

I convinced the group that we would not succeed if we functioned as a Kiwanis organization. Instead we had to make the effort as representatives of the whole community. We promptly set up a statewide organization outside of Kiwanis and called it the Three S Citizens' Campaign: Salvage People, Save Dollars and Shrink the Crime Rate. I was selected as president, and the parent organization was dissolved.

A series of meetings around the state followed. Leaders of many civic, governmental, and religious organizations promised—and ultimately delivered—broad support. Most churches and synagogues in the state were represented. We signed up 6,000 members to participate in defining the problem, educating and motivating their neighbors and friends. Ultimately we influenced the legislature to pass our bills.

I appointed a bipartisan, statewide committee, reaching down to the thirty-seven representative districts of the state, with Democratic and Republican cochairmen in each. The district cochairmen's job was to help at least twelve people in each district become knowledgeable about the corrections problems and the proposed solutions to be defined by the campaign. They were commissioned to educate and motivate the state senator and representative in their districts. I anticipated that there would be strong opposition in the legislature, especially in the senate, to what we wanted to do. Since each senatorial district (nineteen senators) encompassed roughly two representative districts (thirty-seven representatives), we had assigned roughly twenty-four citizen activists to influence each senator. With this army I thought we would be able to gain the support of the legislature. This strategy proved fundamental to our success.

Earlier in 1961, the Prisoners Aid Society had asked Governor Elbert Carvel to establish a Governor's Committee for a State Correctional Program. He appointed Herbert L. Cobin, chairman of the board of the Prisoners Aid Society, as chairman of his committee. Governor Carvel supported our cause enthusiastically.

With financial support ($25,000) from the Delaware Citizens' Crime Commission, of which several Kiwanians (including me) were members, the Cobin committee was able to hire the National Council on Crime and Delinquency to make a professional study of Delaware corrections.

As president of the Three S Campaign, I appointed a seventeen member Technical Committee under Judge Thomas Herlihy, Jr., including Herbert L. Cobin and the top leaders of nearly all the public and private agencies in Delaware involved in correctional problems. Their assignment was to select the recommendations our campaign would adopt for implementation by state agencies and to draft the necessary legislation. We submitted our proposed legislative bills to Governor Carvel who accepted them and arranged for their introduction in the legislature in 1962.

Then we ran into trouble from four top figures from the majority Democratic party in the state Senate: Lieutenant Governor Eugene Lammot, who assigned our bills to unfriendly committees; Senator Curtis W. Steen, president pro tem; Senator Leon E. Donavan, majority leader; and Senator Walter J. Hoey, chairman of the joint finance committee, where several reform bills were buried. Governor Carvel could not influence these strong leaders of his own party. Two years later, thanks to our foresight in building effective activist groups among each legislator's constituents, we were able to obtain the 60 percent vote required by the legislature's rules to force our bills out of Senator Hoey's committee.

At this point, I must give credit to the tremendous, persistent support of the news media, especially *The Wilmington News Journal* papers. For three years they covered our efforts with frequent stories and dozens of favorable editorials.

The people of Delaware were particularly concerned about the way juvenile delinquents were treated. As James H. Snowden, chairman of the Delaware Youth Services Committee, stated during a 1961 Three S Campaign rally:

> Our state has had to handcuff together 14 year olds because our juvenile correctional facilities have no workable security rooms. Our state locks up older aggressive delinquents in the First Offenders Building of our adult prison, and literally throws away the key. Our state houses thirty to thirty-five delinquent youngsters in the three-story, 70 year old dormitories condemned by the fire and health authorities and puts one single man in charge of their custody, their safety, their behavior and their moral conduct.

The National Council on Crime and Delinquency joined the public debate. Its study of Delaware's *overall* correctional services gave the state low grades. Among the allegations they made were: all prison buildings were outmoded and overcrowded firetraps that endangered the health of the inmates; one parole officer, working out of a cubbyhole that also served as headquarters for the state parole board, was expected to supervise all parolees in the state; many inmates were imprisoned who should not have been; supervisory personnel in Delaware prisons were haphazardly chosen and often employed on a part-time basis; and nothing was being done for the rehabilitation of prisoners, either before or after release.

In 1964 I engaged in a running public battle with Senator Hoey. Once again he had managed to bottle up our bills in his committee. As reported by the Delaware news media, he claimed, "That Three S Campaign is just a pressure group. They're trying to run the state from the sidelines. After all, who is running this state?"

In a letter to the editor of the *News Journal* papers I responded, "The citizens of the state have always had the responsibility for running the state. What you have noticed recently is increased exercise of that responsibility. Yes, we are a pressure group—a broad based bipartisan group of citizens bringing the pressure of public opinion to bear on you elected officials to further a worthy cause."

I labelled Senator Hoey Public Enemy No. 1 to correctional reform in Delaware. This led to a much publicized luncheon to which I invited the senator. He continued to snicker at me and called me, "Just a do-gooder." When I told him that nearly all the people of Delaware now appeared to be do-gooders on this issue and he alone was blocking our legislation, he was quoted in the press as saying, "Who me? I'm not out to kill your bill. There's just one or two points in it that should be straightened out." But he could not tell me what the points were. He clearly enjoyed his power and revelled in flouting our program on the front pages.

I immediately called for a mass meeting of citizens to rally for action by the state senate. The response was terrific. Several hundred from all around the state jammed the Unitarian Church building in Newark. The immediate pressure on the Senate was tremendous. "Get that bill out of Hoey's committee," the people demanded.

That is exactly what happened. The Delaware Senate passed the bill and on July 8, 1964, Governor Carvel signed our bill (Senate Bill 323) into law at a gala luncheon of 500 people hosted by the Kiwanis clubs in the Hotel DuPont. The three-year-long bipartisan effort of thousands of Delaware citizens had come to a successful conclusion, and many major changes were made to reform the woefully inadequate system for handling juvenile and adult offenders.

Our correctional system had been generally considered to be among the worst in the nation, and the National Council on Crime and Delinquency's report had confirmed that belief. Rather than doing something to reverse the rapidly increasing crime rate, the system was contributing to the problem. Opportunities to save some offenders from returning to lives of crime were being ignored. Money was being wasted and forecasts of the costs of providing the same kind of inadequate treatment for a skyrocketing prison population were disturbing. A few people had been sounding the alarm for years, but the legislature and the community had not responded.

In the view of the National Council on Crime and Delinquency, the 1961–64 campaign established the basis for building "one of the most effective correctional systems in the nation." A new Department of Corrections was established. Under a legally specified, highly qualified Commissioner of Corrections, it was given responsibility for supervising the custody, rehabilitation, probation and parole of all adult offenders—functions previously handled separately. The diagnosis and treatment of those conditions which brought about criminal behavior was defined as the primary function of the correctional staff. For the first time all probation and parole personnel were required to fulfill certain education and experience qualifications. Probation and parole staff increased by 430 percent. Delaware's notorious practice of holding juveniles and adults in the same institution was terminated. The Youth Services Commission, which operated two training schools and a detention center for juveniles, was given a 47 percent increase in its budget so it could implement seventy-three National Council on Crime and Delinquency recommendations for improving its effectiveness. The commission was able to hire twenty-six highly trained and experienced college graduates to upgrade educational, psychological, psychiatric, and after-care services.

The total operating budget covering the custody and rehabilitation of juvenile and adult offenders was increased by 62 percent. A total of $7,750,000 ($41,500,000 in 1998 dollars) was authorized to build four new institutions. The family courts were moved to new quarters and provided with additional judges. The probation staff for juveniles was increased by 50 percent. However, abolition of the debtors prison had to wait for five years until, as governor, I led a successful effort to eliminate it.

Having accomplished its immediate objective, the Three S Campaign was disbanded, challenging Delaware citizens to maintain vigilance and build on the new foundation that had been established. Probably its most important contribution, however, was teaching Delawareans how to make democracy work—how to organize to bring sustained and effective pressure to bear on a legislative body opposed to acting on a critical community problem.

10

Neighborhood Improvement: Helping the Poor

Near the end of the three s campaign, henry b. dupont, Chairman of the Greater Wilmington Development Council, invited me to join its executive committee. GWDC was an organization of top community leaders dedicated to improving the area's economy, expanding its parking and transit facilities, beautifying its streets and parks, and enhancing its cultural activities.

My main contribution to the GWDC was to convince its members to take on an additional challenge—improving the quality of life for Wilmington's poor, of whom we had many. I developed a plan for providing better jobs, better housing, better health, and better education in three areas of 10,000 people each. Coincidentally, one of the areas was 100 percent black, one approximately 80 percent black, and one approximately 60 percent black. GWDC accepted my plan, raised the $475,000 required, and made me chairman of GWDC's Neighborhood Improvement Program.

We hired James Gilliam, Sr., an intelligent, articulate, neighborhood-savvy African American from Baltimore to head this work. He promptly developed good rapport with the neighborhood leaders and social service organizations. He better defined the most critical needs in the three areas, analyzed the adequacy of the public and private services being provided, and advised us what GWDC might do toward improving the situation. Jim and I spent many evenings together meeting in homes, churches, community halls, and the Walnut Street YMCA with residents of our three neighborhoods—getting to know, to some degree, many African Americans and, to a greater degree, the seriousness of their predicament.

During this period I spoke frequently around the community about "better living through better neighborhoods," paraphrasing

94

DuPont's slogan, "Better Things for Better Living Through Chemistry."

I spoke of the essential need for GWDC's Neighborhood Improvement Program to help people to help themselves and how, toward this end, we were markedly strengthening the existing neighborhood centers in the target neighborhoods. We needed, I claimed, to focus on helping children, especially preschool children, and cited irresponsible parenthood as a principal neighborhood problem. I called for more emphasis on family planning and for cooperation with President Johnson's War on Poverty, especially in finding jobs for African Americans. I cited examples of how some people in Wilmington's poorest neighborhoods were successfully fighting their way to a better education and raising their children to lead lives of dignity and value. These success stories were good reason for all citizens to have more confidence that our poorer neighborhoods could be improved.

We in GWDC learned firsthand how difficult it was to find jobs for young blacks. Most had tried repeatedly to find a job, been turned down time after time, and lost hope of ever finding one. Very few employers reached out to them. Prejudice against hiring blacks was obvious. And when a few young blacks were hired, they were the first to be laid off when an employer reduced his work force. This experience emblazoned on my mind the great injustice that occurs when a young man or woman reaches the age when he or she needs to earn a livelihood and cannot find a job. And when a major inhibiting factor in finding a job is the color of one's skin, the injustice is even greater.

This was—and still is—a major cause of crime in our society. I believe we should all ask ourselves, "What would I do if I desperately needed to earn a living and could not find a job legally? Would I be able to resist the temptation to bend or break the rules in order to make some money?"

We in GWDC made much of the need for more training, but training is an inadequate substitute for a job. One evening a young woman told me she was just finishing the third training session for which she had received a small government stipend. I asked her what she was going to do. She replied, "I'm going to sign up for more training. They never have a job for you at the end of your training session." How true that was! Providing jobs was, and is, the prime requirement.

A few years ago Irenée duPont, who served as chairman of

GWDC back in the mid 1960s, told a group at a large community gathering that I had *saved Wilmington* back in those years. This generous exaggeration stemmed from his conviction that the Neighborhood Improvement Program saved Wilmington during the mid 1960s from riots by young blacks that plagued many American cities at that time. (At a later date in 1968, Wilmington did have a one-day riot, triggered by Martin Luther King, Jr.'s assassination.)

Although our program did make some inroads, it was clear that much, much more needed to be done. Probably our most important contribution was in supporting and establishing centers staffed by neighborhood workers to furnish residents with easier access to services provided by the community for obtaining jobs, health care, better education, and improved housing.

Certainly the Neighborhood Improvement Program contributed to greater understanding of the problems in the neighborhoods and better relationships among many leaders—black and white. On a number of occasions, a dozen or so white leaders, including Irenée duPont, met in the test neighborhoods with a larger number of primarily young, black leaders. Some young blacks were initially quite hostile toward us, especially toward Irenée DuPont, who served as our lightning rod. He kept coming back, however. His persistence paid off, and their hostility was gradually replaced with constructive discussion.

I believe all of us went away from that experience more motivated and better equipped to use our authority and resources to help mitigate the social problems in Wilmington's poor neighborhoods. I know it influenced me when I was governor.

My main conclusion from that experience was that the community needed to provide many more opportunities for disadvantaged people to release their substantial potential for helping themselves, since this potential is the only national resource large enough to free them from their predicament.

11

Reorganizing Delaware's Republican Party

IN THE EARLY 1960S I BECAME INVOLVED IN THE ACTIVITIES OF THE Republican party. Soon I was deeply concerned about the gross inequity in the way delegates were allocated to the Delaware State Convention, the body that governed the state party and nominated all candidates for statewide offices. The party was divided into four districts: 1, Wilmington; 2, New Castle County outside Wilmington; 3, Kent County; and 4, Sussex County. The delegates were equally divided among the four districts, fifty delegates each for Districts 1 and 3, fifty-one for District 2, and fifty-two for District 4. This was irritating to the much more populous District 2 which, at that time, provided 55 percent of the Republican vote on election day. That was almost five times the Republican vote provided by Kent County, for example.

Reducing this inequity was no easy chore. Any decision to change the allocation of delegates would have to be made by the Republican Convention. And delegates from Kent, Sussex, and Wilmington would have to vote to give up a major share of their district's influence in state party affairs.

I travelled up and down the state, trying to sell delegates on supporting the change. A typical response came from a Sussex County delegate, who said, "You must be out of your mind, Peterson. We're not going to vote away our power."

Downstate Delaware, the area south of the Chesapeake and Delaware Canal, including Sussex and Kent Counties and southern New Castle County, had only 30 percent of the state's population, but had long dominated Delaware government. Approximately 70 percent of both the members of the legislature and the commissioners who then ran the executive branch came from downstate.

The U.S. Supreme Court's one-man-one-vote decision had recently corrected the inequity in the legislature, to the irritation of

many downstaters. This encouraged downstate Republican leaders to dig in their heels and fight further deterioration of their
power. At the same time, the District 2 Republicans were encouraged by the Supreme Court decision to extend the one-man-one-
vote principle to party affairs. They faced the fact, however, that
downstate delegates had the votes to control any reapportionment
of delegate strength.

To resolve this confrontation we knew we would have to appeal
to the sense of fair play among grassroot Republicans throughout
the state, encouraging them to lobby their local leaders to support
a more equitable allocation of delegates. I began to build a statewide organization with this goal in mind. It was headed by a committee of twenty-four prominent Republicans. Office holders
elected statewide agreed to help. They did not want to antagonize
the Republican power house in District 2.

Recognizing that it would be extremely unlikely, if not impossible, to gain the votes to base reapportionment of delegates
strictly on the basis of Republican voter strength as District 2
wished, we agreed on a compromise proposal to base 50 percent
of the delegate strength on a geographic basis (an equal number
from each district) and 50 percent on the relative number of
Republican voters. This was of major importance to achieving our
final results.

U.S. Senator John Williams from Sussex County was probably
the most influential Republican in the state. He was known
throughout Delaware as "Honest John" and in Washington as
"The conscience of the Senate." I went to see him in his ocean-
side summer home in Rehoboth Beach. He was very friendly and
promised to help influence the Sussex County delegation. I
thanked him and left thinking I had made a major coup that day.

At the next convention we introduced our resolution for reap-
portioning delegates, confident we had the votes to pass it. Before
the voting started, I received word that the Sussex County delegation was going to vote unanimously against the resolution. This
would sink us. Using a telephone extension on the convention
floor, I called Senator John Williams in his Washington office to
ask for his help. He asked me to bring the chairman of the Sussex
County delegation to the phone. I did so. After the chairman
hung up, he immediately called a secret caucus of his delegation.
When they broke up, one of the delegates told me that the chairman had announced that he had just spoken to Senator Williams,

who asked that they vote against any attempt to reapportion the delegates. That is what they did—unanimously. Our resolution failed.

Now we redoubled our efforts to appeal to Republican leaders' spirit of fair play. Harry G. Haskell, U.S. Senator J. Caleb Boggs, Walton Simpson, and Frank Grier played key roles in this effort. Of special importance was the help of John Rollins, Sr. John was a self-made wealthy businessman who had been a lieutenant governor of Delaware and a major financial supporter of the Republican party and its candidates for office. He spent many hours personally contacting his many friends around the state and gaining their support.

By the fall of 1964 it appeared we had the votes we needed, so we arranged for a special party convention to be held on December 14, 1964. This time the convention was harmonious. In spite of a few bitter speeches about how the northern part of the state wanted to dominate the party, and in spite of the need to convince a few delegates who were wavering about keeping their promise to vote for the resolution, the convention overwhelmingly voted for it. Clearly we had done our homework well.

Again it was demonstrated that when people are informed and organized, they can be counted on to do what is right. Unfortunately, my leadership in this cause gained me the enmity of a number of downstate Republicans. Their anger resurfaced a number of times in my subsequent campaigns for the governorship. In retrospect, however, the risk was worth taking.

IV
Governor of the First State

12

Getting Elected as a Political Newcomer

By the mid 1960s the Delaware Republican party was in a shambles. After the darling of Republican conservatives, Barry Goldwater, had been seriously trounced by President Johnson in the 1964 presidential election, many Delaware Republicans were disillusioned—conservatives because their man had been so badly beaten, liberals because the party's national convention had nominated such a conservative candidate. The principal donors to the Delaware Republican Party were especially unhappy and threatened to withhold their future support.

In the midst of this philosophical confrontation between conservatives and liberals, I intensified my public speaking about what I labelled "Reasoned Progression." It called for citizen action to define the most important community problems, analyze them, identify the best solutions, and then organize and provide the resources to get the job done.

This approach is no different from that applied in the free enterprise system when companies solve problems such as how to launch a new venture. Yet, when it is applied in the public arena, many self-styled conservatives from the business sector label it a "damn liberal program," and in the process disassociate themselves from contributing to the improvement of the community.

Can you think of a more liberal activity than launching new businesses such as manufacturing airplanes, automobiles, television sets, computers, or pharmaceuticals? What a major impact each of them has had on society, disrupting age-old practices, providing great opportunities, creating major social problems. Yet the captains of such major liberal ventures call themselves conservatives.

In 1965 I repeatedly spoke about the bad habit of labeling activities as liberal or conservative. At this juncture I was asked by several so-called conservative and liberal Republican leaders to

103

become state finance chairman and to do what I could to strengthen the party. Before this I had had only three assignments for the party. I had chaired the successful 1959–60 statewide effort to recruit new members; I had been a delegate for Nelson Rockefeller to the 1964 national convention in San Francisco; and I had led the highly controversial but successful reapportionment of delegates to the state convention.

I accepted the finance chairman position with the understanding that I would have complete charge of how the money was spent. Then I announced that money would be disbursed only by check, thereby stopping the long-term custom, heretofore practiced by both parties, of providing large sums of cash for use by local party leaders on election day—so called "walking around money." The big donors approved stopping this practice, but many local party leaders were outraged. They had previously received large amounts of cash that they passed out to their workers with no record of how the money was disbursed. Now each worker was paid by check and no money was available to pay people to vote for Republicans. Despite the initial animosity, by the time of the 1966 elections, we were able to build harmony in the party and raise the money we needed.

Now people started to talk more and more about my running for office. In the past when this subject had been raised, I promptly disowned interest. I was a scientist, still enjoying my challenging job with DuPont. I did not want to get into elective office. But now I found myself speculating on how much I might achieve on the major problems about which I was concerned if I had the authority of a major elective office.

One day in 1967, State Senator Reynolds duPont asked me to come to his home after work for a drink with him and another key Republican leader and donor, Harry G. Haskell, Jr. They told me they wanted me to run for governor in 1968, that they thought I was a better bet to get the liberal and conservative factions in the party to pull together than the others being considered, that my record as a citizen activist would draw considerable support from Democrats and Independents, that the fact I had never run for any political office before could be made into an asset, and that they would see that adequate funds were raised for my candidacy.

I went home and talked it over with Lillian. We considered that the governor's salary would be only one-third of my DuPont salary, and my job security would be much less than with DuPont. And then we decided to accept the challenge.

We also considered the impact of my decision to enter politics on our four children. Like most parents, we were very proud of our offspring and anxious that they have a satisfying life. Glen had graduated from college and was teaching art. Peter had left college and launched into his in-depth study of religion. Kristin was a senior in college. Elin was in sixth grade. We decided that if we handled a political career well, it could only enhance their lives. In any event, they strongly supported us.

Immediately I started to study how a relative unknown like me might get elected. I did not realize how few Delawareans knew about me. My statewide activities and the substantial publicity I had received made me think I was fairly well-known. But later, when a poll was run to check my name recognition against that of the incumbent, Governor Charles L. Terry, Jr., it showed he had 96 percent name recognition and I had only 9 percent.

Name recognition is very important in politics. Politicians like to say, "I don't care what you call me, but be sure you spell my name right." Moreover, Governor Terry had been a leading Delawarean for decades, holding nearly every key position in the Delaware Judiciary, and running for the governorship when he was chief justice of the Delaware Supreme Court. In contrast I was a long-term, prominent research director within the confines of the DuPont Company, for which I received essentially no publicity, and a volunteer activist on a few community issues.

I knew that I was not very popular among some party leaders. My involvement in party reapportionment had irritated downstate delegates. Many local leaders throughout the state did not like my having stopped the provision of "walking around money." Some were not enamored with my having headed the Three S Citizens' Campaign for prison reform which they saw as coddling prisoners. Many long-term office holders and contenders for political office did not like the idea of a newcomer vaulting over them for the choice political office in the state.

I decided to call upon my experience in organizing the Three S Campaign—by involving hundreds of people throughout the state, by reaching into every community. This would be separate from, but in addition to, the regular party organization. I called it People for Peterson and asked my two friends, Dr. Andrew J.

Knox and his talented wife Sally, to head it. Andy was a Research Chemist with DuPont. He and Sally were deeply interested in community affairs. We signed up many husband-and-wife teams, including many scientists and their wives, who were long-standing friends of mine. They were Republicans, Democrats and Independents, all volunteers. Nearly all of them had no prior experience in a political campaign, but they knew how to organize. They did a terrific job—raising money, enlisting workers, establishing People for Peterson headquarters around the state and producing campaign literature. Whole families became involved. The esprit de corps was great. Today, thirty years later, members of the team still talk of the exciting and rewarding experience they had. Without them I never would have won that election.

At first the regular party organization thought People for Peterson was infringing on their territory, but, as the months went by, they came to respect People for Peterson. After all, the regulars, too, wanted to win.

The harmony that resulted was due to the superb organizing and personal relations ability of William Campbell, the overall chairman of my campaign. He was a DuPont engineer and a friend whose abilities I came to admire when we worked together on an earlier statewide citizens' project. He pulled together all aspects of the campaign, working long hours strictly as a volunteer, with substantial help from his wife, Ginny.

My own family was a major help, especially Lillian. She spoke on my behalf at dozens of coffees, entertained hundreds of supporters, and advised me regularly.

Early on I travelled around the state, trying to gain the support of prominent party leaders. It was hard going at first, but eventually I signed up nineteen. Since I knew that such commitments early in a campaign could be quite fluid, I invited all nineteen to my home for a strategy session. I asked each one of them to comment on my candidacy. Everyone expressed strong support. Having done so openly in front of many of the party leaders, they appeared locked into my candidacy.

One of them was Robert Short, a prominent Sussex County farmer who had his own aspirations for the governorship. At a previous meeting with several local conservative Republican leaders in Brandywine Hundred, I told them Bob Short was behind me. They called me a liar, saying Bob was definitely going to run himself and they were going to support him. So I was pleased when, in the subsequent meeting in my home, Bob expressed his support for me.

Two weeks later, however, Bob publicly announced he was running for the governorship. His candidacy went nowhere, and in a few months he withdrew. No doubt his untrustworthy performance at my home in front of eighteen top Republicans hurt his campaign.

Conducting a statewide political campaign was expensive. My many volunteer supporters provided invaluable assistance, but could afford only modest financial aid, so I reminded Reynolds duPont and Hal Haskell of their earlier promises to help. They brought Henry B. duPont, Lammot duPont Copeland and Irenée duPont to the family room in Andy Knox's home, the headquarters of People for Peterson, where I presented a chart talk on what I would like to accomplish if I became governor. After I had answered a few questions, Reynolds announced that Hal and he had each agreed to raise $25,000 for my campaign and wanted the other three to do likewise. They all agreed and each subsequently raised the funds to fulfill his commitment. Without that funding, I doubt I could have won.

It is interesting to note that not one of them ever asked for a single favor when I was governor. And they all raised the same amount for my bid for reelection in 1972, with Emily duPont substituting for her deceased husband, Henry B.

John Rollins, Sr. also proved to be a major supporter. It did not start out that way, however. One evening at a cocktail party in his home, John made it known that he was going to support David Buckson for governor. John Rollins was a power in the Republican Party. He had been a lieutenant governor, had unsuccessfully run for the governorship, and had been a major financial supporter of party candidates and activities for years. He would control many votes at the convention that nominated the candidate for governor.

Dave Buckson himself was a perennial candidate for governor. He had run unsuccessfully four years before, had been lieutenant governor, had served eighteen days as governor when Governor Boggs resigned to be sworn in as a U.S. Senator, and now was running again.

During the party Lillian told off John Rollins, reminding him how many times I had helped him, had worked until 2:00 or 3:00 A.M. on his 1960 campaign for governor, and had taken on the difficult job of finance chairman at his request. When we returned home later that evening, Lillian received a call from Linda Rollins, John's wife. She said they wanted to come to see us the next morning.

Over a cup of coffee John told us he had changed his mind and he would support me. He did in a major way, both financially and in lining up delegates to support me at the convention.

Hal Haskell was another major power in the party. He had been Delaware's Congressman for one term and an unsuccessful candidate for governor. He had financed many candidates and party activities and was a popular candidate for mayor of Wilmington in 1968. As a result, he had the allegiance of the delegates from Wilmington to the State Convention. They, too, supported me. Consequently the nomination was easily won. Now we had to focus on beating the Democratic candidate, the incumbent, Governor Charles L. Terry, Jr.

My campaign was based on my ability to get people to work together and on the philosophy that people working together can solve almost any problem—provided they have the kind of leadership that helps them pull together. I promised leadership that would offer hope to all Delawareans for a better future— leadership that placed progress ahead of politics, opportunity ahead of opportunism, involvement ahead of indifference and faith in people ahead of fear of people. Working together we could make Delaware a model state in our nation.

This message was well received. Polls conducted by both the Terry and Peterson teams showed I was running ahead of Governor Terry. Then the biggest issue of the campaign began to dominate the contest—the National Guard's patrolling African American neighborhoods in Wilmington.

Frustrated black youth in Wilmington, like blacks in other cities, had found hope for a better future in the leadership of Dr. Martin Luther King, Jr. Some had gone to Washington to hear Dr. King's memorable address at the Lincoln Memorial and had come home singing, "We Shall Overcome." Then on April 4, 1968, Dr. King was assassinated by a white man and their symbol of hope was gone.

Five days later, on April 9 in Wilmington, Delaware, the growing anger of the young blacks burst into rioting, following the pattern set in major cities all over America. Homes and shops were burned in the rioters' own neighborhoods. Almost any governor

would have called out the National Guard, but would have removed them in one, two, or three days after the rioting was over,
as happened elsewhere in the country. But Governor Terry kept
National Guardsmen patrolling black neighborhoods in Wilmington for over nine months, the longest such patrols have ever been
used in America.

By mid-April I started calling on Governor Terry to remove
the National Guard. He adamantly refused, telling people that
young blacks had more guns than the National Guard. He predicted future rioting. Good friends told me they wanted the
Guard on patrol, that their safety depended upon it, and that
they were no longer planning to vote for me. Another friend told
me she was too frightened now to take her dog out for a walk at
night. A niece of the Delaware Superintendent of Police, driving
from Dover to a Young Republicans' meeting at which I was to
speak north of Wilmington, told me how her uncle advised her
to drive *around* Wilmington, because it was too dangerous there.

Fear spread throughout the state. Polls now showed I was ten
or more points behind Governor Terry. I decided to hit him
harder and harder on the issue, accusing him of spreading fear
and failing to solve our problems. Gradually I reduced the gap.
Then, one month before election, Terry had a mild heart attack.
Yet, he was back campaigning in ten days. What this meant to the
final outcome of the election, I do not know. Some people told
me they felt sorry for Terry and now would vote for him on that
basis, the so-called sympathy vote. Some certainly voted against
him because of concern over his health. But one other factor had
a major favorable impact for me during the last three weeks of
the campaign: my use of television.

In 1968 Delaware had no commercial television station. To use
television, a political campaign had to buy advertising time on one
or more of the Philadelphia channels—CBS, NBC and ABC. The
signals from these channels reached about 80 percent of the
homes in Delaware, and the cost per minute of advertising was
the same as for someone who wanted to reach all of metropolitan
Philadelphia. We decided to save our money for TV until the last
three weeks of the campaign when we would use a one-minute
ad and a five-minute story about the life of Russ Peterson.

Throughout the campaign, to get better known, I worked hard
at greeting people in shopping centers, at plant gates and at sports
events around the state. I always said, "Hello, I'm Russ Peterson.

Return Day, November 1968, Georgetown, Delaware. Winners and losers ride in parade two days after election. Courtesy of the author.

I'm running for governor. Hope I can have your vote." Most smiled, shook hands and moved on, probably wondering who I was. Some scowled and refused to accept my hand. A few said, "Get lost." It was unusual when anyone came over to meet me. But when my TV ads started running, I was a celebrity. People now gathered around me. "Saw you on television," they said. "It was great. Let me shake your hand."

This was an impressive demonstration of the power of television. It almost certainly had a positive impact on the voters. But I will never know the relative impacts of Governor Terry's heart attack, my TV campaign and my Fear and Failure attack on my opponent. In any event, I won by a small margin. And I even got known in Philadelphia.

One hour after I was sworn in on January 21, 1969, I ordered the National Guard removed from the streets of Wilmington.

The next four years were an exciting, rewarding, and productive period in my life. My hope as a citizen activist—that with the power of the governor's office I could lead the state to face up to

Peterson removes the National Guard from the streets of Wilmington. Jack Jurden, *The News Journal*, January 1969. Courtesy of the author.

some of its opportunities and critical problems—was fulfilled. Some people have considered those four years as one of the most progressive periods in Delaware history. Clearly much was accomplished.

In retrospect, I think several factors contributed to this. First, I consulted with community leaders and likely leaders of the incoming legislature. Then, using what I learned from them and what I had gained as a long-time student of state government, I developed an agenda for action before I was sworn in. I was strongly committed to it and determined to carry it out without worrying about its impact on my getting reelected.

My stellar staff, under the superb leadership of Chris Perry, and I enlisted thousands of citizens to help make Delaware a model state. We made volunteering for public service the *in* thing to do. And the leadership of both the senate and the house worked closely with us in the planning, selling, and passing of critical legislation. Fortunately, both houses and the governor's office were controlled by the same party, thereby minimizing partisan obstructionism.

Special attention was given to five areas: furthering educational opportunities, extending justice and equality to all Delawareans, reorganizing the executive branch, protecting the environment, and reducing the crime rate.

Funding by the state for education from kindergarten through graduate school was increased by 63 percent. Delaware Technical & Community College, which was started by my predecessor, was expanded from one to four campuses, thereby offering post-high school educational opportunities for 5,000 live-at-home students. The operating budget of the predominately black Delaware State College was increased by 125 percent and its capital budget markedly expanded. Its student body doubled. At the same time the University of Delaware increased the number of African Americans in its entering class from 1.0 percent to 7.6 percent.

Supplemental funding for school districts in low-income neighborhoods was provided for the first time. Kindergartens were established statewide. A Community Coordinated Child Care Program (4-C) was created and charged with maximizing effectiveness of public funds in early childhood education. The first special education programs to help children with learning disabilities were established. State funds were provided to Delaware Adolescent Program, Inc., to help unwed pregnant adolescents continue their high school education.

To help keep restive young people off the streets, I urged Delaware schools to unlock their doors and facilitate use of their indoor and outdoor facilities evenings and weekends by community organizations for educational and recreational programs for young people. Many schools did so, especially in Wilmington.

While national chairman of the Education Committee of the States in 1970–71, I became deeply involved in advocating expansion of vocational education. For this effort I received a special citation by the American Vocational Association.

We in Delaware markedly expanded our support for vocational-technical facilities in high schools, increasing the number of students involved sevenfold during my administration. We became the first state to fund efforts of vocational student organizations (FFA, FHA, DECA, VICA, DBC). As a result of this I was invited to speak in San Antonio on April 17, 1971, at the national convention of DECA (Distributive Education Clubs of America). What a thrilling experience! Over 5,000 students were present. They organized and ran the affair. The discipline and order they maintained in their hotels as well as at the convention center was impressive. And their pride in their vocational training shone brightly.

When I was introduced by their president, Linda Ford from Delaware, as the first governor to attend a DECA convention, I received a tremendous welcome—a beating of drums, a round of cheers and sustained applause. I had worried about speaking to so many young people, but now I felt at home. It was fun working with them. I had gone the more traditional path in receiving my education. Now I found these young people, upon receiving their diplomas, every bit as excited as I had been when I received my Ph.D. How good for America, I thought.

I recalled John W. Gardner's speech as secretary of health and welfare where he pointed out that if society continues to exalt the philosopher, no matter how shoddy his training, while scorning the training of plumbers, it will "have neither good plumbing nor good philosophy. Neither its pipes nor its theories will hold water."

Being interested in producing excellent philosophers too, we also strongly supported the University of Delaware. It was becoming a first-class university with a substantial private endowment. We increased its state funding by 60 percent in four years.

I personally worked closely with University Vice President George Worrilow in supporting expansion of the marine science program into the College of Marine Studies and the establishment of a major marine science campus on the Delaware coast at Lewes.

Convinced that Delaware could not afford its own full-fledged medical school, I worked with University President Arthur Trabant and the Delaware Medical Society to establish and fund the Delaware Institute of Medical Education and Research (DIMER). This institute allied with Jefferson Medical College in Philadelphia which agreed to accept an annual quota of students from Delaware. Within three years, seventy-six Delaware students were enrolled there. This move was calculated to alleviate the shortage of medical doctors in lower Delaware.

My administration's second major goal was to extend justice and equality to all Delawareans. For the first time African Americans were appointed to many key positions, including the state police force and the University of Delaware Board of Trustees, as well as the downstate magistrature. Better housing, more jobs, and service centers were provided in low-income neighborhoods. Open housing legislation was passed. The debtors' prison and the whipping post were abolished, and changes were made to provide more just and equitable treatment of offenders. Although Delaware's first merit system for state employees was established during the previous session of the Delaware General Assembly, my administration was the first to implement it. And, as described earlier, several changes were made to insure more equal opportunities in education.

My administration also reorganized the executive branch of our state government, brought much needed change to the criminal justice system, and played an important role at the dawn of the environmental movement—reducing air and water pollution, saving open spaces, implementing the nation's first comprehensive program for recovering solid waste, combining all natural resource and environmental control programs in a single department, taking the first enforcement case under the federal Clean Air Act all the way to the U.S. Supreme Court and winning. But our biggest contribution was passage of the Coastal Zone Act in 1971.

Delaware leaders paying respect to Caesar Rodney at Statuary Hall, U.S. Capitol, 1971. Mayor of Wilmington Harry Haskell, U.S. Representative Pete duPont, U.S. Senator Caleb Boggs, U.S. Senator William Roth, Governor of Delaware Russ Peterson. U.S. Senate Photo.

Russ and Lillian Peterson with King Gustaf VI Adolph of Sweden at Sofiero, his summer palace. *The News Journal*, William P. Frank, August 1971. Courtesy of *The News Journal*.

Governor Nelson Rockefeller campaigning in Delaware for reelection of Governor Peterson and U.S. Senator Boggs, 1972. Courtesy of the author.

Jack Jurden, *The News Journal.* **1972. Courtesy of** *The News Journal.*

13

Changing Delaware's Archaic Commission Form of Government to a Cabinet Form

Delaware's executive branch of government had always consisted of commissions appointed by the governor. By 1968 the
number of commissions had grown to 142, with a total of over
1,200 commissioners. Each commission consisted of five to twenty-
five members serving staggered four-year terms. It took a full,
four-year term before a governor could appoint all commissioners. These commissions were autonomous and could ignore the
governor, as they did from time to time. Each one selected its own
chairman from among its members and hired its own executive
director. Each appealed to the legislature and the governor for
funding.

Over the years several attempts to reorganize this inefficient
and unresponsive government had met with no success. In the
two-year period 1969–70, during only one session of the legislature, we changed this government to a streamlined cabinet form
with only ten departments, each headed by a secretary appointed
by and serving "at the pleasure of the governor," and confirmed
by the senate.

Overnight the governor's office was transformed from a weak
one to a powerful one. Since then the cabinet form of government
has performed well and been endorsed by successive governors,
legislatures, and the community at large.

The history of this major change in government provides a
good lesson in how the governor and the legislature working together can successfully plan, organize, and execute an effort to
resolve a major long-standing, controversial problem. Let me tell
you that story.

In 1960, during Governor J. Caleb Boggs's last year as governor,
he launched the latest of a number of attempts to reform the

executive branch. He called it, "A New Day for Delaware." It was the brainchild of Harlan Wendell, a public relations executive for the DuPont Company; Rodney Layton, a young lawyer; and Hal Haskell. The plan called for replacing the commissions with a cabinet.

Governor Boggs asked me to help find witnesses to testify before the legislature on the merits of his proposal. I first tried to convince several prominent chairmen of the larger commissions to testify. They refused, as they thought the commission form was excellent and did not want it changed. Each one liked chairing a commission. Furthermore, no one had consulted them about changing the government.

Then I tried to sign up some executive directors. They, too, were uncooperative. They did not want to buck the wishes of their commissioners, and in addition were afraid of losing their jobs in a consolidation of the commissions.

Eventually I signed up seven witnesses. Governor Boggs personally appeared before the legislature to present his program. Several legislators made it clear that they were opposed, because they would retain more power with the commissions than with a powerful governor. My witnesses were not well prepared. The legislators were quite rough with the governor. After all, the majority were Democrats, it was an election year, and Republican Governor Boggs was running for the U.S. Senate. His New Day for Delaware failed.

Having become convinced of the importance of reorganizing the executive branch, and having learned of some of the crosscurrents involved in doing so, I decided, eight years later when I was elected governor, to give high priority to creating a cabinet form of government. During the twelve weeks between election day and my swearing in, I developed a detailed plan of how to do this. Fortunately the Republicans had gained control of both the house and the senate. Those likely to be in leadership positions in both houses accepted an invitation to meet in my office, including Reynolds duPont, who would become president pro tem, and William Frederick, speaker of the house. I encouraged them to work together with me on the reorganization. They were pleased to be included in planning this effort. They agreed that they would establish a joint committee of the senate and the house on the reorganization of the executive branch. The president pro tem of the senate and the speaker of the house would be chairman and vice chairman respectively. In this way we could make sure that all of our legislative proposals would go to that committee, instead of to an uncooperative committee. They also agreed to authorize me to appoint a task force to prepare recommendations for the reorganization. We met twice more to consider the nature of a cabinet form of government.

A few weeks after I was sworn in on January 21, 1969, I invited the chairmen and the executive directors of all 142 commissions to meetings at the state conference center, Buena Vista. I told them of my plans to reorganize the government and asked for their suggestions and help. Several of them spoke in favor of the reorganization.

On April 25, 1969, the General Assembly created a Governor's Task Force on Government Reorganization, with members to be appointed by the governor. The legislation stated: "It is declared to be the public policy of this State that the commission form of government shall be abolished and a cabinet form of government shall be adopted so that the Office of Governor shall possess the supreme executive power vested in it by the Constitution of this State."

Then I issued an executive order appointing nine citizens to the task force representing both parties and all three counties. A Republican lawyer, E. Norman Veasey (now chief justice of Delaware Supreme Court), was made chairman and a Democratic lawyer, Charles K. Keil (later a family court judge), who had been a legislative assistant in Democratic Governor Elbert Carvel's administration, was made vice chairman. Robert L. Halbrook, Jr., Esq. was appointed executive director of the task force, which hired the University of Delaware's Department of Urban Affairs Under Staff Director Dr. James L. Cox for research and consulting support.

The task force was given specific dates for submitting reports to the governor, all calculated to permit completing the total reorganization before the end of the current two year session of the legislature on December 31, 1970. After the next election no one could be sure what the support in the legislature might be.

The leaders of the legislature established the Joint Legislative Committee on Reorganization, advising it to bring recommendations from legislators to the task force, receive legislation related to the reorganization, conduct public hearings on the proposals, and report its recommended legislation to the Delaware General Assembly.

It was of major importance that the overall reorganization not be called for in one piece of legislation, as Governor Boggs had done. Then the opponents of reorganization from all of the commissions being reorganized could bring the maximum lobbying pressure against the act. Accordingly I asked that separate bills be introduced for each department. We selected the largest department for the initial bill—Health and Social Services. It consolidated twenty-six agencies.

That this strategy was important was demonstrated when the Health and Social Services bill passed. Many people lobbied against this bill, nearly all connected with one or more of the twenty-six agencies being consolidated. As a result, the bill barely passed. But then, nearly all these lobbyists, who had little if any interest in the other agencies to be reorganized, gave up. They were replaced by a smaller group of lobbyists who worked against the next bill which created the Department of Natural Resources and Environmental Control. It consolidated only fourteen agencies and passed easily.

I signed the first two bills into law in 1969. The other departments were established, one by one, in 1970 with little opposition.

On August 5, 1970, the last of the new secretaries took the oath of office in Delaware's House of Representatives. Then my cabinet and I marched behind the Colonial Fife and Drum Corps to the new Townsend Building where the first cabinet meeting was held. *Wilmington News-Journal* columnist, William P. Frank, marked the occasion with a moving speech about the historical significance of that day.

During my four-year term I had the honor of sitting in the governor's seat before and after the reorganization. That seat became a lot hotter under the cabinet form of government!

Under the old setup, if the governor's office received a call from a citizen about a highway problem, the citizen was told the governor had no authority over that problem. The caller was told to contact the Highway Commission which met, for example, on the third Thursday of the month. But after the reorganization, the citizens knew the governor had the authority directly through his cabinet secretaries, so they expected action from that office.

Now the governor could act efficiently. To illustrate, let me relate an example. I had tried repeatedly under the commission form of government to get the superintendent of state police, who reported to the Highway Commission, to put some African Americans on the state police force. He claimed he could not find any who were qualified, and the chairman of the Highway Commission strongly backed his claim.

When the cabinet was formed, I told General Fred Vetter, the new secretary of Public Safety, to whom the superintendent of State Police now reported, that he would not receive any more funding for training sessions for new candidates to the state police unless the next class included six African Americans. Secretary Vetter reacted promptly; six well qualified blacks graduated with that first class.

After the cabinet was established, downstaters awakened to the fact that they had lost some of their earlier power. Under the commission form, Delaware citizens below the Chesapeake and Delaware Canal constituted 30 percent of the state population, yet occupied 70 percent of the seats on state commissions, including most of the chairmen's seats. Now under the cabinet form, each department secretary represented the whole state and served at the pleasure of the governor who was elected by the whole state.

Nearly everyone in Kent and Sussex Counties had a relative or friend who once served on a commission, a prestigious position in most circles. They did not like losing that prestige. This was probably the most significant factor in my getting clobbered downstate when I ran for reelection.

Today, twenty-five years later, there is general agreement that the cabinet form of government is far more effective than the commission form ever was. Certainly no governor would consider returning to the commission form now that he has the authority commensurate with the responsibility vested in him by the Constitution.

The risk in changing the government was well worth taking.

14

Saving Delaware's Unspoiled Coastal Zone

IN A WAY, DELAWARE'S COASTAL ZONE ACT BEGAN WITH MY SON, Peter, whose interest in birds proved to be contagious. Starting at the age of nine, while walking with his mother and me in the woods, Peter could point out the difference between a hairy and a downy woodpecker, a cardinal and a towhee, and could identify many birds by their songs. To further his interest, and at his mother's suggestion, I took him and his brother, Glen, on a tour of the Everglades. We saw sixty species of birds we never knew existed.

Soon our whole family became hooked.

On weekends or holidays we would be out early in the morning, binoculars at the ready, tromping through woods or strolling along a beach. Sometimes we made a game of seeing how many species we could identify in a given time. To find more birds, it became necessary to visit more habitats. We extended the range of our outings to the unspoiled wetlands, forests, bays, and rivers that make Delaware so special.

We also joined trips with expert ornithologists. As an inveterate organizer, I roped friends and colleagues into our sport. The competition escalated into a kind of Olympic Games each year, when we would roam up and down the Delaware coast, each individual and team striving to identify, by sight or by ear, the greatest number of species in a 24-hour period.

I remember one day in May 1984, between 4 A.M. and midnight, when I achieved my personal best, logging 153 different species of birds. Our marathon started in Cedar Swamp, where we heard and saw an amazing variety of warblers serenading each other. At Little Assawoman Bay we watched whistling swans fly twenty feet over our heads as they descended for a splashdown into the bay where they joined an assortment of diving and dabbling ducks. On Rehoboth Bay we watched birds going about their different

123

ways of making a living, the ospreys and terns hovering, diving, and then hitting the water; an osprey rising with a fish in its talons; a tern carrying the prize in his bill. We saw herons and egrets stalking their food in the shallows, and we watched a black skimmer skimming the surface of the bay, its lower mandible knifing through the water.

At Little Creek, a peregrine falcon power-dived to snatch a dowitcher in flight. At Port Mahon ruddy turnstones feasted on the eggs of horseshoe crabs. At Bombay Hook National Wildlife Refuge, two bald eagles soared overhead; at sundown, barred owls hooted in their imitable way, "Who cooks for you, who cooks for you-all?"

Canada geese in the thousands came honking in over the marsh, then dropped down to roost on the tranquil water or disappear in the spartina grass. Then we watched the aerial mating ritual of the male woodcock, and though it did not count in our bookkeeping, we saw a red fox move across the field. Before heading home we heard a great horned owl.

It was a memorable experience, and not only because I had identified more birds than ever before in a single day. We had been out in the fresh air from before dawn until after dark, amid natural beauty and wild creatures, exhilarated by the diversity of the life and the landscapes. On this and other birding adventures around the Delmarva Peninsula, we were struck with the richness of the region—the biological richness, and the wealth of recreational opportunities provided by our coast. We saw how many different ways people enjoy this captivating place where our continent meets the bay and the sea.

But we also saw things that concerned us. When you return to the same places over the years, you notice changes that are occurring—a marsh filled in, a forest cut down. Over time we noticed more *No Swimming* signs, more litter on the beaches and trash along the roadsides, more tar balls on the sand.

As birders, we became concerned about the use of pesticides by farmers, especially after reading Rachel Carson's *Silent Spring*. Over the years we saw fewer ospreys on our outings, then finally no ospreys at all. Rachel Carson had shown us the connection. Chemicals were poisoning the environment. The ospreys were on their way out, victims of the DDT that made their eggshells so thin that the eggs broke during incubation. Reproductive failure threatened extinction for this species, but the problem was not limited to ospreys. The threat was far more pervasive than that, extending to all living things, including *Homo sapiens.*

The more I became involved in watching birds and studying their behavior, the more I began to recognize something that another Peterson—Roger Tory Peterson, the dean of American birders—had discovered early on in his career. The birds serve as a barometer, measuring the health of our ecosystem. They are the indicators of environmental quality. When their health is affected, when their numbers diminish because of habitat loss and pollution—these cues tell us that our entire life-support system is hurting, and that we are all victims. Through birding I had come to see what a good thing we had in southern Delaware—a relatively unspoiled paradise in contrast to the heavily industrialized Delaware River in northern Delaware and Pennsylvania. I saw, as well, what an economic blessing our coasts and our bays represent.

Delawareans were not the only ones who enjoyed the quality of life of the Delaware shore. Tens of thousands of visitors came each year from Philadelphia, Baltimore, and Washington. Rehoboth Beach has been called the nation's summer capital because so many Washington-area residents vacation there, attracted by the peace and beauty, by the swimming, boating, fishing, hunting, and birding, as well as by the string of parks and wildlife refuges—in short, by the special quality of life.

Our coastline and deep-water bay together formed the state's number-one natural asset and, as such, also served as a magnet for heavy industry. In the 1950s, a refinery and petrochemical complex had been built by Getty Oil Company at Delaware City, thus spreading industrial development south of Wilmington to where the Delaware River widens into Delaware Bay. The Getty refinery produced a sulfur-laden coke that was burned in Delmarva Power Company's new electric-generating plant built close to the refinery, and which, in turn, emitted huge quantities of waste material—sulfur dioxide and particulate matter—into the air.

In 1961, the Shell Oil Company applied to New Castle County to rezone 5,000 acres of agricultural land the company had purchased for a refinery site farther south on Delaware Bay, at the mouth of the Smyrna River near Woodland Beach. The new Shell refinery would be built almost adjacent to the Bombay Hook National Wildlife Refuge.

Where crude oil is refined, other petroleum-related industries tend to move in, as they did in Delaware City. If Shell's new refinery were allowed, it, too, would become the stimulus for a complex of other industrial plants.

When Shell applied for a zoning change to the New Castle Levy Court (a legislative body despite its name), environmentalists organized to fight the move. The opposition was led by Edmund H. (Ted) Harvey, a conservationist who headed Delaware Wild Lands, Inc., a private organization that purchased land in order to preserve it. Harvey's new group wisely named itself Delawareans for Orderly Development (DOD) to show they were not against all development by any means, only that which undermined public values and destroyed the natural and cultural attributes of the region. It was a question of compatibility, and DOD declared that an oil refinery on Delaware Bay, in what was essentially virgin territory, would not be a good example of compatible land use.

But the county, to no one's surprise, agreed to the change. As county, city, and town governments usually do, they saw the refinery as a boon to the tax base and a source of new jobs for an expanding population—a population that would, however, expand much faster with a new refinery and industrial complex.

Next, DOD took its fight to the Delaware courts and lost there, as well. In 1962, the state's supreme court upheld the county's decision to alter its zoning to accommodate Shell. The battle had been lost, or so it seemed. Shell was free to build. Fortunately for the future of the Delaware coast, the company then decided to delay its building plans.

All I knew about the issue in those days was what I read in the paper. At that time most of my spare hours were taken up with our Three S Citizen's Campaign to reform the state's prison system. I might have sent $25 to DOD in response to a mail appeal; if so, that was the extent of my involvement.

For the rest of the 1960s, nothing very dramatic happened to the coast below Delaware City. But big plans were in the works by the time I became governor in 1969. Shell was about to drill water wells as a first step in construction. In addition to Shell's proposed refinery near Woodland Beach, three other oil companies had purchased three square miles of land at Big Stone Beach, just a few miles north of the Prime Hook National Wildlife Refuge. At that point, their plans were still secret.

Zapata Norness, a bulk shipping and storage company started by George Bush, who was then a Republican congressman from Texas, planned to build a 300-acre island in the bay, later to be doubled in size, where coal destined for world markets and iron ore shipped in for domestic markets could be stored. The hills of coal on the new island would be higher than the highest natural promontory in Delaware.

Unknown to me and most other Delawareans at the time, the U.S. Secretary of Commerce had been working quietly with a number of oil companies, and with Zapata Norness and other huge, ocean-going transportation companies, to make Delaware Bay the premier supertanker port and industrial center in the East. From industry's standpoint, it made good sense. Delaware Bay was one of the few bays deep enough, with a little dredging, to handle the huge new transport ships. Most of the existing refineries in the East were on the Delaware River, mainly in New Jersey and Pennsylvania. Most of the oil shipped to our Atlantic coast already came up our bay.

A few weeks after taking office, I met with the State Council on Planning. The council was considering what kind of a future was best for the state and what problems we ought to be facing up to. Such long-range thinking is rare in government, but it is obviously of paramount importance to the future generations who will inherit the natural bounty—or the ecological devastation—that we leave behind.

In addressing the council, I said:

> Concern yourselves with the kind of state we want to pass on to our children and grandchildren. We have two great opportunities right now, but we can't capitalize on both of them. They are incompatible. One choice is to participate in one of the world's most rapid industrializations, build a series of refineries and port facilities, and live with all the growth and benefits and problems they will bring. The other choice is to leave most of the coast as it is, so people can enjoy the hunting, boating, fishing and peace and quiet, the quality of life the coast now affords us. I believe the second way is the better way. But let's have a statewide discussion of the choices.

Governors usually embrace whatever new enterprise will produce new taxes and new jobs. They compete with one another to attract industry—any kind of industry—to their states. The kind of rapid industrial development that was about to come to Delaware would bring billions of dollars in investment to our state. Yet here I was, the new governor, questioning whether this was what we wanted.

That nobody took my musings very seriously is reflected in the news coverage of that meeting. The reporter who attended that informal affair wrote nothing about the choices I mentioned. The other subject discussed that day, the need to change the state's administration from an antediluvian commission form of government to the much more efficient cabinet form, a system that the federal government and most other states had long since adopted, was the only subject covered in the news story.

I cannot fault the reporter for this. My speculation about the future of our coast probably seemed no more than good intentions and wishful thinking. Yet of the two major initiatives of my term in office, government reform and coastal protection, it would be the latter—the law banning heavy industry from the Delaware coast and establishing state controls over all other industrial development in the coastal zone—that would be remembered more vividly and continue to be contested more than a quarter of a century later.

It is certainly true that the radical change in the way we governed the state had been fiercely resisted. But once it became law, and once the initial kicking and screaming had subsided, this change was broadly accepted, and from then on taken for granted as the right way to go.

My proposal that we protect rather than industrialize our coast received almost no public attention during 1969, my first year in office. Privately I studied its ramifications and developed a plan of action. In January 1970, in the Governor's Future of the State speech to the legislature, I spoke of my intention to develop a master plan for the coastal zone.

Then I took a big step, one that some advisers said I had no right to take and which would get me in trouble. By executive order, I called a moratorium on all new industrial development in Delaware coastal areas, including the refinery Shell was ready to build. My only authority here, it turned out, was the power of public support for the new governor's leadership. No one challenged it.

The moratorium would remain in effect until my task force on Marine and Coastal Affairs, whose creation I also announced to the legislature, had completed its report. The task force would study the situation and come up with recommendations about how we could better protect our coast.

From what I had learned as a citizen activist, I knew several steps must be taken to change the status quo in a way that benefits the public. As early as possible, it is important to get influential political leaders in your corner. For example, to work for change at the state level, it helps to get the governor on board as early as possible, and this is usually accomplished through citizen pressure. In this case we were lucky, since the governor was clearly on board from the outset. But I also needed to involve the leadership of the house and senate, to bring them into the process before the task force reported and legislation was drafted.

In such a campaign it was also likely that we would need to raise money, assemble good data on which to base our case, rally a variety of citizen groups behind our cause, and get ample press coverage and strong editorial backing from the news media. Therefore, my next step involved raising the money to cover the cost of the task force and the salary of a distinguished chairman. Fundraising is essentially a matter of arguing persuasively to the right person. In this case, the person was Baird Brittingham, a Delaware financier and conservationist, and at that time chairman of the Oceanic Foundation which was building a kind of Sea World in Hawaii. Dr. James H. Wakelin, a distinguished oceanographer and research scientist I had known from my DuPont days, then worked for Baird as president of the foundation. I knew he would be the perfect chairman for my task force. Jim agreed and so did his boss who generously provided Jim's services to the state of Delaware for $1 a year. Baird also agreed to raise $100,000 to help finance our study.

The first hurdle had been cleared. The task force, with staff and volunteers in place, included a terrific executive director named Amor Lane, also on loan from the Oceanic Foundation; a blue ribbon board that included William Gaither, dean of the new College of Marine Studies at the University of Delaware (who several years later would join with industry to attack the Coastal Zone Act); Ted Harvey, the champion of orderly development who led the earlier fight to keep the coast refinery-free; Austin Heller, head of the state's new Department of Natural Resources and Environmental Control (DNREC); and David Keifer, the state planner.

With this stellar starting lineup, the study began. And with the moratorium in place, the pressure was temporarily off the coast. We were a little surprised, however, that nobody had yet challenged this edict. ("You're nuts," is what some of my colleagues told me when I decided to impose it. "By what authority," they asked, "can the governor ban all new industry on the entire coast of a state for at least a year?") No such action had ever been taken anywhere else that we knew of.

If my own staff resisted that step, then why was there no resistance from the powerful interests affected by the moratorium and by whatever controls might stem from the study? Why did Shell, DuPont, Zapata Norness, and the whole gamut of heavy industry interests waiting in the wings remain quiet?

I think, in part, they were reassured by my background. I had been at the DuPont Company for twenty-six years, deeply involved in research, manufacturing, and sales. I had gone almost overnight from my last assignment at DuPont, identifying and launching new business ventures for the company, to undertaking new ventures for Delaware as its Republican governor.

So far, at least, DuPont and the rest of the state's industrial establishment looked upon me as one of their own. Throughout 1970, as the task force gathered its data, there was little public debate on the issue, and no noticeable opposition. Business and industry had, for the time being, adopted a "wait and see" attitude.

The Confrontation Begins

That attitude changed abruptly on January 3, 1971. The occasion was my third Future of the State message. I explained that the task force would be submitting its report within a month and that the findings seemed to point in one direction. I told the legislature I would be pushing for passage of a Coastal Zone Act prohibiting all new development of heavy industry in the coastal zone that the task force had delineated as roughly two miles wide and 115 miles long, covering the shores of Delaware Bay, the Atlantic coast, and the little bays on the leeward side of Delaware's barrier islands in the south.

At that point the battle lines were drawn. I would now be regarded, by many influential people in Delaware, as a traitor to my former employer, to the industrial world from which I had sprung, to my political party, and to the president of the United States (the Nixon administration would oppose our efforts). In view of at least some of the president's men, I would be considered disloyal to the country.

On February 9, the executive committee of the Delaware State Chamber of Commerce voted unanimously to oppose our initiative. All the major companies in Delaware were represented on the executive committee, including DuPont, Hercules, General Motors, and Atlas. Max Colson, the Chamber's president, wrote to me expressing their opposition. A permanent ban on heavy industry would, he said, stifle the economy, deprive a growing population of needed employment, and give the state a reputation of being antibusiness.

I worked hard on my reply to the Chamber, staying up until 2 or 3 A.M. for the next couple of nights, applying pen to pad, writing, crossing out, searching for the right detail, trying to be factual and reasoned and hard-nosed because I was writing to business leaders. But as I wrote I also knew that it was the *emotional* appeal of our proposal that would gain the public support we needed to counteract the tremendous power then coalescing against us. We *had* to convince all concerned that this was our last opportunity to preserve the natural beauty and wildness and way of life we cherished. We *had* to make the Chamber believe it would be a great legacy to our children and our children's children.

We had already stated the many reasons for protecting our coast, but we had not yet pulled them together into one coherent statement. How clearly and convincingly we did this now would make all the difference. Moreover, we had to be absolutely un-equivocal on one key point: we favored *both* business and environ-mental protection. By preventing our coast from being destroyed by shortsighted development we were preserving, instead of fore-closing, future options; by controlling industrial development in the coastal zone, we were helping, not hindering, the state's econ-omy; by encouraging tourism and recreation and compatible de-velopment, we were fostering the creation of more, not fewer, jobs.

My letter to Max Colson ended up to be five pages, single spaced. Looking back, it was obviously worth the effort. But mak-ing our case in writing to our chief critics was not enough. To influence events, the letter had to reach a much wider audience than the Chamber of Commerce, and in this cause the news media fully cooperated. *The Wilmington Morning News* ran the letter in its entirety (February 17, 1971) starting on the front page, and columnists and editorial writers praised our position.

We also had to make clear that our bill, which had yet to be drafted, would not prohibit all industry from the coastal zone, as my moratorium did. The bill would ban new heavy industry, to be defined in the bill, and it would ban offshore terminals that would turn Delaware Bay into a major port for supertankers. All other industrial uses would be allowed so long as they were *compatible*—a key concept—with recreation and tourism. Expansion of existing heavy industry would also be allowed, within certain limits.

The letter made a point that cannot be made too often: a wild, beautiful, healthy, unpolluted shoreline will help maintain a quality of life that will attract desirable economic growth and provide the best kind of jobs.

"I am well aware of the need to provide an adequate number of jobs for our growing population," I wrote Max Colson. This can be done "both through the expansion of our present enterprises and the attraction of additional ones."

"We have much to offer new businesses," my letter continued. That means "we can and must be selective in attracting those which can contribute the most to Delaware. Jobs are very important to our people. But so is the overall quality of our environment—and not just the quality of our air, water and land, but also the quality of our life."

If I were writing that last sentence today, I would be even more emphatic about the link between jobs and the environment. Too often, the issue is represented as jobs *versus* the environment. If we preserve our rivers and bays and Atlantic coast for recreation, we can have more employment. I would have also emphasized, as I did later in my reelection campaign, that heavy industry is highly mechanized and provides a relatively small number of jobs.

I also knew it would be helpful in making the case for coastal zoning or in any other effort to protect or restore biological health, to put the issue in perspective: to call attention to how much has been lost and how little remains, to draw the line and refuse to let happen here what has happened elsewhere.

My letter put it this way:

> We have in Delaware a unique and very valuable asset in our ocean and bay fronts and their accompanying wetlands, streams and open

spaces. Delaware is a very small area of 2,000 square miles, which is only 5/100 of 1 percent of the United States. It is a playground for millions of people from our neighboring states. It provides us with one of our most profitable industries—tourism—and great enjoyment for our own people.

We have been fortunate that man has seen fit to ignore most of our little peninsula, leaving it pretty much in its natural beauty.

But now our turn has come!

Strong economic forces in our modern world point to Delaware Bay as the most attractive place on the East Coast for building a major transportation and industrial complex. The operators of the huge marine vessels now being built around the world to provide low cost transport for oil, coal and iron ore find that Delaware Bay offers the best deep-water port on the East Coast. A consortium of the largest oil companies in America wants to build a huge artificial island on which to unload oil to feed existing refineries and the seven new ones required in the East in the next 10 to 20 years. Shell is currently scheduled to break ground in 1973 for the first of these on the 5,000 acres it owns near Smyrna.

Zapata-Norness, Inc. has requested permission to build an island in the Bay on which to store millions of tons of coal for transshipment to Europe and Asia. Subsequently, they would like to enlarge the island to several square miles to store mountains of iron ore for transshipment over a causeway to the mainland to feed steel mills.

What do you think would happen on the wide-open undeveloped lands along our Bay with, in effect, a coal mine, an iron ore deposit and a river of oil at their front door?

Our bay and rivers would be lined with refineries, steel mills and allied industries, converting what we now have to the Marcus Hook-to-Philadelphia pattern. Does the State Chamber of Commerce really think Delaware will be better off as a result?

One of the most compelling arguments for protecting a particular place or way of life is to compare it with another place nearby which once shared these same attributes but has now been overwhelmed by *progress*. To make this point, I suggested to Mr. Colson that, "some summer day you take all of your board of directors on a helicopter flight from Fenwick Island (at the southern tip of the Delaware coast) to Philadelphia and back. I will be surprised if anyone steps out of the helicopter not anxious to work with me to keep our bay and adjoining areas below the Chesapeake and Delaware Canal free from the industrial complex now proposed to be planted there."

If anyone did not get the message after that experience, I suggested, there was something wrong with them.

Now we needed to present a desirable alternative and a happier vision of the future. If we were going to oppose business as usual, we had to *propose* something better in its place. By taking a protective approach to our coast, and by working with our neighboring states to do the same, I argued, "we can clean up the Delaware River and its tributaries so that by 1980 the Delaware Bay can once again be lined with fishing, boating, and picnicking areas, and thousands of Philadelphians and Wilmingtonians can come by river steamer to enjoy a day in the open and spend their tourist dollars here."

I acknowledged that refineries and steel mills are important, but so are recreational areas: "The key question is not whether refineries, for example, are good or bad, but are they the best use for the land involved?"

The time had come to make a choice. "We are heading full steam ahead toward the industrial complex. Without prompt action, this choice will win by default. I intend to do all I can to lead the State into preserving the bulk of our Bay and coastal areas for recreation and compatible commercial and industrial uses."

The letter then responded to the accusation that ours was an antibusiness proposal. "You imply in your letter that Delaware's image as a home for new industry has been damaged by my position. I don't believe this. On the contrary, I am confident that my position will strongly encourage most industry and businesses to want to come to Delaware. We intend to make this (our unspoiled coast and related quality of life) one of our principal selling points in attracting selected industry."

The Chamber of Commerce had charged me with "extreme discrimination" against refineries and other heavy industry. Now I turned that argument around: "To fail to do what I propose," I told Mr. Colson, "would be discrimination against the people of Delaware. I have been elected to represent their interests to the best of my ability."

The letter concluded with a list of the various forms of economic activity that should be promoted—agriculture, transportation, corporate headquarters, research facilities, auto assembly plants, breweries, industrial parks. We needed to capitalize on all of our natural and man-made assets to plan our economic future.

I reminded Mr. Colson that, "our favorable corporation laws, attractive living environment and expanded educational training make our state a good bet to attract such enterprises."

"We have much to offer," the letter concluded. "We can afford to be selective."

Though the Chamber's executive board had voted unanimously to oppose us, that did not mean that everyone in the business community would be against the Coastal Zone Act. Privately, many business leaders and partners in the law firms that were representing the oil companies, and particularly their spouses, believed in what I wanted to do. At a social function it was not unusual for the wife of a business executive to tell me to "keep up the good work" on behalf of *our* coast. She and many others knew what I knew: that her family, along with most other families in Delaware, present and future, would be the beneficiaries.

A week or so after my letter was sent to the Chamber of Commerce, a copy was circulated among executives in the DuPont Company. Years later, a friend of mine at the company came across the letter and sent a copy to me. Scribbled in the margins were notes from those executives to C. B. McCoy, the company's president, to help him decide what public position (if any) DuPont should take on the issue.

The comments revealed the soul-searching that went on behind the scenes. The coastal-zone issue had the makings of a popular cause, and DuPont, justifiably proud of its reputation as a good corporate citizen in Delaware, was reluctant to take a position that could tarnish its image.

"This is one of the best letters I have ever read," wrote one reader. "I endorse the contents wholeheartedly!"

A division manager wrote: "Superb letter. Do *not* agree with view we should avoid being involved. Instead, think we should get DuPont into picture via positive suggestions, responsive to the Governor's request. As for appearing to cop out on the Chamber's position, the quicker we do that the better."

Another wrote in the margin, "Letter is a political winner. Whatever happened to our stand on major public issues?"

The assistant general counsel was more cautious: "The Governor's position as outlined in this letter appears rather strong. I am still of the opinion that if we can avoid being involved, we will be much better off in the long run."

The head of the Public Relations Department agreed: "We believe DuPont should stay as far away as possible from this controversy and we hope you can avoid comment."

In 1971, I received no word from the DuPont Company, pro or con, on the Coastal Zone Act. I learned, however, that DuPont was being pressured by the oil companies to join the attack on our proposal. The oil companies were important customers of DuPont's lucrative tetraethyl lead, which was added to gasoline to prevent "knocking." And DuPont was a principal customer of the oil companies, as it depended on hydrocarbons for making chemicals.

A few days after I wrote to the Chamber of Commerce, Shell's president, Denis Basil Kemball-Cook, came to see me in my office in Dover. He was about 65 years of age, white-haired, and had a wonderful smile. It was easy to like him.

I remember how he complimented me on Delaware's great environment and commended me for what I was doing to protect it. He acknowledged that oil companies had done a poor job of designing refineries in the past. Then he tried to convince me that Shell knew how to build a clean refinery. "It won't harm your environment, Governor," he said.

I thought of when I was put in charge of developing Dacron for DuPont and how proud I was of the heavy-industry facilities we built. And I remembered when, as a young chemist, I visited modern chemical plants. They looked beautiful to me, especially at night with the lights on their high stacks. I could understand how the president of Shell felt about his state-of-the-art refineries.

I told him I shared his enthusiasm for building cleaner refineries. But I explained that even the cleanest and most modern refinery would not be compatible with our undisturbed coast. An oil refinery just did not belong in a beautiful, undisturbed natural area that was best suited for recreation and wildlife. And a refinery, because it was growth-inducing, was just the beginning. I explained that such development diminished our potential for tourism, also an important industry in Delaware. I suggested he consider expanding existing refining facilities to get whatever future capacity might be needed, rather than encroach on virgin territory in our coastal zone.

He replied that his company had spent many millions of dollars to prepare to build a refinery in Delaware—that for the past ten years they had been working in and out of the courts to gain permission to build, and now when they had all the permits they thought they needed, Delaware said *no*.

Clearly he was trying to convince me to change my mind.

I said I was sorry, but the answer was still *no*.

At about that time the Commercial Development Association (CDA) honored me at a black tie dinner in the Waldorf Astoria Hotel in New York City. They had decided to give me their annual award for the work I had done at DuPont in launching new business ventures. (CDA consisted of large industrial companies, of which DuPont was an influential member.)

It seemed ironic that Russ Peterson, the maverick Republican governor who intended to ban heavy industry from the Delaware coast, should be honored by this group. I figured their decision had been made well before my January speech to the legislature, by which time it was too late to change their minds and give the award to someone else.

At the reception preceding the dinner, I found myself surrounded by oil-company executives. Basically they were complaining about what we had been doing in Delaware. They were all trying to talk me out of my opposition to their plans for the Delaware coast. I proposed to them, as I had to the president of Shell, what seemed a better alternative: "Why not increase the capacity of your existing refineries on the Delaware River? If you do that, you won't have to build in an unspoiled area." I told them that at DuPont we had doubled, tripled, and quadrupled capacities in some of our existing plants rather than build new ones.

In the end, that was what these oil companies did. When higher gas prices forced the country to conserve energy, the predicted demand for petroleum never materialized. Years later, at a conference in Texas, where I was criticized for my actions in Delaware, I pointed out to my oil company critics, whose refineries were then operating well below capacity, that they should pay Delaware a bonus—a percentage of what they saved by not building new refineries there—for keeping them from wasting their money.

At the CDA dinner I sat at the head table next to Edward Heston, the president of Cities Service Oil Company. I knew that his company, along with two others, had purchased 1,800 acres at Big Stone Beach where they planned to build a refinery. What I did not know, and what Mr. Heston told me that night, was that Cities Service had also formed a consortium with a dozen other oil companies. Their intent was to build refineries up and down the coast and to construct a huge floating dock, six miles out in the bay, to berth supertankers bringing crude oil to the region. Two pipelines would run the crude oil to the shore, where the consortium planned to build a storage tank farm from which onshore pipelines would feed the petroleum to refineries.

Mr. Heston explained this would be an economic boon to my state and in the best interest of the people of Delaware, and he hoped I would reconsider my position. But I knew it would be Delaware City all over again, this time where the river opened into the estuary near the Woodland Beach Wildlife Area and the Bombay Hook National Wildlife Refuge.

It was hard to enjoy my big night in the big city with all the lobbying going on.

Edward R. Kane, the vice president of DuPont who became president two years later, introduced me. He generously praised my work with his company and as governor, including my "progressive work in pollution control." But he did not mention the controversy with the oil companies. Later in the evening, I noticed oil company executives in vigorous discussions with Ed, but in our own talks together that evening, neither he nor I raised the issue.

Back in Dover, I received a call from Michael R. Naess, president of Zapata Bulk Systems, Inc., an affiliate of George Bush's company. He had just given a speech to the Delaware Chamber of Commerce about his plan to build a 300-acre island for coal transfer in Delaware Bay. The company planned to spend $160 million. He told me that the Delaware Chamber thought his plan was a good one, that his proposed island might fall outside the proposed coastal zone. He asked to come to see me.

"Certainly you may come to see me," I told him. "But you should know that I am completely opposed to bulk product transfer along our coast. We intend to prohibit it. I don't think you have a chance of building an artificial island in Delaware's best fishing grounds."

He decided not to meet with me.

That February, the Building and Construction Trades Council of Delaware, an AFL-CIO affiliate, came out in favor of Shell's proposal. Although a modern refinery hired few people once it was going, the construction project would provide thousands of jobs. The workers, hard hats in place, picketed the next morning in front of the governor's house. As I waved to them on my way to work, they scowled and booed. Later that morning Lillian and her housekeeper, Florence Crossan, took trays of coffee and donuts to the men. They were much more friendly to the women. Nearly everyone had a snack, and then they all left.

Having labor as well as management against us strengthened our opposition. To counteract the impression that working people opposed strong coastal protection, we needed to persuade some other unions to speak out on our side. Our best bet seemed to be the United Auto Workers.

The UAW had worked against me in my 1968 election campaign. When I visited Chrysler and General Motors plants, the workers would not even shake my hand. They seemed to assume that because I was a Republican and a former DuPont executive, I would be unsympathetic to their interests. But what could be more in their best interests than preserving Delaware's greatest recreational asset? Knowing as well that Walter Reuther, the national head of that union, was a man of foresight and liberal views, I sensed that the UAW would be a natural ally in our cause.

So I called the union and talked with the man in charge of environmental programs. That someone there had such a title was already a good omen. The environmental director seemed pleased that a governor would take the time to call him. He said he thought our plan was terrific. It would, he agreed, protect the natural resources for workers and their families, most of whom enjoyed the kind of pleasures provided by an unspoiled, unpolluted coast. Even though most UAW members could not afford to live near the beaches, they could still benefit from their glory. The ocean and the bays were for everyone to enjoy—and anyone who lived in Delaware was never very far from the water.

It is satisfying to recall that during my reelection campaign, when I greeted UAW workers at the gates of the Chrysler and General Motors plants, their leaders stood in line with me and every man shook my hand.

I also contacted AFSCME, the American Federation of State, County and Municipal Employees, a large and potent organization. As with the UAW, it did not take much convincing to involve them in our campaign. They were well aware that protecting the coast protected the interests of their members.

It felt like my old volunteer days with the Three S Campaign, only now instead of prison reform it was environmental protection, and instead of being a volunteer citizen organizer, I had the advantage of sitting in the governor's chair. This seemed a reversal of the way things usually worked, when citizens rallied to put pressure on the governor and other political leaders to force them to act in the public interest. Now the governor was going all out to mobilize the citizens. For me, those hectic, heady days of 1971 were an activist's dream come true!

I contacted the Delawareans for Orderly Development, who had mobilized against Shell a decade earlier, and they were soon back in action, reconstituted under the leadership of cochairmen Elbert Carvel, a former governor and staunch conservationist, and Mrs. Clement W. Theobald, mother-in-law of my son Peter.

Wisely, they invited an equal number of prominent Republicans and Democrats to join their board, an indication that the future of the Delaware coast was a bipartisan concern.

Ted Harvey's Delaware Wild Lands, the Sierra Club, and a fishermen's group, added their voices. I asked leaders of the American Association of University Women and the Federation of Women's Clubs to meet in my office; they, too, agreed to support the initiative.

As part of my effort to involve young people in government, I had created the Governor's Council on Youth, made up of outstanding high school and college students. The group had grown from fifty students to well over 300, with a full-time, paid director whom the students had the final say on hiring.

Now I told them I needed their help. It seemed a perfect issue for these eager young idealists, coming in the wake of the first Earth Day, at a time of growing interest in ecology and growing national awareness of the need to protect our air, land, and water.

Many of these students did become active in the campaign for the coastal zone. They raised money from merchants (many of whom officially opposed our initiative as members of the Chamber of Commerce) to print brochures promoting coastal protection. As the legislative session progressed, the students became keen lobbyists, helping to counterbalance the oil-company lawyers working on the other side. It was heartening to see young citizens caught up in this issue, handing out literature and talking with legislators, but I must admit to wondering sometimes if they were skipping school.

In April the Task Force on Marine and Coastal Affairs released its preliminary report. They had done pioneering work, analyzing the biological, cultural and economic significance of the Delaware

Coast. For the first time our state government was taking a careful look at what we had, what was at stake, and how we could capitalize on our resources in a way that would benefit Delaware residents far into the future. Though the phrase had not yet been coined, what we were after was *sustainable development,* the kind that uses our resources without using them up, that meets the needs of the present generation without shortchanging the future.

The report provided a solid, scientific basis for the impending legislative battle. In its summary, the task force went right to the heart of the matter: "It is widely believed that the existing development along the shores of the upper Delaware River from the Chesapeake and Delaware Canal to Philadelphia exemplify the ultimate fate of substantial portions of the shoreline from the canal to Cape Henlopen—*unless a rational program for land and water use is instituted.*"

In some passages, the task force appealed to the emotions as well as the intellect, as it set the scene in poetic terms. "Only those people who have directly experienced the wetlands that line the shores of our bay can appreciate their mystic qualities. The beauty of rising mists at dusk, the ebb and flow of the tides, the merging of fresh and salt waters, the turmoil of wind and weather—all unite to create an environment that man has only superficially explored."

The task force unconditionally recommended that the coastal zone be dedicated to active and passive recreational use and be compatible with other uses of an agricultural, commercial, industrial, or educational nature. They emphasized that development of a deepwater port in Delaware Bay would lead inevitably to development of an incompatible heavy-industry complex and the potential for catastrophic spills. As an alternative they recommended that the state help local communities develop additional recreation areas and shoreline access in order to provide adequate public facilities for tourists.

The task force recommended against any more heavy industry in a narrow area extending the full length of the coast, and it recommended against the approval "at the present time" of any deepwater port facility or offshore islands.

The Coastal Zone Bill, soon to be drafted, would strengthen that recommendation by prohibiting heavy industry and artificial island terminals not only at the present time but perpetually, for as long as the statute prevailed, by setting up a permit system to

help determine what future industrial development, other than
flatly prohibited uses, might be carried out in the coastal zone.

The Legislative Phase of the Campaign

In January 1971, I assigned my counsel, Fletcher (Sandy)
Campbell, Jr., to write the Coastal Zone Bill. He was assisted by
David Kiefer, the state planner who had worked closely with the
task force.

We knew the statute had to be carefully crafted to survive the
legal challenges that lay ahead. It had to be clear, simple, and
tightly written. Because certain kinds of industry had never before been blocked from a state's coastal zone, we knew that such
a law would be attacked as unconstitutional.

Heavy industry had to be carefully defined and the coastal zone
precisely delineated. The bill would allow heavy industry to expand where it presently existed, subject to the controls of a permit
system. Other kinds of industry could locate in the coastal zone—
subject also to permit requirements.

As the bill explained, this was a balancing act. "While it is the
declared public policy of the State to encourage the introduction
of new industry into Delaware, the protection of the environment,
natural beauty and recreation potential of the State is also of
great concern."

Andrew Knox, a new member of Delaware's House of Representatives, sponsored the legislation. Andy was a research chemist
and former DuPont colleague. He and his wife, Sally, had headed
the citizen group, People for Peterson, which helped to get me
elected. Now Knox and the house leadership lined up twenty co-
sponsors, a majority of the thirty-nine-member body. The legislation was introduced as House Bill 300 on May 12, 1971.

Republican leaders in the legislature swung into action. President pro tem Reynolds duPont in the senate and Speaker George
Hering in the house, both of whom I had consulted while planning the legislation, worked in their caucuses to persuade colleagues. They negotiated several clarifying amendments, one of
which placated the county governments who were initially opposed to the bill because they feared it preempted their zoning
authority. The amendment made clear that the only place their
zoning power would be superseded by the state involved the ban

on heavy industry; the counties would be involved in the permitting process for any other industrial development plans, and other land uses (commercial, residential, resort) would continue to be locally controlled.

Two future governors supported the bill—Michael N. Castle, who played a key role as a member of the state senate, and Pierre S. duPont IV, then in his first term as congressman from Delaware.

Next, the legislature held public hearings around the state. A strong showing at these meetings was crucial to our success. The state's lawmakers, many of whom tended to side with the wealthy corporate interests, needed to see that their constituents—the people who elected them and had the power to remove them—wanted this bill to pass. This was another critical moment in our campaign when good organizing by citizen activists made a difference.

The hearings were well attended, and by an overwhelming margin, the large audiences spoke in favor of the bill.

Then the oil companies weighed in, led by Shell. On May 21, 1971, John Pratt, manager of Shell's refinery in Houston, the company's national headquarters, told the *Wilmington Morning News*, "This arbitrary prohibition against our industry and some others, and the arbitrary establishment of a coastal zone boundary, is not in the best interests of the state or the people of Delaware." He argued that the Coastal Zone Act "completely overlooks the contributions these industries can make to the economic well-being of the people of Delaware." He also picked up on the idea of compatibility. "Time and again we have stated publicly our desire and pointed to our ability to build a facility that will be compatible with the area," he said.

The company insisted that it could build a clean refinery that would not in any way harm the natural environment. To prove its point, Shell invited members of the task force and the legislative committees considering the bill to visit two of its model refineries, an installation near New Orleans, nominated that year for a conservation award from the Louisiana Wildlife Federation, and the Anacortes facility on Washington's Puget Sound.

Austin Heller, the task-force member who also served as secretary of the Department of Natural Resources and Environmental Control, accepted Shell's offer and visited both refineries. "They were quite well maintained," he reported, "but they were not pollution free by any means." (*The Wilmington Morning News*, March 16, 1971)

But even if Shell's refinery near Woodland Beach were as clean as a computer-chip factory, other good reasons compelled us to keep oil refineries from proliferating along the coast. That there were environmental consequences quite aside from pollution was a point that our opponents could not or would not acknowledge. "We can only speculate as to the overall impact of this bill on the further development of the state," Mr. Pratt told the press. "For instance, the prohibitions against bulk cargo or transfer facilities along the Delaware River and Bay will preclude development of one of Delaware's greatest economic assets."

Development, of course, is in the eye of the beholder. One company's development can be a state's cancer.

The oil industry wanted to develop the Delaware coast in a way intended to benefit each company's bottom line, but in the process it would have altered the natural character of Delaware Bay and left future generations with much less than we have now. Our hope was to develop in the true sense of the word, to realize the potential of the state's coastal zone by protecting it for people and wildlife, for recreation and tourism, and for other nondestructive activities.

At that point the Nixon administration entered the fray. George Bush's company, Zapata Norness, recruited the Departments of Commerce and Treasury to fight the ban on its proposed offshore terminal. "Unless the United States is able to receive these (oceangoing) bulk carriers, our ability to compete will be seriously damaged," wrote the assistant secretary of the Treasury Department in a letter to the Delaware House of Representatives. He urged the legislators to vote against the Coastal Zone Act.

Then the Commerce Department submitted written testimony opposing the bill on grounds that "it might damage the nation's trade position and undermine President Nixon's program to assure United States leadership in shipping." That blast came from the department's assistant secretary for maritime affairs.

The next day I received a call from this fellow's boss, Commerce Secretary Maurice Stans, asking me to come to Washington to see him. Stans, I knew, was very close to President Nixon, having been the principal fund raiser in Nixon's 1968 campaign, for which he had been rewarded with his present post. (Early in 1972 he would step down from the cabinet to become finance chairman of the

Committee to Reelect the President, a role which led to his much-publicized prosecution by the Watergate investigators for alleged criminal activities and his subsequent acquittal.)

When I arrived at his huge office on June 4, he and twenty-five members of his staff were waiting for me. If his intent was to impress me with numbers, he succeeded. The sampling of senior staff members he had assembled for that occasion was about four times the size of my entire executive staff in the governor's office.

At first Secretary Stans was courteous enough. He introduced his staff and explained that they had spent the past ten years preparing to make Delaware Bay a major center of maritime commerce. When his staff finished telling me of their plan for the future of the Delaware coast, a plan never presented to the people of Delaware, Secretary Stans took over. After emphasizing how important this plan was for America, he stood up, looked straight into my eyes and said, "We think you are being disloyal to our country." I will never forget those words.

I stood up and replied, "Hell, no. I am being loyal to future generations of Americans."

I noticed that a smile crept onto the faces of some others in the room. Were they amused by this governor from a tiny state acting so big? Or did they enjoy seeing this confrontation with their boss?

Then Secretary Stans moved to his fall-back position. "How about at least amending the bill to allow a deep-water port in the bay?" he asked.

I told him I could not be very encouraging about that, but I would think it over and get back to him. Everyone in the room shook hands with me as I left. Suddenly it felt as if I were being treated like the governor of a large state with many electoral votes. All the way home, I thought about Stans' request, and I communicated my answer to him the following day. I said *no*.

Next, we heard from Richard Nixon's environmental adviser, Russell Train. He had just been appointed by the president as chairman of the newly created Council on Environmental Quality (CEQ). To my surprise, Mr. Train expressed opposition to Delaware's Coastal Zone Act. The Nixon Administration, he told me, did not want any coastal zone management laws enacted individually by the states at this time. He said we should wait until a national land-use policy act was passed. That way there would be a framework for coordinated national planning.

Whatever the merits of his argument, which seemed dubious,

it would have been a long wait. That bill never came close to being enacted—it lacked the necessary support from the Nixon and later the Ford administrations—and its prospects seem dimmer with each passing president.

Later, when I succeeded Russell Train at CEQ and he became head of the Environmental Protection Agency, I asked CEQ staff members why he had publicly opposed our coastal initiative. I had always regarded him as a committed conservationist. "Russ is a politician first," they told me. When the Nixon administration decided to oppose the Coastal Zone Act, it became a question of party loyalty. "Russ Train would never buck his party or disagree with the president," a former colleague of his replied. Ironically, years later Russ Train and I worked together on many national and international environmental causes. Over the years he became widely recognized as one of the world's most effective conservationists.

One of the best things we had going for us in Delaware was the support of the news media. We maintained close relations with the press, briefing key editors and reporters, feeding them useful information, meeting frequently with their editorial boards. Two key staff members, my executive assistant and my press secretary, were former journalists who maintained an excellent rapport with the press.

All of the state's daily newspapers supported our drive to protect the coast. As HB 300 came up for consideration, a stream of newspaper columns and editorials urged favorable action. On June 4, 1971, after well-attended hearings on the proposal, John D. Gates, an editorial writer of *The Wilmington Morning News* wrote:

> Call it what you will, a superb brainwashing job by ecologists and conservationists or a sudden public awakening to the dangers of environmental destruction. No longer will major development decisions be made without active public participation.
>
> That's progress. Those decisions do not affect only the principals involved, they influence the way of life and the nature of Delaware. The public deserves a voice, a loud voice, in their making.
>
> Now that business and industry are being forced into public accountability, now that the Establishment or whatever one wants to tag it, must justify itself, the whole American system stands to benefit.

As the bill was taken up in committee, our opponents focused their attack. The oil-company lawyers drafted an amendment that would remove the outright prohibition on new refineries, steel mills, paper mills, petrochemical complexes, and bulk-transfer facilities offshore. The crux of Shell's argument was that the proposal was arbitrary and discriminatory because it banned industry by class. The oil companies proposed, instead, that each industrial project be judged on its merits. They wanted each application to be reviewed by an appointed commission and approved or disapproved on the basis of its potential impact.

As a citizen activist and a student of the commission form of government, I knew that this would be deadly. An appointed body would be highly susceptible to lobbying by narrow interests. To get his way, the appointing official, whether a governor, supervisor or mayor, need only appoint amenable commissioners. Shell and its allies favored such a system because they knew they could manipulate it. After all, that was how Shell had won permission for its new refinery a decade earlier from the Levy Court of New Castle County. A single appointed body was too weak a reed on which to anchor something as important as the future of the Delaware coast.

Another problem with the case-by-case approach was that it promoted the kind of piecemeal development that ignored a fundamental principle of environmental protection—the need to consider the cumulative impact of past, present, and projected activities when considering the specific proposal at hand. No one development project, no matter how damaging, will by itself ruin a natural coastline or bay; it is the *accumulation* of environmental insults that eventually destroys a coastline or kills a bay.

The bill came up for a vote on June 21. The house leadership and Andy Knox, the prime sponsor, had done a good job of preparing, and they handled the debate masterfully. Legislative Hall was jammed. Many young people were there, lobbying along with the professionals. Reporters were all over the building.

Debate proceeded well into the evening, with frequent recesses for caucusing and for house leaders to meet with me in my office. Several legislators who had been supporting the bill were now wavering.

Sherman Tribbitt, the Democrat who would succeed me as governor, led the attempt to gut the bill. He was seen frequently

with industry lobbyists who represented much of the power structure in the state.

Several minor amendments were approved. The critical amendment prepared by the oil companies came up at 9:30 P.M. I was
in the balcony watching the proceedings. It was an exciting, nerve-
wracking moment. I held my breath as the votes were counted.
We won by one vote: twenty nays and nineteen ayes.

The final vote on the bill came at 10:45 P.M. Having lost the key
vote on the oil companies' amendment, seven Democrats switched
their votes in order to be on record as favoring a popular bill.
The final tally in the house showed twenty-eight of the thirty-nine
members supporting the measure. We had cleared the first of our
two hurdles.

The next day the action moved to the senate, comprised of
thirteen Republicans and six Democrats. Three of the Republicans were adamantly opposed. They joined with the Democrats
to try to persuade one more Republican to join them, giving them
the 10 votes needed to defeat the bill. Republican leaders in the
Senate, Reynolds duPont and Frank Grier, along with Lieutenant
Governor Gene Bookhammer and I, worked to hold our ten votes.
Lobbyists cornered senators every time they left the sanctuary of
the senate chamber. By dinner it appeared we held only a bare
majority of the votes.

After dinner an aide rushed into my office to say that two Republican senators had been turned around by lobbyists during
dinner. That meant the opposition now had eleven votes to our
eight. I asked those two senators to meet with me and the senate
leadership in my office. We impressed on them the need to maintain party unity, to respect the will of the people, to remember
who elected them to office and who could send them packing, to
consider the well-being of future Delawareans.

After about an hour, the two agreed to support the bill.

When the senate went back into session, I was watching again
from the balcony. Shortly before 11 P.M., the final vote came. It
was sixteen to three. The margin in our favor seemed overwhelming, but this was an illusion. As in the final house vote, many of
the senators, when they saw which way the vote would go, joined
the winning side in what had become a motherhood issue. But
motherhood or not, the reality was that our bill had eked by, in
both chambers, with only one vote to spare.

It was a grand occasion. The conventional view of *progress* and *development* had, at least momentarily, been reexamined and redefined. The people of Delaware had opted for environmental quality and compatible development in place of what had been happening elsewhere for the last hundred years.

Writing a year later in the magazine, *On the Shore,* David Nevin offered this perspective: "Considering the industrial boom of the last two decades and the ravished stretch from Wilmington to New York City, it's miraculous that the Delaware coast survived; the Coastal Zone Act saved it in the last moments of its last chance."

It had been such a close call that almost everything done on behalf of the Coastal Zone Act had been decisive: the support of environmental groups; the coverage and support from the press; the letter to the Chamber of Commerce justifying our position; the backing of the auto workers and civil service unions; the involvement of young people; the rebirth of Delawareans for Orderly Development; the participation of citizen groups not necessarily associated with environmental causes, such as the American Association of University Women and the Federation of Women's Clubs; the active support of respected political figures, including ex-governors and political leaders whose last name happened to be duPont. Every action and every supporter made a difference.

Our efforts were successful because they had grassroots support that was so strong that elected officials, at least a majority of them, could not turn their backs on it. Our opponents had the power of money; to compensate for this, we sought and won the power of the people. We had shown that when enough people are motivated and organized, they can make the public interest prevail over special interests.

It was a delicious moment, one that many of us involved in the victory still savor. We were soon to discover, however, that the fight had just begun.

National Wildlife Federation award, Mexico City. Jack Jurden, *The News Journal,* **1971. Courtesy of** *The News Journal.*

15

Bringing More Justice to the Criminal Justice System

MY TEN YEARS OF EXPERIENCE AS A VOLUNTEER ACTIVIST CON-
cerned with the injustices of our criminal justice system led me,
as governor, to devote a major effort in this area. Many problems
defined by the Three S Campaign still needed attention, and I
was determined to reorient Delaware's criminal justice efforts toward the causes of crime, not just the symptoms. Among my
achievements were working with the legislature to eliminate Delaware's two anachronisms, the whipping post and the debtors'
prison.

The whipping post had been Delaware's most notorious treatment for offenders in earlier years. Prisoners were shackled to a
post and lashed with a cat-o'-nine-tails. Delaware was the last place
in the industrialized world to use this punishment; the last lashing
occurred as recently as 1952. Other whippings were ordered by
lower courts after that, but higher courts overruled them. Although Delaware law still required there be a whipping post in
each county, lawmakers apparently were so ashamed of this anach-
ronism they made it illegal to photograph a whipping post. When
I ordered the posts taken down, champions of the lash screamed,
"The governor is breaking the law!"

"Not so," I replied. " Each county still has one." I even offered
to show the complainers where they were stored, but no one took
me up on this offer. But it was not until 1972, when I signed
Delaware's new criminal code into law, that this practice was officially abolished.

Today a few Delawareans still call for the return of the post,
contending that public whipping will put an end to crime, that
it will keep troublemakers from the big cities around us from
overrunning our state. There is no evidence to support those con-

Peterson abolishes Delaware's notorious whipping post. Jack Jurden, *The News Journal,* **1972. Courtesy of** *The News Journal.*

tentions. There is also no evidence that the solution to our crime problem is to get tough on criminals. Robert G. Caldwell, a former University of Delaware professor, wrote the only definitive history of Delaware's whipping post, popularly known as Red Hannah. His 1947 book concluded that whippings did not deter crime.

In earlier centuries, when whipping was a common practice, it drove offenders to more serious antisocial acts against a hated community. Today sociologists tell us that whippings by an angry and abusive parent can drive children to more rebellious acts. And surely the recent slaughter in Bosnia shows that the severest punishments, such as beating, rape, and murder, do not deter anyone from similar and repeated acts of revenge. Still, some people believe—despite all indications to the contrary—that brutal punishment discourages criminal behavior.

We also brought an end to the debtors prison. No longer would anyone be sent to prison for failure to pay a fine, thereby acquiring a prison record which would be a major handicap in getting a job. The fine could be paid in a number of ways, including by installments or by working for an appropriate number of hours for the state. (Later the U.S. Supreme Court declared it unconstitutional to send a person to prison for failure to pay a debt.)

With these two archaic practices out of the way, we began to focus on updating the corrections system. To better prepare an offender for life after prison, my administration significantly increased work-release, a program that permits an inmate to work for a private employer during the day and return to prison for evenings and weekends. Sometimes an inmate would continue in the same job full-time after being released from prison. At the very least, work-release provided a prisoner with skill and experience to help him find a job on the outside. Although we were pleased by the success of the program in getting some releasees employed on an ongoing basis, the program was curtailed by my successor before sufficient data were acquired to obtain any meaningful quantitative measure of the impact on recidivism.

We also made major changes in the adult and juvenile corrections departments by bringing in managers trained in the behavioral sciences. These people were committed to salvaging offenders. For example, the old Youth Services Commission had been run by a former professional football player and eight of his former teammates. Their competence was illustrated by the way they dealt with any juvenile delinquent who ran away from

Ferris School. They would assemble a posse of youth under detention in the school to help scour the community for the escapee.
When they caught him, the posse was allowed to beat up the
runaway. Escapes increased until behavioral scientists came in to
redesign the program. The new team emphasized education, co-
operative work assignments, professional counseling and a variety
of organized sports and recreation. Escapes dropped to zero; recidivism declined.

Under the next governor, however, most of the successful supervisors left or were fired. Soon after, the Division of Corrections
was removed from the Department of Health and Social Services
and made a separate department. Thus it was no longer served
by personnel with the rehabilitation skills and motivation of
Health and Social Services and reverted almost exclusively to the
traditional custodial services.

To focus on reducing crime, I established the Agency to Reduce
Crime and placed in it leaders from the criminal justice system
and from education, labor, welfare and recreation. Then we set
an ambitious but attainable goal: cutting Delaware's rate of violent
crime in half within ten years.

Initially our efforts caused a downturn in the crime rate, but
then the rate resumed its upward climb. The agency developed
many ideas for reducing crime, such as providing jobs in low-
income neighborhoods, but there just was not enough money in
the tight state budget to carry them out. The lesson was obvious:
unless we could put money where our good intentions were, they
would come to naught. Therefore, I decided to try to get financial
help from the federal government.

I began to work closely with Elliot Richardson, secretary of the
U.S. Department of Health, Education, and Welfare. I convinced
him that Delaware would be a good national laboratory for running social experiments. We had essentially all the problems of
the big states. What better testing ground for experimental programs that could be run statewide for relatively small federal and
state outlays? If a program failed, only a small amount would be
lost. If it succeeded, the program could be replicated nationwide
with good assurance of success.

Initially we planned to focus on youth in low-income neighborhoods—to provide more incentives and opportunities for vocational education, to move people off welfare to self-sustaining

jobs, and to further drug and alcohol rehabilitation. Secretary Richardson anticipated having discretionary funds available for some of these programs. But before our plans could be implemented, he was moved to another position in President Nixon's cabinet, and I failed to get reelected. Our successors did not follow up on this promising idea, and Delaware never became a national testing ground for crime reduction, though it still has great potential to do so.

Several years after I left office, the title of the Agency to Reduce Crime was changed. This name had become an embarrassment, because crime continued to increase. The state went back to processing and warehousing more and more offenders.

On another front, the National Governors Association made me chairman of its Committee on Public Safety and Criminal Justice for two years. Our committee convinced the governors to launch a nationwide effort to get at the causes of crime and to adopt Delaware's goal of cutting the rate of violent crime in half within ten years. While the governors did pass unanimously a resolution to this effect, it was only words on paper and carried little weight. The Association of Governors itself had neither the authority nor the funding to back up these good intentions.

The Riot at Smyrna

On the evening of September 2, 1971, as I was returning from a TV interview in Salisbury, Maryland, I received an urgent call from Director of Corrections John Moran telling me a riot was underway at Delaware's main prison near Smyrna. John, who had been recruited from outside the state, was a highly competent criminologist. He understood the importance of rehabilitating offenders. I told him I would join him at the prison and then asked my aide, Art McGee, a state police lieutenant, to drive me there at high speed.

Many guards were in the control room, and reinforcements from other shifts had been called in. I found John Moran among them. He was calm as he explained that the riot was in the maximum-security building. Inmates had overpowered the three guards on duty there, taken their keys and opened all cells. Then they went on a rampage, destroying nearly everything they could, even tearing the guards' toilet out of the floor. Water was pouring over the floor.

Moran had been negotiating with the prisoners by telephone. They were threatening to kill the guards, but it was not clear what they wanted. (Later we learned that they had put three guards in a utility maintenance pit below floor level and threatened to pour motor oil on them and ignite it.)

As John and I made our way to the warden's office to meet with his key people I said, "I'm here to back you up, John, not to tell you what to do."

We discussed the best course of action to pursue, and the officers explained that among the rioters were three very dangerous men who were kept under sedation. They worried what those three might do once the sedatives wore off. The consensus was that prompt action was critical. As shillelaghs and gas masks were passed out, I talked to several of the guards. They were frightened.

"I don't want to go in that damn place," a six-foot-four, two-hundred pounder said. "But what other choice do I have?"

A short, thin man who appeared to be in his twenties complained, "We have a terrible job. There aren't nearly enough of us."

"I agree with that," said a much older, balding officer. He complained that there were not enough guards, and as a result they got frustrated and said things that antagonized their charges.

At that point, John Moran called everyone together to explain that they would march to the back entrance of maximum security, where they could put on their gas masks. When Moran's assistant, Harry Towers, opened the door, Moran would lead them into the building. The guards would first lay down a curtain of tear gas and then propel the rioters into the cells—any cells—and slam the doors. As soon as they found the three captive guards, they would remove them and then open up the building to air it out.

"Any questions?" Moran asked.

I put up my hand.

"Yes, Governor," he said.

"Does anyone have a gun?" I asked.

Two men put up their hands.

"You shouldn't take them," I advised.

John Moran told them to turn in the guns. A senior officer locked the guns in a drawer.

"Let's go," Moran barked and led his men out of the control area toward maximum security.

I walked out onto the edge of the large, well-kept, grassy yard, which was surrounded by the several buildings that made up the Smyrna prison.

Two years earlier, in 1969, I had spoken here at the opening of this institution—the modern prison that resulted directly from the Three S Citizens' Campaign. We had hoped that this model prison would turn out offenders better prepared to live and work in the community.

Now, as I stood outside the control area, I observed the maximum-security building on my left. Next to it was the medium-security building and further on, the minimum-security building. To my right, was the work-release area, from which men were transported to work in the community during the day. Our earlier plan had called for assigning offenders to these buildings according to the seriousness of their offenses and providing for their promotion to a less secure building with more privileges when and if they responded satisfactorily to education, work, and other rehab assignments. I wondered what this riot would do to our plans.

It was strangely peaceful. There was no obvious sign of action in the vicinity of maximum security. I wondered where Lieutenant McGee, my security officer, was and decided he was probably worrying about where I was.

Then a man outlined in a barred window in medium security started hurling invectives at me. His foul words reverberated around the courtyard. He screamed them over and over. I was sure he had no idea who I was.

Suddenly the door of maximum security opened and several guards burst out of the building. One of them ran straight at me. When I realized he was heading for the control area, I hollered at him, "Stop! I want to talk to you."

"To hell with you," he yelled back. "I'm getting out of here." He disappeared into the building. He was one of the guards who had been held hostage, and he kept his word—he quit and never came back.

Still alone, I walked toward the maximum-security exit where the guards had taken off their gas masks and were excitedly comparing notes.

John Moran stepped aside and told me that all three hostages were safe and all the inmates were locked up. "We shoved them into the nearest cells. Now we're trying to air out the building."

"May I go in to see what happened?" I asked.

He replied that the building was full of tear gas.

"Let me borrow a gas mask," I said. John found one for me and offered to go along.

When I entered, I could not see much. I did see several men in one cell, heard men coughing and cursing, and saw some broken furniture. But the gas mask given me was contaminated with tear gas on the inside and soon my eyes were watering so badly I could barely follow John out of there.

During the next few days we tried to find out what had caused the riot. On September 9, my assistant, Jerry Sapienza, and I met with 21 inmates—three from each of seven areas in the prison. John Moran had arranged this at my request. No guards or prison administrators were with us.

It was an orderly meeting. The men spoke freely. Two from maximum security claimed to have been beaten severely on the head during the riot and to have bled profusely. I asked them to come forward, and I looked at their heads but saw no wounds. They then claimed their wounds had healed during the seven days since the riot. As the meeting went on, we learned that the main cause of the riot was that the classification and award system they had been promised in the new prison was being violated. Smyrna was so crowded that some new inmates imprisoned for minor, nonviolent offenses were placed in maximum security, and the movement to less secure buildings as an award for good behavior had been suspended.

One man imprisoned for life for killing a policeman spoke up. "I've been in prison for eight years, first at the old New Castle prison and now here at Smyrna. Every year at the end of August we have a riot or serious disturbance," he said.

"Why do you think that is?" I asked.

He told me it was because the whole Superior Court shut down for vacation in August. Consequently, the prison became overcrowded during the hottest and most humid time of the year. Later I checked into this and found it was true. With the court on vacation, all offenders apprehended during August were stored in the prison, waiting for the court to return to consider their cases.

Prison officials knew about the Superior Court's vacation policy, but felt powerless to do anything about it. Neither they nor the Superior Court judges connected the overcrowding of the prison in August with the annual uprising that same month. It took an observant prisoner to do that. And it took someone with authority to listen and to request that the court stagger vacations throughout the year. (Later the court agreed and the legislature provided more judges to reduce the backlog.)

We also listened to the guards' contention that a shortage of guards contributed to unease in the prison. We belatedly added seventeen additional guards. All this reminded me of Abraham Maslow's statement that "happiness stems from the progressive realization of a desired goal." When an offender is imprisoned, chastised by the community by having his freedoms taken away, he will value the promise and nurture the hope of being rewarded for good behavior by being moved to a more favorable prison environment. Conversely, the inmate will be seriously let down when such a hope is shattered. For public officials to keep their word is very important, even when dealing with "the least of these, thy brethren."

In hindsight I now see that I must share in the blame for the uprising. Enamored with our brand new prison and the enlightened rehabilitation program planned for it, I failed, in the heat of the state's annual budget debate, to listen to the urgent request of the Department of Corrections for additional funds to cope with the burgeoning prison population. Without more resources they could not do their jobs.

On September 9, 1971, one week after the Smyrna riot—and at the same time I was meeting with inmates at Smyrna—a riot occcured at the penitentiary in Attica, New York. The inmates took employees hostage and went on a rampage. They demanded to speak directly to Governor Nelson Rockefeller; he declined. (Requests by inmates to talk to governors are not infrequent, especially in a large state like New York which has many prisons.) After four days of unsuccessful negotiation between State Corrections Commissioner Russell Oswald and the rioters, and with threats to the hostages increasing, Governor Rockefeller ordered state police to storm the prison. They went in firing. In the process they killed eleven hostages and twenty-eight inmates, making this one of America's bloodiest prison riots.

Later, when I lived on the Rockefeller estate in Pocantico Hills, New York, I asked Nelson Rockefeller at dinner one night to tell us about the Attica event. This was a painful subject for him. All he said was that he wished he had gone to the prison. And then he changed the subject.

In 1987 a national meeting of corrections authorities was held in Washington, D.C., to discuss prison riots. They concluded that officials have two choices when confronted with an uprising. Either they go in promptly to retake the prison while the rioters are disorganized, or they wait and wait, and talk and talk, as long as hostages appear safe, avoiding the use of force as long as possible. I would add that if the rioters have no guns, as in the case of the Smyrna riot, the retaking of the prison should be done without guns. In the excitement, fright, and anger of a riot, a gun can be used too readily, creating a problem worse than the riot. A riot should be recognized as a signal of the need for management reform, not the need for harsher treatment.

Fighting Crime on the National Scene

In 1971, U.S. Attorney General John Mitchell invited me to lunch in his office. He asked me to chair a National Advisory Commission on Criminal Justice Standards and Goals, pointing out that President Nixon considered crime the most serious domestic problem in America. The administration wanted to establish a national commission of leaders from all over the country, and from all branches of the criminal-justice system, to determine how to reduce crime. The commission's mandate would be to establish standards of excellence for police, courts, attorneys general, corrections, probation and parole officers, and to set goals for each of these units. The commission would be funded and staffed by the Law Enforcement Assistance Administration (LEAA), then headed by Administrator Jerris Leonard.

I asked, "Would we be free to report on what we thought was required to reduce crime regardless of how controversial it might be?"

Mitchell told me we would—that our objective would be to reduce crime. I accepted, neither of us knowing that he, the attorney general of the United States, and his boss, the president, would soon be adding personally to the nation's crime statistics.

Dr. Peter J. Pitchess, a lawyer serving his fourth four-year term as sheriff of Los Angeles County, who ran on both the Democratic and Republican tickets and received over 70 percent of the vote, was appointed vice chairman of the National Advisory Commission. He was a tremendous asset. A tall, handsome man with a warm smile, he looked more like a college professor than a supercop. He understood the criminal justice system inside and out, and he was articulate and forceful when he talked about it.

Commission members included Governor Forrest Anderson of Montana; the chiefs of police from Los Angeles, Omaha, and Dallas; Chief Justice Henry McQuade of Idaho; leaders in corrections and education; the Reverend Leon Sullivan; Attorney General Gary Nelson of Arizona; the mayor of Indianapolis, Richard G. Lugar, and the district attorney of Philadelphia, Arlen Specter. (The last two later became U.S. senators and presidential candidates.) Tom Madden, who had been general counsel of the LEAA, became our executive director. Although most of the commissioners hailed from conservative jurisdictions in the West, all endorsed the commission's quite radical recommendations and worked to define what was needed to reduce crime, not what was needed to get someone reelected.

We called our final report *A National Strategy to Reduce Crime*. It established a goal for America—to cut the rate of high-fear crimes, such as murder, rape, and mugging, in half in ten years time. Earlier the nation's governors had voted unanimously to adopt the same goal.

We knew that America had the know-how and the resources to accomplish the goal—all that was needed was the dedicated leadership to commit the funds to implement the know-how and provide the necessary resources. We identified two steps necessary for reaching this goal: reforming the criminal justice system and preventing at-risk individuals from getting into trouble in the first place. Reforming the system involved dealing with the way the offenders were treated after they were arrested and convicted; prevention involved identifying and working to eliminate the causes.

The Commission also recommended that we should:

- Organize the criminal justice system as a total unit concerned with rehabilitating the individual offender rather than passing him along as a number from one entity to another.
- Reduce the time interval from arrest to trial to less than sixty days. (We noted that some offenders were out on bail commit-

ting a second and a third crime while awaiting disposition of
the first. Clearly we were recycling criminals.)

- Establish the patrol officer as a protector and friend of the
neighborhood, responsible for controlling crime in a specific area.

- Abolish plea bargaining within five years. (We condemned
plea bargaining as an institution. We asked how we could
expect offenders to respect justice when prosecutors encouraged them to plead guilty to a lesser crime they had not committed in order to avoid being charged for a greater crime
they had committed.)

- Develop a national commitment to make corrections an effective instrument for reintegrating into the community the vast
majority of offenders who are neither dangerous, nor practiced criminals.

- Exclude incarceration as a penalty for such victimless crimes
as marijuana use and possession, prostitution, pornography,
and sexual acts between consenting adults in private.

- Increase citizen involvement in helping people to live within
the law.

- Provide enough choices, including career education, within
our school system so everyone who leaves school does so with
a job offer or acceptance to another institution of learning.

- Make jobs available to everyone so they can earn the means
of satisfying their basic needs—with government providing
jobs when the private sector cannot. (This was probably our
most important recommendation.)

- Outlaw the possession, manufacture, and sale of handguns in
the United States. (In countries where such laws exist, almost
zero deaths from handguns occur per year, while in the
United States, 50 such deaths occur every day on the average.)

Our revolutionary conclusion was that our criminal justice system perpetuates crime.

Our report, *A National Strategy to Reduce Crime,* was published
by the government and widely circulated, though the national
news media paid little attention to it. All 50 states, with financial
help from the LEAA, carried out extensive studies of their own
criminal justice systems, using our report as a stimulus. The re-

port was also published as a paperback by Avon Books in 1975. Twenty-four years later it is not apparent what influence, if any, the report has had.

By the time the report was finished, Elliot Richardson had become United States attorney general. I sent the report to him and then visited him in his office to discuss it. He agreed that it was a good comprehensive report, but asked why we had included so many controversial recommendations. I remember being shocked when he told me that the report was so full of political dynamite that the administration could not do much with it.

"We weren't asked to produce a politically safe document." I reminded him. "We were asked to recommend a strategy to reduce crime. Until the president and other political leaders have the guts to face up to the problem as we did, crime is going to continue to increase, not decrease."

Others shared my view. Here is how Professor of Law Isidor Silver, at the John Jay College of Criminal Justice in New York, described the reaction of the Nixon Administration to our report in his introduction to the paperback version of our report.

> The Nixon administration—which had found itself in the embarrassing or even ludicrous position of appointing some of the previous crime commissions only to disdain their findings—could reasonably have believed that the new "Crime Commission" would render a safe law-and-order report. When that body formally tendered its main findings (in a 318 page document) on August 9, 1973, Attorney General Elliot Richardson was only slightly less flabbergasted than was the president himself. Richardson could only note that "federal government is neither enforcing nor opposing the goals contained in this report." With a sure instinct for finesse, he hastily added that the document was of "uncommon importance." And so it is.

Shortly thereafter Elliot Richardson resigned in the Saturday Night Massacre when he refused to carry out President Nixon's order to fire the Watergate Special Prosecutor Archibald Cox.

I have followed criminal statistics in the criminal justice system over the past twenty-four years and have entered the national debate on more than one occasion. In this same period, crime has continued to escalate, with only occasional downturns. I continue to believe the nation invests far too little in fighting the causes of crime.

16

Losing My Bid for Reelection as Governor

THIS IS A CHAPTER ABOUT HOW NOT TO MAKE IT HAPPEN.

In June 1971, after two and a half years as governor, I was riding high. The legislature and the governor's office, working closely together, had passed a long stream of major legislation including the Coastal Zone Act. State government had been changed to a cabinet form. The governor's office was now a powerful one with the governor, for the first time in Delaware history, clearly in charge of the executive branch. Finances appeared so sound that I had triumphantly announced that there would be no need for any tax increase in the remainder of my term. Close observers of the political scene predicted that Governor Peterson's reelection was a sure thing. The future could not have looked brighter.

Then on June 26, just four days before the end of the 1971 fiscal year, a dark cloud suddenly appeared. The secretary of finance advised me that instead of a modest surplus at the end of the year, we would have a deficit of $5.2 million. This resulted, he explained to me, from a shortfall in the income from the corporate franchise tax paid by the large number of companies incorporated in Delaware.

The budget bill for the 1972 fiscal year, based on an anticipated surplus in 1971, had just been passed by the legislature. According to Delaware law, the governor cannot sign the budget bill unless enough revenue is anticipated to cover the projected expenditures, a sharp contrast to federal law which permits billions in annual deficits. But now, due to the shortfall, it was necessary to amend the budget by a reduction in expense, an increase in taxes, or some combination of the two. On June 28 I went before a joint session of the legislature and reported the bad news. I said, "The problem stems directly from my error in estimating franchise tax income. I was dead wrong."

Was this admission that I had made a mistake a politically naïve act, as many would later claim? Perhaps. Certainly it would have been more politically astute for me to fire my secretary of finance and play down the problem. However, having so strongly argued that the governor needed more authority when I led the campaign for a cabinet form of government a few months earlier, I now decided the governor should take the blame. This opened the door for an all-out attack on me personally.

"He, himself, said he was to blame," my opponent would say many times over during the year-and-a-half remaining in my term.

The estimate of the state's revenues had been made by the governor's bipartisan Economic Advisory Council of nineteen members chaired by Eugene R. Perry, president of National Vulcanized Fiber Company. When I became governor, I had established this council by executive order, following the practice of the state of California in taking the official estimate of revenue out of the governor's hands. To their credit, the council's first forecast for fiscal 1970 had proven accurate. For the next year the council projected a substantial increase in the franchise tax income, based on new legislation making conditions more favorable for companies to incorporate in Delaware. This legislation did pay off in later years, but too late for me to win a second term.

Each month I plotted, on a chart kept in my desk drawer, the revenue coming from the state's several taxes. By the end of April 1971, the plot showed no growth in the franchise tax income over that of the previous year. I asked the chairman of the Economic Advisory Council to reconsider the council's forecast before the governor and the legislature finished the budget for fiscal year 1972. He appointed a special committee to study it. On May 15, 1971, Chairman Perry came back with a reassuring report. "Relax," he said in effect. "The franchise tax forecast is sound."

During this time both the secretary of finance and the secretary of state, who administered the franchise tax, strongly supported the advisory committee's forecast. I should have believed the chart in my desk.

Within five weeks after becoming aware of the two-percent deficit for fiscal year 1971, the legislature and the governor, through a combination of reduced expense and slightly increased taxes, corrected the problem. At the end of fiscal 1972, the state had a modest surplus as projected. But our prompt correction of the problem did little to reduce the criticism caused by the miscalculation in the first place. This was well illustrated at the Blue and Gold football game which took place shortly after the fiscal problem was resolved.

Each summer star high school football players from all over the state participate in the well-attended Blue and Gold game played in the University of Delaware stadium for the benefit of disabled youth. It is the tradition for the governor to sit on one side of the field during the first half and to walk across the field to the other side between the halves, the crowd vigorously applauding their governor. At the 1971 game, when the announcement was made that the governor and his fifteen-year-old daughter, Elin, would now cross from the Gold side of the field to the Blue side, a loud, sustained boo echoed and reechoed in the stadium. Tears ran down Elin's face as we started to walk across the field. Her tears hurt more than the boos. I took her hand and squeezed it. She smiled back, and we continued hand-in-hand across the field.

It was now clear that a new day had arrived.

My announcement of a financial problem had already brought my political opponents out in the open. David Buckson, former lieutenant governor and attorney general, immediately challenged me for the Republican nomination. Heretofore the gubernatorial candidate was nominated by a majority vote at a state convention. But this year the process was different because—in one of my good-government moves—I had persuaded the legislature to provide for primary elections. If a leading candidate at a political party's state convention failed to get 67 percent of the vote, his top challenger could call for a primary election.

At the 1972 convention I failed by one delegate to reach the 67 percent level, and Buckson called for a primary. Although I went on to win the primary, Buckson's months-long attack during the primary battle had weakened my support among Republicans, especially downstate where Buckson was popular.

Downstaters were already unhappy with me for pushing through the cabinet form of government, causing them to lose control of the executive branch which they had dominated for decades. Buckson, and later the Democratic candidate for governor, Sherman Tribbitt, effectively fanned this flame.

One day during my campaign, Lieutenant Governor Bookhammer, State Senator Hickman, and Republican Party Chairman Bunting came to my office to let me know I was in deep trouble in Sussex County, their home territory. They told me that if I did not start playing politics, I would lose the election.

I told them, "I came to this office to solve problems, not to get reelected. I am not going to play politics as you mean it—by giving special favors to supporters."

Bunting then asked how I expected to solve problems if I were not reelected.

"At least I can have one productive term in office," I said. "I refuse to be a typical politician, perpetually working to get reelected, and never getting around to solving any real problems."

Bookhammer told me that at least I could be friendly with Bill Murray. He asked me to come down to Sussex and go out with the three of them and Bill Murray in Murray's boat. He said that Bill was bad-mouthing me all over downstate Delaware.

Bill Murray was a wealthy man who had sold his Murray Feeds to a national company and put much of the proceeds into land in Sussex County. He had worked hard for me in 1968, and I had appointed him to the old highway commission.

Now, in 1972, he wanted the state to dredge a shallow creek on his land, which would give him access by boat to Indian River Bay and the Atlantic Ocean, thus markedly increasing the value of his land. State biologists told me the creek was an important nursery ground for shell and fin fish and should not be dredged.

I agreed to go out on his boat. After a drink, some snacks, and friendly conversation I found myself alone in the bow with Bill. He reminded me that he had gotten 400 votes for me in my first election.

"I know," I said, "you were a great supporter. Thank you very much."

Jabbing his finger at me, he told me that if I did not get that creek dredged I would lose those 400, plus 400 more.

I replied, "Bill, I told you the biologists say that creek is a valuable nursery ground for fish. I can't do it."

He kept his word, becoming a major opponent in my own party. Although my action demonstrated how not to get reelected, I still derive much satisfaction from having stood up for one of Delaware's important fisheries.

The most frustrating experience in my campaign was my opponents' success in keeping the 1971 financial problem on the front pages of Delaware newspapers for the next sixteen months. No matter what the story, even about such minor events as cutting a ribbon at a new store opening, the reporter managed to weave in my administration's earlier financial problem. One who was particularly adept at this was John Schmadeke, a reporter for the *Wilmington News-Journal* papers. He seemed to have a vendetta against me for reasons I just could not fathom.

After I lost the election I received a letter from him apologizing for what he had done. Later, when I was chairman of the Council on Environmental Quality, John, who was then with another paper, visited me in my Washington office. He came in with a nice smile, admired my office, and commended me profusely for what I had done as governor. Then his expression changed. He said he was sorry for some of the stories he had written about me when I was running for reelection. Tears actually ran down his face. He told me that if he had known I might lose the election, he never would have done that.

This was a strange but moving experience. Here was a proud and generally competent journalist coming to meet me face-to-face to apologize for harming a cause he really believed in. It took both courage and humility to do this.

I said, "John, I appreciate your coming to see me, but please don't be so rough on yourself. There were many reasons why I lost that election."

As he left he thanked me for seeing him and said it was a relief to get this off his mind. In trying to understand John's behavior, I have speculated that his writing about me was influenced by someone higher up in the paper, perhaps someone who took a particular dislike to what I was doing as governor. I must hasten to add, however, that the editorial page of both *News-Journal* papers strongly and consistently supported me.

A few years ago former governor Elbert Carvel, a Democrat who preceded me in office and who was a trustee of the University of Delaware, and the former president of that University, Dr. Arthur Trabant, each told me separately that I lost my reelection bid solely because of all-out opposition of one member of the university board of trustees. I told them I knew that several members of that board were unhappy with me, but no one person was responsible for my defeat.

Their antagonism stemmed from one of my first acts as governor. I had called a special meeting of the board, of which I was an ex-officio member, to tell them the board was not representative of the people of Delaware. I bluntly said that a change was required. I took this action because, during the campaign, many faculty and students had told me of their irritation at the board's insensitivity to faculty and student views. They were particularly upset by the board's perception that the duPont family, which had six highly influential representatives on the board, acted as though the university were its private preserve. Students were already seething, as on other campuses at that time, about the Vietnam war, civil rights, racial inequality, degradation of the environment, and poverty. The trustees' repeated refusal to allow even one student representative to meet with them exacerbated the problem.

When I met with the trustees in President Trabant's home, I related these concerns and said that I shared them. I pointed out the large representation from the duPont family, the absence of young people, blacks, Hispanics and people of modest means, and the presence on this board of only one woman. I suggested we work together to change the makeup of the board.

Immediately I was attacked. One member of the duPont family was furious. He claimed I had insulted the family after all they had done for the university. President Trabant reported to me years later that some of the trustees "were so angry they could have eaten nails."

After the meeting we adjourned to a large sunroom where drinks were to be served and where a table of delicious hors d'oeuvres was laid out—a reception planned for the new governor. But nearly all the trustees left the house right after the meeting and skipped the reception. Only former governor Carvel and Daniel Hermann, a justice of the Delaware Supreme Court, remained with President Trabant, his aide and me. Then Carvel and Hermann left, leaving only three of us with all the refreshments. The next day the message permeated the community—the university trustees would never support Governor Peterson again.

At this point I went to see my friend, Henry B. duPont, with whom I had worked well in GWDC. He was also a trustee. He said he agreed with me and that he would work with me to help change the make up of the board, but that I should not have been so brutal.

"You have to hit the donkey over the head to get his attention," I said.

"You got our attention, all right," he responded.

Still he continued to be a strong supporter.

Shortly thereafter a vacancy opened on the board when Henry F. duPont died. He was the founder and owner of the famous Winterthur Museum and had been a trustee of the university for over fifty years.

I appointed Arva Jackson to succeed him. Arva was young, brilliant, and the first African American on the board. Her other distinctions included being the youngest member, the second woman, and lowest-income trustee. Soon a second African American, Dr. Luna Mishoe, president of Delaware State College, and three young white men were appointed. The times were "a changin'," as Bob Dylan then sang.

A few months later at a meeting of the trustees, the perennial request for permission for a student to address the group came up for a vote. Similar requests had been repeatedly defeated in the past. This time it passed easily, with a number of the former opponents of such action supporting it. That noon when we walked from one building to another for lunch, the sidewalk was lined with hundreds of students, some in trees and some atop a building. They had planned a major demonstration that day, but upon learning that the trustees had agreed to listen to a student representative at the afternoon meeting, the students called it off.

To what extent my early actions with the board contributed to my reelection failure I do not know. I do know that some of them spent large amounts on my opponent's campaign. But several other trustees contributed generously to my campaign, so perhaps it all balanced out.

The six largest contributors to my first campaign, all businessmen with reason to be upset by a number of my actions, came through again, with equal generosity for the second campaign. I will never forget visiting one of them, Irenée duPont, in his office. "Why should I support you?" he asked me point-blank. He reminded me that I had done much against his interests, including passing the Coastal Zone Act, which he had publicly opposed. He also blamed me for raising the personal income tax and business taxes.

"There is one good reason, Irenée," I replied. "You are interested in the welfare of your children and grandchildren."

He thought for a minute, then he asked how much I wanted. And he raised the money I requested.

Some people, especially downstate, were unhappy with me for what I did in support of African Americans. But I made many black friends in the process. Before I was sworn in as governor, I met with twenty-five young blacks who were recognized as the leaders in their community. Telling them I wanted to help in solving their problems, I asked that they prepare a list of their concerns.

They invited me to meet with them the day after I became governor in a building that the police had advised me to stay away from. In fact, I met with them alone the day after I had ordered the National Guard to stop patrolling African American neighborhoods. Bob Hallman had been selected as the group's leader. He and I sat behind a small table facing about twenty-five other black leaders who had produced a mimeographed list of their concerns. We spent two hours going over them. All their requests were reasonable.

During the next six months, the legislature and the governor took care of many of them. Laws that forced people who could not pay a fine to go to jail (the debtors prison) were repealed; funding for educational programs that particularly benefitted blacks was markedly increased; the first blacks were put on a number of agencies, including the University of Delaware Board of Trustees and downstate magistrate courts, and open housing legislation was passed.

Bob Hallman called a public meeting to celebrate the changes and to call for further action. At the same time some whites were incensed and privately labeled the governor a "nigger lover."

After I signed the Open Housing Bill at a Governor's Prayer Breakfast in a downstate school and was departing the building, a man walking in front of me said to his companion, "Imagine that son-of-a-bitch signing open housing legislation at a prayer breakfast." I tapped him on the shoulder, smiled and asked, "Can you think of a better place to express brotherhood?" The startled man said nothing and accelerated his departure.

My efforts to help blacks were sincerely motivated by my long-term desire to remove the man-made obstacles to their getting ahead and to provide opportunities for their doing so, and were not consciously undertaken to gain their support at the polls. On the contrary, I believed my advisors' appraisal that these actions on behalf of an oppressed black community would cost me many votes among non-blacks. However, I was greatly disappointed when the black community voted strongly against me in 1972. This really hurt. The vote was close enough that they could have easily turned the election in my favor.

Yet on reflection, their reasons for voting against me were clear enough. I was a Republican; black voters were highly motivated to support a Democrat. My campaign organization and I did far too little to inform black voters of my record.

It was especially disappointing that Democratic Senator Herman Holloway, the only African American in the state senate and a friend who worked closely with me on numerous programs to support blacks, worked hard to get his people to vote a straight Democratic-party ticket.

Twenty years later, however, Senator Holloway organized a large dinner party in his church to honor me for what I had done as governor. He told the guests that night that the African American community had failed over these many years to recognize all I had done for them when I was in office. He said, "We hope to make amends for that tonight by awarding you this Martin Luther King, Jr. Humanitarian Award." It was an evening I continue to cherish.

The award reminded me once again how important it is for elected officials to work to solve community problems. That is where their focus should be, not on getting reelected. Working incessantly to get reelected is a disease that hampers effective leadership and infects the political process. The news media contributes to the problem by playing up an official's skill in getting reelected as a measure of his competence as an officeholder. The champion vote getter becomes a celebrity like the football player who scores the most points. Neither accomplishment is of much consequence to the community.

In facing up to problems, elected officials are bound to antagonize some voters. The more problems they deal with, the more opposition they will have. So to get reelected, the incumbents embrace the conventional wisdom which calls for avoiding controversial issues. Political parties exacerbate the problem: their primary goal is winning elections, not solving problems.

Sometime later, when I worked for the U.S. Congress heading the Office of Technology Assessment, I visited the offices of a great many senators and representatives and saw firsthand that a high percentage of the activity in their offices was directed toward getting reelected. In fact, representatives and senators from both

parties have told me that when new members report for duty
their leaders call them together and tell them something like this:
"If you think you came here to solve problems, you are mistaken.
You came here to get reelected."

News commentators and columnists, and even many reporters,
find it hard to refrain from judging every elected official's moves,
not by the public benefit of such actions, but rather how they will
affect the next election. This is especially true for the president,
the most important political problem solver in the nation.

It is of little long-term significance to a community if a given
elected official is not reelected. What matters is what that official
did in office. If all elected officials faced up to critical problems,
helped solve them, and then got thrown out of office, what a boon
that would be for America! There are plenty of other good people
to replace them. But when elected officials spend most of their
time working to get reelected and very little time on solving problems—and as a result keep being reelected—that is a sad day for
America. The problem could be mitigated by establishing term
limits for all elected office holders.

Polls show that voters in nearly all congressional districts believe
the Congress as a whole is doing a poor job while their own con-
gressmen and senators are doing a great job. Both of these ratings
cannot be true. Could it be that the voters judge Congress on its
true record but are conned by their own elected officials?

Some friends and supporters have said that maybe I was too
eager to change everything overnight, that I moved too quickly,
and thus stepped on too many toes during my one brief term as
governor. Had I gone more slowly, they said, I could have spent
a second term doing more of what needed to be done. Who
knows? The fact remains that we accomplished a good deal, some
of it of enduring value, in only four years.

Moreover, temporary setbacks can open the way for even
greater challenges and rewards. For example, if I had not been
denied a second term as governor of Delaware, I would not have
gone to work with Nelson Rockefeller and become chairman of
the President's Council on Environmental Quality.

V

Follow-Up to My Role as Governor

17

Saving and Re-Saving the Coastal Zone Act: The Need for Eternal Vigilance

THE EARLY 1970S WERE HEADY TIMES FOR THE ENVIRONMENTAL protection movement. Increasingly alarmed by the abuse of our natural world, more and more people had begun to challenge the traditional notions of progress and best use.

In Delaware, the people said "no" to business-as-usual along their precious coast and bays, and reaffirmed the importance of wildness and beauty and natural diversity to future generations as well as their own. This was a reaffirmation of values *other* than economic—yet the economy could only benefit from such a decision. By choosing to preserve the coast for plants and wildlife as well as for people, Delawareans had also chosen to maintain a way of life that made Delaware a desirable place to live and do business.

Other states were also moving to secure their natural legacies. In New York, another Republican governor, Nelson Rockefeller, led the charge for the Adirondack Park Agency Act. This landmark law created a zoning authority for an area the size of Vermont, a vast state park of private and public land that was threatened by real estate development, just as the Delaware coast was endangered by a proliferation of heavy industry and supertankers.

Vermont enacted a permit system to help preserve its rural areas and way of life in the face of growing pressures to subdivide and suburbanize. California, faced with runaway real estate development along much of its magnificent coastline, established a system of zoning commissions to preserve the remaining resources and insure continued public access. To save its rich farmland and open spaces from suburban sprawl, Oregon was about to protect its Willamette Valley through some of the nation's strictest land-use controls. Hawaii set up statewide zoning to keep its remaining pineapple plantations from becoming resorts and retirement communities; Wisconsin moved to protect its lakeshores and water quality; and Massachusetts enacted regulations to save what was left of its wetlands.

The United States Congress considered, but did not pass, a National Land Use Policy Act which would have provided financial help to the states to encourage land-use planning and zoning. The President's Council on Environmental Quality released a report entitled *The Quiet Revolution in Land Use Controls.* In the introduction, Chairman Russell Train expressed the view that land use was the most important environmental issue remaining substantially unaddressed as a matter of national policy.

This "wave of the future" would soon crest and break, however, and the pull of a strong undertow would be felt for much of the next generation—through the presidencies of Ronald Reagan and George Bush, into the congressional leadership of Newt Gingrich and the rise of a shrewdly misnamed "wise use movement."

Starting in the mid-1970s, the battle to save our resources, and the new laws intended to protect them, turned defensive. Citizen activists worked hard to maintain the gains of the early 1970s, as can be seen by Delaware's successful defensive actions in warding off repeated assaults on its Coastal Zone Act.

In the summer of 1971, this act was widely heralded. Glowing newspaper and magazine editorials appeared in other parts of the country, including the college town of Madison, Wisconsin, where I had spent my student years. Dozens of other states followed our lead by enacting coastal protections, though none went so far as to ban incompatible uses as Delaware had done.

On October 18th of that year, an international perspective was introduced. At a large dinner in New York's Waldorf Astoria, attended by conservation leaders from many countries, the World Wildlife Fund (WWF) recognized our victory in Delaware. WWF cited our state for prohibiting heavy industrial development of our unspoiled coastal area, a habitat of international importance for bird life and marine life. For this they gave me a special award, their Gold Medal. In presenting it, Prince Bernhard of The Netherlands, then president of WWF, pointed out that this was the first time that any community had ever won a fight against a major oil company. His enthusiasm for this accomplishment might have struck some observers as odd, since Shell Oil was headquartered in The Netherlands, and the Dutch royal family had large hold-ings in the company. But Prince Bernhard was clearly a conserva-tionist as well as a capitalist.

This dinner provided me with three splendid opportunities.

The first was meeting Prince Bernhard, a distinguished conser-vationist as well as a hero who led the Dutch forces when the Allies invaded Europe toward the end of World War II, helping to free his homeland from the Nazis. (His mother-in-law, wife and daughter have successively served as queen of The Netherlands.) Over the years I would work closely with him on world conserva-tion issues.

The second benefit of that dinner was the chance it gave me to share the spotlight with the people of Delaware. It was their vic-tory over the oil companies, not Russ Peterson's, that was really being recognized. In receiving the award, and at every chance I had after that, I explained that this gold medal had been pre-sented, through me as governor, to the citizens who had per-suaded their legislators to enact that law.

The dinner also gave me the chance to shake hands with my childhood hero, Charles Lindbergh, who was on the board of the World Wildlife Fund and, like Prince Bernhard, a dedicated conservationist. It was exciting to be with these world-famous con-servationists and to know they cared about Delaware's coast.

On receiving the WWF medal, I talked about the need for eter-nal vigilance. As many at the dinner knew from personal experi-ence, our gains in defending natural areas would have to be defended continually. Such battles can be lost only once. One hun-dred times we can prevent the damming of the Grand Canyon, the clearcutting of a rainforest, the extinction of a species, the loss of a cherished way of life. But if we lose the 101st battle, that defeat is likely to be permanent.

During this upbeat celebration, I could not help reflecting on another dinner in that same grand ballroom seven months earlier when the Commercial Development Association had given me a very different award for other innovative endeavors. Surrounded by the CEOs and other top executives of America's largest compa-nies, I had been cited for my work in launching new business ventures during my career with DuPont. That celebration had been cooled by the oil company representatives who lobbied me at every opportunity, urging me not to sign the Coastal Zone Act. When the Act was passed later that year, they and their allies—

the very same people who were praising my entrepreneurial efforts on behalf of DuPont—led the fight for the next twenty years against our innovative environmental protection.

My call for eternal vigilance at the World Wildlife Fund gala was a call that thousands of Delawareans and I would respond to many times over in the years ahead. The first assault came right after New Year's Day in 1974. The forces that had opposed the CZA from the start now mounted a concerted attack on the two-year-old statute. And from where they stood, the timing could not have been better. The new governor, Sherman W. Tribbitt, sided with them in their campaign to remove the ban on heavy industry in the coastal zone. The country was in the grip of an energy crisis, with long lines forming at gas stations. And rising unemployment had become a national concern.

The CZA provided a good scapegoat. Opponents claimed it gave Delaware an antibusiness image and contributed to the downturn in the state's economy. It was time to fix the act, they said, to make it more responsive to changing conditions. So as not to scare people, they professed to seek only a modest amendment.

On the surface, their approach sounded reasonable. They sought to replace the blanket ban on heavy industry by judging each application case by case, "on its merits." If an oil refinery or chemical plant were judged to be environmentally benign, if it met clearly defined standards for air and water quality, it would be approved. Otherwise, no permit would be issued.

On the surface, who can dispute the desirability of judging a development project—or anything else—on its merits? But there are fundamental problems with that approach. One problem is that such judgment is narrowly focused on one project. Think of those appointed to assess the costs and benefits of a single project favored by powerful financial and political interests. Will the judges seriously weigh the long-term consequences of the project, say a refinery or oil port, against the qualities that make the Delaware coast attractive for recreation and tourism? Will they weigh the future growth in other heavy industries that a single refinery or oil port will stimulate? Will they consider the cumulative effect of a succession of approvals of single projects?

Perhaps. But based on experience elsewhere, I would not count on it.

The other questions were *who* would judge the merits of the case? *Who* would decide whether a particular refinery, pulp mill, coal-storage island, or oil-tank farm is or is not compatible with the current use of the coastal zone? To Shell Oil or DuPont, a "clean" new refinery and the petrochemical complex it would spawn, seem wonderfully compatible. And to a young research chemist, as I had been in the 1940s, a new chemical plant, no matter where it is built, can be a beautiful thing.

Under the CZA, all heavy industry is deemed incompatible with the coastal zone. For this reason no new heavy industry is allowed there—period.

To change this law requires a majority vote of both houses of the state legislature and approval by the governor. If oil and chemical interests succeeded in removing the blanket prohibition on heavy industry, it would be the governor's appointed committee, the Coastal Zone Industrial Control Board, that decided on the merits of each particular proposal. In the case of Sherman Tribbitt, who shared industry's view that the Delaware coast was a place for refineries, chemical plants and super-ports, the likelihood was great that any review board he appointed would become a rubber stamp for approving such projects.

In fact, if this amendment to the CZA had succeeded, all that would have been left of the act would have been a zoning commission. Under such a system, the oil companies would never have lost. They might have been delayed for a short time, but eventually, they would have gotten their way. Almost any big developer who promises new jobs for a community and new taxes to the local government, is welcomed with open arms, no matter how detrimental the long-term consequences of that development might be. That is precisely what occurred in 1962 when New Castle County approved Shell Oil's request to build a new refinery.

On January 3, 1974, the first shot was fired. Charles B. McCoy, who had just stepped down as DuPont's CEO and now headed the company's finance committee, declared in a speech before the Wilmington Rotary Club that the CZA was too restrictive and contributed to "an anti–industry image" that impeded Delaware's economic growth. That same day the Building and Construction Trades Council mailed pamphlets to nearly every home in Delaware, claiming that the CZA cost jobs. In referring to McCoy's speech, DuPont's new CEO, Irving S. Shapiro, explained that the time had come for DuPont to speak out on the issue.

On January 8, Shell Oil announced that it would still build its refinery in the Delaware coastal zone if the CZA were relaxed.

Governor Tribbitt said, "It might not be a bad approach to go the case-by-case route." He had proposed this same amendment in 1971, as minority leader of the general assembly, before the bill was passed. The following week, the state's labor secretary, who served at the governor's pleasure, blamed the law for rising unemployment. The week after that, the business-oriented Committee of 100 criticized the "prohibitory" law for giving Delaware an "anti-business, anti–industrial image."

The contention that the CZA cost jobs, hurt the economy, discouraged new business, and gave Delaware a bad name would be repeated regularly for years thereafter. As always, the press rallied to the defense of the act. Ever alert to political zigzagging, Joe Smyth, editor of *The Delaware State News*, wrote an editorial on January 9, 1974, that recalled Sherman Tribbitt's statement when he was running against me for governor in 1972: "I am opposed to the construction of oil refineries in the coastal zone and oil off-loading facilities in the river, the bay or anywhere else off Delaware's coast. I have hunted on the wetlands, fished the streams, and enjoyed the beaches of Delaware. My children enjoy them, and I will do everything in my power to make sure that my children's children will do the same.'"

Then Smyth wrote,

> Okay, Governor, break your most solemn campaign promise. Sell your soul to Big Labor, Daddy DuPont and Big Oil. Violate the trust Delawareans placed in you.
>
> But what about your children's children? What will they think of you?

Not surprisingly, Governor Tribbitt made no attempt to answer that question.

The Philadelphia Inquirer weighed in (January 1974) with an editorial headlined, DESTROY DELAWARE TO SAVE IT? The writer referred to the pamphlet circulated by the Building and Construction Trades Council, in which the Council's president, Theodore W. (Toby) Ryan, Jr., declared the time had come to rewrite the CZA.

"Our amendment," explained Ryan, "will say that industry

should be allowed in the coastal zone as long as it meets any pollution standards the state wants to set." The state needed this kind of development for jobs and economic growth, Ryan said, because "no state can survive with an anti–industry image."

The Philadelphia Inquirer responded:

> But what about tourism and fishing? Aren't those industries, too? And what about space and scenery and solitude? Aren't those values to be protected, too? Must every square inch of America's dwindling open shoreline be sacrificed to industrial growth?
>
> The question, it seems to us, is not whether Delaware will survive, for it will, but how its citizens will live. To destroy forever the livability of a place is not our idea of the way to save it.

Business Week (March 2, 1974) put the issue in a national context. "As in 1971, the Delaware vote may again be an important portent" of whether or not the nation's coasts "will be free to fulfill their ecological and recreational functions."

The New York Times, (April 6, 1974) under the influence of John B. Oakes, its conservation-minded editorial page editor, added more perspective to the debate. "Delaware occupies only one-twentieth of one percent of this country's area—and the strip involved is a narrow fragment of the state. In the East Coast megalopolis that strip is a relatively unspoiled oasis, free alike of industrial complexes and honky-tonk tourist traps."

The *Times* also noted that "only oil refineries, petrochemical plants, steel and paper mills and marine terminals are specifically barred from the ocean and bay fronts, wetlands and open spaces. Small non-polluting enterprises are approved and welcomed; tourism is profitable and the hope is that by 1980 the entire bay can be a center for fishing, boating and picnicking. Unemployment, long below the national average, should become even less significant."

A little later, when we both presented testimony at a legislative hearing, Toby Ryan lit into me. "Governor Peterson did not defeat big business," he said, "because they're still in business. But he did defeat the working men and women of Delaware because unemployment has gone up since his little gift [the Coastal Zone Act] to the state, and the people recognized it, because they defeated him at the polls." Though he was dead wrong about why I lost the election, Ryan was right that unemployment among his members was high at that time, having reached 20 percent in early 1974.

But new refineries are not the only answer to unemployment. In its report on the Delaware debate, *Business Week* also quoted an executive at National Cash Register, which employed 1,300 people in southern Delaware. "The quality of life is a big plus," he said. "Our people who come from other states appreciate the beaches and recreational facilities."

About that time, the Delaware Chamber of Commerce announced jubilantly that "the pendulum is now swinging from ecology to the economy"—as if human beings (including Chamber of Commerce executives and oil company lawyers) can exist apart from the rest of creation, as if maintaining a healthy, beautiful environment is at odds with our economic well-being.

It was clearly an orchestrated attack by the most powerful interests in Delaware. Grace "Bubbles" Pierce called me in Washington, where I was now serving as chairman of the Council on Environmental Quality, and brought me up to date. I must come back to Wilmington, she said, and help to mobilize the troops.

Bubbles is a diminutive, dynamic, beach-loving activist whose husband once told her she would probably organize hell if she ends up down there. The name Bubbles goes back to her school days, and it captures perfectly her irrepressible, effervescent quality. But it does not do justice to her other striking qualities—a keen analytical sense, a super-salesman's ability to persuade and persist, and a bulldog's determination not to let go. During the unending battle to save the coast and the law that protects it, Bubbles Pierce has been the epitome of eternal vigilance.

The next day I responded with a press release to the Delaware papers and sent a similar statement to each legislator. Subsequently I made several speeches around the state. The key, as always, was to put the issue and the arguments in perspective. Unemployment *was* high in the construction industry in Delaware, as it was in other states, but the overall unemployment rate had been lower in Delaware than the national average for each of the previous five years.

Therefore, when they insisted that the state now suffered from an anti–industry reputation, the Chamber of Commerce and Du-Pont were themselves doing the state a disservice. Naturally, Delaware had a bad image among the oil and petrochemical companies who wanted to develop our coast but now could not do so. But the CZA was giving the state a good image almost everywhere else.

The point we hammered on was this: managers of companies that might be considering a move to Delaware tend to look at the quality of life that they and their employees can have here. Our beautiful oceanfront and bays, easily accessible and wholly conducive to the pure enjoyment of life, are an attraction to business. Furthermore, the jobs produced by the recreation industry greatly exceed the number of jobs an oil company can provide, simply because the oil industry is highly automated. As in any such debate over the need for environmental protection, we turned the jobs argument around.

During my term as governor we had convinced the Scott Paper Company to build a plant in Dover, the state capital. We made much of the fact that Scott had stated publicly that one reason they came to Delaware was the attractiveness of our unspoiled coast. The Scott plant provided as many jobs as three operating oil refineries would have. Andrew G. Knox, the state representative who had been the CZA's prime sponsor, again jumped to its defense, an act of some courage on his part considering that he was a DuPont research chemist, and the company was working to weaken the law.

As always, some of the strongest supporters of the coastal protection fight were members of the duPont family, who disagreed with the company's party line. For example, State Representative Thomas L. duPont, a Republican from Westover Hills, was quoted by *The Philadelphia Inquirer* on January 13, 1974, as saying it was "hogwash" to contend that neutralizing the Coastal Zone Act would improve the economy. He warned that the opponents were using the energy crisis as a crutch to destroy the Coastal Zone Act.

And Emily duPont joined with former governor Elbert Carvel to lead the newly resuscitated Delawareans for Orderly Development in the fight to keep the coastal protections in place. Mrs. duPont was the widow of Henry B. duPont, a former chairman of the finance committee of the DuPont Company. She was a colleague with whom I worked closely on community projects and who, along with her husband, was a generous financial supporter during my campaigns for governor.

Perhaps the most courageous performance of all came from my wife, Lillian, who always kept a watchful eye on developments in Delaware. In my absence, Lil agreed to speak at several public hearings on behalf of the Coastal Zone Act. Though she was as strong and unswerving in her beliefs as anyone I've ever known, public speaking made her uncomfortable. When we campaigned together in my race for governor, she spoke around the state to many groups, but I knew it was a job she did not relish. (However, I was told she did a better job than I in discussing the state's finances.)

Now, as she testified at a public hearing on the amendment to gut the Coastal Zone Act, construction workers in the audience heckled and booed her. What had previously been merely uncomfortable had turned into an ordeal, but she held her ground and made her points. If anyone deserved a gold medal from the World Wildlife Fund, it was Lil.

It was like old times, that winter and spring of 1974, with Andy Knox and Bubbles Pierce and the Delawareans for Orderly Development lobbying to save the law. At least a dozen other citizen groups jumped back into the fray. The state's United Auto Workers again rose to the occasion, counteracting opposition from the construction workers union, and once again the UAW was right on target. They cited the group's national president, Leonard Woodcock, who had warned against "an industrial strategy of playing on the economic fears of workers and communities to create widespread political opposition to cleaning up the environment" at a hearing before the U.S. Senate Committee on Public Works on June 23, 1971. The Delaware UAW declared that the Coastal Zone Act should be seen as an asset that made the state more desirable for industry's workers, executives, and their families, and that the only amendment to the Coastal Zone Act that could be tolerated would be one that strengthened it.

In March, State Representative Kermit H. Justice, a supporter of the act in 1971, now introduced the industry coalition's bill in the house, thereby removing the prohibition of heavy industry. Senator Robert J. Berndt, a chemist with DuPont, introduced a similar bill in the state senate.

Justice distributed a memo throughout the state, explaining why he had switched his position. The law, he said, was "unecological" and was "exerting a pernicious, strangulating effect on Delaware's economy." Concerning the ban on refineries, steel mills, and other heavy industry, he offered the following insight: "The narrow-mindedness of this approach is not only stupid but, if

I may be permitted a maudlin bit of patriotism, un-American as well."

It may be that Kermit Justice truly believed that a Shell refinery near Woodland Beach would have helped to solve our energy problems, though it is hard to imagine how, recalling that Delaware's one existing refinery was then operating well below capacity. Several years later, when serving as state transportation secretary, Justice seemed to recant. He told a reporter that his strong language in 1974 was intended to gain attention for his argument that the antibusiness image projected by the CZA was damaging the state's economy. He assured readers he supported the act then and that he still did.

At the same time, however, he assigned one member of his staff in the Department of Transportation to develop a plan for building a major port in the coastal zone. This would have been a clear violation of the CZA, but not unsurprising for someone who was known as a friend of developers. (Years later, in 1993, a federal court found him guilty of extorting money from developers. He received the maximum prison sentence of twenty-seven months.)

When the bill to amend the Coastal Zone Act was introduced— an amendment that would have essentially repealed the CZA—it was supported by a majority of legislators in both Houses. But when public hearings were held, the people again made clear that the patriotic duty of their elected representatives was not to open the coast to oil refineries and petrochemical plants but to save it for the enjoyment of future generations. The amendment died in committee. The Coastal Zone Act had survived its first attack.

Three years later, in 1977, another new governor presented another opportunity to undermine the law. When Pierre S. du-Pont IV replaced Sherman Tribbitt as the state's chief executive, legislators, businessmen and state officials saw their chance and again joined forces. The oil-company lawyers drafted new legislation—essentially the same bill that failed in 1974.

Governor duPont had been an early supporter of the Coastal Zone Act. He had also established a good environmental record as a U.S. representative. But in his last year as representative, while campagning for the governorship of Delaware, he jumped the fence to join the oil interests and the DuPont Company in opposing the CZA. Why the switch? Political analysts figured this was an early move to change his image in preparation for his subsequent campaign for the GOP presidential nomination. It had served him well to champion coastal protection in 1971, when he represented Delawareans in Congress; now it served his purposes to be a champion of unrestrained free enterprise.

Once again the press sprang to the defense of the act.

"The coastline has been protected," wrote Joe Smyth, editor of *The Delaware State News* (April 27, 1977), "but not a single desirable industry has been prevented from locating in Delaware." He then went on to write:

> If Delaware's economy has suffered, it is only because the chemical and oil industries, aided by the big-business oriented State Chamber of Commerce, have continually complained about Delaware's so-called 'anti–industry image.' If there is such an image, they've created it.
>
> Your representatives in the state legislature have been weakened by months of wining, dining and intensive lobbying by an unholy alliance of Big Oil, Big Daddy DuPont and even a few misguided Big Labor leaders.
>
> Having heard from all those organized pressure groups, your legislators need to hear from you.

Smyth even offered a suggestion about how the lawmakers should be dealt with if they caved in to heavy industry.

"If Delaware's legislators ruin the state's Coastal Zone Act," he said, "the entire bunch of them should be strapped to a dunking stool and dipped into a big vat of oil."

In April the bill to amend was introduced in the house. As reported on April 23, 1977, in *The Wilmington News Journal,* it had twenty-three co-sponsors. Only twenty-one votes were required for passage. House Majority Whip William J. Gordy stated that passage of the bill was virtually assured.

Once again, the legislature held hearings around the state; once again, citizens mobilized and the testimony overwhelmingly favored keeping the CZA as written.

I came home from Washington and spoke in the house chamber in Legislative Hall on May 11, 1977. It felt good to be back and to see the galleries crowded with people who loved the Delaware coast and were not going to let the CZA be compromised. As I ran through the litany of arguments for a strong act—and responded to the arguments of the oil companies for gutting it—I think it began to dawn on the lawmakers where their constituents stood. The cheering crowd in the galleries conveyed an unmistakable message.

The latest ploy of the oil companies was tied to the energy crisis. The prohibition on heavy industry should be removed, they argued, to allow development along the bay to receive the flood of oil they expected to discover from drilling off the coast. In my speech to the legislature I responded, "Before changes are made in a law that is considered landmark legislation around the country, let's wait to see if there's any significant amount of oil on our continental shelf."

Then, I suggested, we needed to answer a few important questions.

- Where will the oil come from?"
- Where will the pipelines be run?
- Who will benefit and who will be hurt by the pipeline route?
- How can we justify spending hundreds of millions of dollars for a new oil transport system when the one we now have in place has been working well and providing more jobs than the new one would?

The most persistent of our opponents' themes also had to be addressed directly and given some fresh perspective. Here in this familiar setting in Legislative Hall, I was able to draw on my experience since leaving the governor's office to counter the standard argument against the CZA:

> Delaware does not have an anti-business image. It has a pro-business image. In fact, it is frequently called the "corporation state"—run by and for corporations. This is not true, but it is a prevalent view around the United States.
>
> I have talked to hundreds of large audiences and met with thousands of people all over the country during the last few years—visiting 50 states—and have never heard anyone (except here at home) say Delaware has an anti-business image. The people of Delaware should censure the State Chamber of Commerce and their associates for spreading this false propaganda, especially for contending that the Delaware Coastal Zone Act gives our state a bad image. On the contrary, every place I go people know about our Coastal Zone Act and consider it a positive factor—making Delaware a *more* desirable place. In fact, it helps to counterbalance the image of Delaware as being the captive of corporations.

In considering the attractiveness of Delaware to outsiders, one should check the population growth rate over the last six years in the mid-Atlantic area. Between 1970 and 1976, Delaware's population increased by 6.2 percent—definitely ahead of our neighboring states and ahead of the national average. New Jersey's population grew only 2.3 percent. It is hard to find any evidence of any industry rushing to locate in the Marcus Hook area, the industrial wasteland north of Wilmington, for example.

A study made several years ago by the Sussex County Council showed that companies considering locating in that county rated the Coastal Zone Act an attraction—not a deterrent.

Instead of spreading misleading propaganda about our coastal protections, I encouraged the legislature to pass a resolution urging Governor duPont and his staff, the Chamber of Commerce and the labor unions to capitalize on the *good image* the Delaware coastal zone gave the state. You should all work together, I suggested, to attract businesses and jobs to Delaware, for it is a highly desirable place to work and live.

Mindful of the need to propose preferable alternatives, I suggested the state use the University of Delaware's College of Marine Studies' campus to attract national governmental and private laboratories and marine-based businesses to that area. And finally, I suggested that the legislature study the jobs, business earnings and tax receipts that would be lost to Delaware if the coastal zone below the Chesapeake and Delaware Canal changed its image from an oasis for tens of thousands to a haven for heavy industry.

These points, of course, needed to be heard beyond the chamber where I was then speaking. Thanks to the Delaware press, my testimony was reported throughout the state the following day.

In the end, it was an organized and outspoken citizenry pressuring their elected representatives who carried the day. Gradually the bill's sponsors withdrew their support. The ban on heavy industry remained in effect.

Perhaps the most outrageous proposal for the Delaware coast came from a former colleague who, initially, had been at the forefront of the campaign to protect the coast. Dr. William Gaither, a stalwart member of my Governor's Task Force on Marine and Coastal Affairs which had produced the report providing the scientific basis for the CZA, experienced a dramatic change of heart.

For many years he had been dean of the College of Marine Studies, which we had envisioned as a center for research and teaching, dedicated to enhancing the natural values of the coastal zone. Economically, educationally, and ecologically, the development of this institution seemed the best possible use of our natural resources. Thus we were stunned to learn that Bill Gaither, who had led this institution during its formative years, was proposing dredging huge quantities of sand from the best fishing area in Delaware Bay to build a pair of thousand-acre islands as the terminus of a major deepwater port, connected by a causeway with a new highway and railway running the length of the state. With this infrastructure in place, the coastal zone would become a center for power generation, steel making, ship building, oil importing and refining, and the export of coal and grain. This extreme proposal ran headlong into the law of the state and went nowhere.

A more serious threat loomed in 1985 in the form of a legal challenge. Though Sandy Campbell and Dave Kiefer had worked overtime to make the Coastal Zone Act as challenge-proof as possible, we knew that sooner or later some prohibited industry would raise the constitutional issue.

The challenge came from Norfolk Southern, a railroad and van line company. Their lawsuit stemmed from the company's plan to use the Big Stone Anchorage, an area well offshore in the mouth of the bay, to lighter or transfer coal from smaller vessels to super-collier transport ships, the equivalent of the petroleum industry's super-tankers. One of the largest American exporters of coal, mostly through the Port of Norfolk, Norfolk Southern argued that the Big Stone Beach anchorage was the only protected transfer point on the U.S. coast between Maine and Mexico that was deep enough to accommodate the big ships. They claimed that it provided the best way for them to expand their ability to attract world markets for coal. The company also claimed that the additional export business would create 2,000 jobs in coal-producing states.

The heart of the corporation's legal argument—the first time any state's coastal zone protections had been so challenged—was that Delaware's prohibition of offshore transfers of bulk materials such as coal, violated the commerce clause of the U.S. Constitution, effectively usurping Congress's right to regulate trade crossing state borders.

As in 1971, the federal government joined the side of heavy industry. At that time, the Nixon administration had fought enacting the ban. Now the Reagan administration hoped to lift the ban through court action. Both the U.S. Justice Department and the Department of Commerce filed supporting briefs that included the following statement: "While the U.S. recognizes and takes most seriously the importance to Delaware of maintaining its recreational beaches, tourism and fishing industries, we believe that these concerns do not outweigh the burden to interstate commerce."

Having the federal as well as the state executive branch working against us was certainly not helpful. To counterbalance that bad luck, however, we had some good luck in the form of Michael N. Castle, Pete duPont's successor as governor of Delaware. On June 10, 1985, Castle fired off the following telegram to Commerce Secretary Malcolm Baldrige: "I understand the profit motive driving Norfolk Southern, but I find it disturbing that such corporate tunnel vision is shared by the federal agency responsible for administering the nation's Coastal Zone Management Act."

In successfully combatting attacks on the Coastal Zone Act in the legislature, a network of activists mobilized hundreds of others to write, call, visit and otherwise pressure their lawmakers, while the spotlight of publicity illuminated the issues and the interests involved. This time a long, costly legal defense lay ahead. A different strategy was needed.

Regina Mullen, deputy attorney general for Delaware who would be handling the case, told me of her limited resources. Compounding the problem was the lukewarm support of her boss, Attorney General Charles M. Oberly, who had earlier sided with the decision by John E. Wilson III, secretary of the Department of Natural Resources and Environmental Control, to give Norfolk Southern a permit for the proposed lightering operation. (When Wilson's decision had been reversed by Delaware's Coastal Zone Industrial Control Board, and Norfolk Southern sued, Oberly and Wilson were named as the state's reluctant defendants in the case.)

The defense of the Act rested entirely with Regina Mullen. Without help, this one attorney, with little backing from the state agencies run by Oberly and Wilson, faced a potentially overwhelming struggle against Norfolk Southern and the federal government. As bright, energetic, knowledgeable, and dedicated as Regina Mullen was—and she possessed all these virtues in abundance—her task was daunting.

What we needed, as in any major court battle of this sort, was legal support from national citizen groups and financial support from their members to help pay for a prolonged lawsuit. As I was then president of National Audubon Society, I was able to arrange for three national groups with expertise in coastal issues to inter-vene as defendants—Audubon, Sierra Club, and a highly profes-sional, no-nonsense outfit of lawyers and scientists who specialized in such cases, the Natural Resources Defense Council (NRDC).

NRDC, which had an impressive record in winning cases in federal courts, was joined by two other defendants: the Delaware Wildlife Association and the Delaware Saltwater Fishing Associ-ation, the two citizen groups that had initiated the appeal revers-ing the permit decision, thereby triggering Norfolk Southern's lawsuit in the first place. Additional briefs were filed by Governor Castle, the state's congressional delegation, and four friends of the court: National Wildlife Federation, Delaware Nature Education Society, Delaware Wild Lands, and the California Coastal Commission.

John Adams, who heads NRDC, assigned Lynne Edgerton as its staff attorney in the case. Lynne, in turn, arranged for the New York law firm of Weil, Gotshal and Manges to assist in the case. For three years, as the suit made its way through the courts, Lynne provided valuable support to Regina Mullen, the lead attorney in the case.

At the time John Adams agreed to intervene, I offered my help in raising funds for the costly litigation. In early 1985 we wrote joint appeal letters to NRDC's membership that raised over $100,000, the best return the organization had ever received in this kind of fund appeal. By portraying the threat to Delaware's Coastal Zone Act as a threat to all coastal areas, the letters struck a nerve with NRDC members throughout the country.

The four page letter from John got right to the point:

> Dear Concerned American:
> I want to bring to your immediate attention a terribly threatening lawsuit brought by the giant Norfolk Southern Corporation against the people of Delaware.
> If Norfolk Southern wins this federal case, oil and coal companies across America will have what they always wanted: a constitutional right to industrialize seashores, regardless of state laws that protect the natural beauty of coastlines and provide for their use as recre-ational areas.

My note supported John's argument in a more personal way:

> Dear Friends of the Environment,
>
> One of my proudest achievements as governor of Delaware was the passage in 1971 of America's first state coastal protection law.
>
> When I heard of Norfolk Southern Corporation's suit to take away our right to protect our coasts, I immediately called my friends at the Natural Resources Defense Council to ask for their expert help.
>
> At stake is the very future of America's beautiful coastlines. Should Norfolk Southern win, you can bet that every coal and oil giant in America will use that victory to their advantage.

The federal district court eventually ruled in favor of Delaware. When Norfolk Southern appealed, the U.S. Circuit Court of Appeals also found for Delaware. In September 1987, the company announced it would not appeal to the U.S. Supreme Court. The CZA had withstood the long-awaited constitutional challenge.

While this court battle was being waged, another challenge came from a different direction. Three days before the end of the 1985 legislative session, a bill was introduced, at the request of Governor Castle's administration, to amend the Delaware-New Jersey Compact that had created the Delaware River and Bay Authority (DRBA). This agency owns and operates the Delaware Memorial Bridge and the Cape May-Lewes Ferry. Both Delaware and New Jersey wanted to change the bi-state agreement so that each state could separately spend some of the money earned by the two facilities.

Governor Castle's goal was to tap into these ample cash reserves to finance transportation and related projects in Delaware. Under the new bill, the DRBA could undertake projects which, "in the judgment of the Authority, are required for the sound economic development of the area," such as refineries, chemical plants, paper mills, and supertanker ports. The DRBA would simply take their projects one-by-one to the state legislature for approval.

If this bill were passed, it would, because it followed the Coastal Zone Act, supersede the earlier law. The semiautonomous group of appointed commissioners on the DRBA would become a dominant, virtually unaccountable force for industrializing the coastal zone. To many veteran defenders of the CZA, the strategy seemed both shrewd and sinister: if you cannot neutralize the act directly through amendment, and if you cannot beat it in the courts, then you just pass another law that circumvents it.

Governor Castle insisted he intended no such thing, and I believed him. Ever since he had been a state senator and supported passage of the CZA, he had strongly supported it. But now the actions of some key people in his administration did not reflect a similar commitment.

Kermit Justice, by now the state secretary of transportation, was soon to hire Booz, Allen and Hamilton, a management consulting firm, to study port development in other states. For Delaware, Justice moved to establish a Port Advisory Committee to look into the possibilities of a large port at Big Stone Beach in defiance of the Coastal Zone Act. To spend state dollars on such a study was in direct conflict with his oath of office to uphold the laws of the state. Some of us began to wonder whether he was in collusion with the Philadelphia-based developers who persistently pushed for port development in our coastal zone.

And then there was Michael Harkins, the governor's secretary of state, who told *The Wilmington News Journal* that the Delaware River and Bay Authority should purchase 1,750 acres of waterfront land opposite the Big Stone Beach anchorage. Still owned by the consortium of oil companies, this tract formed the centerpiece of Dr. William Gaither's scheme for industrializing Delaware Bay.

Harkins also directly recruited legislative support for the governor's bill giving carte blanche to the DRBA. Harkins listed as cosponsors an astounding thirty-nine of forty-one representatives and seventeen of twenty-one senators. Then he arranged for introduction of the bill three days before the end of the legislative session and pushed for its passage in that short time.

Gwynne Smith, a state representative, explained Harkins' method of lining up sponsors. She told me that Harkins had informed the legislators that unless he heard from them, he would put their names on the bill. Not having heard from most of them in the busy, concluding weeks of the session, he added their names as sponsors.

Alerted by Lillian, I came home to Delaware from my Audubon office in New York City to meet with editors and reporters of the Wilmington newspapers. The next day they reported my concern, and editorial writers and columnists also sounded the alarm. The governor and legislators now realized they were being watched, and press coverage also alerted conservationists throughout the state.

The next morning I arranged for a letter to be placed on the desk of each state representative and senator, urging them to defer action on the bill. Many legislators removed their names as cosponsors. The bill was tabled.

When this same bill resurfaced in 1989, we environmentalists were ready for it. I sent a letter to the governor asking that he amend the bill by stipulating that it not take precedence over the CZA. Then I joined several others in a press conference denouncing the bill as it had been written.

Governor Castle sent Secretary Harkins to my home to discuss the matter. After expressing his irritation about my blocking his bill, and after he had told me he was the only friend I had left in Delaware, he listened to my position and agreed to take an amendment I had written to Governor Castle. The next day the governor accepted it. The Delaware River and Bay Association would be treated under the Coastal Zone Act as any other developer would be. With that safeguard in place, the bill became law in 1990.

Although attempts to scuttle or weaken the Coastal Zone Act had failed in the legislature and in the courts, the Chemical Industry Council of Delaware and Delmarva Power & Light Company managed until recently to stymie the implementation of one important provision of the act: regulations for administering it. Regulations were required to serve as guidelines in deciding how and where the law applies, when a permit might be granted, and what administrative procedures needed to be followed. They would help remove possible ambiguities and avoid inconsistencies.

For seventeen years after passage of the act, no significant effort to develop the regulations was made by successive secretaries of the Department of Natural Resources who administered it. This inaction was due to persistent and successful lobbying of the secretary and the governor. Industry lobbyists did not want comprehensive guidelines that weighed factors such as the cumulative impact of new developments on the quality of the environment in the coastal zone. They wanted each application for a permit considered on its specific merits. They knew from experience this was a more certain way to gain approval from a sympathetic administrator.

Finally, in 1990, Governor Castle appointed a nationally known environmentalist, Dr. Edwin "Toby" Clark, to head DNREC. Over a two-year period, and with extensive input from industry and the community, Clark submitted his proposed regulations, as required, to the Coastal Zone Industrial Control Board. The board, in turn, held a series of hearings, made some final alterations, and adopted a set of regulations that became law on July 25, 1993.

The Delaware chemical industry and Delmarva Power challenged the new regulations on a technicality. The control board, they said, had not allowed the necessary time between a private executive session, when the final regulations were considered, and a public session, where they were officially voted on. Next, the state's business court, the Court of Chancery, declared the regulations null and void on the basis that the Administrative Procedures Act had not been followed properly. With one judicial flush, three years of conscientious work, and thousands of hours of public input, went down the drain!

The secretary of DNREC and the Coastal Zone Industrial Control Board could have solved this problem easily by replaying the last steps of the approval process, carefully following the requirements of the Administrative Procedures Act. But by this time a new governor, Thomas Carper, had appointed replacements for Toby Clark and the longtime chairman of the Coastal Zone Industrial Control Board, Donald Crossan, a former dean of agriculture and vice president of the University of Delaware. Their successors let business have its way.

Three years later, in 1996, Governor Carper announced his determination to see that the regulations were established. He asked DNREC Secretary Christophe Tulou to pursue this goal. Tulou hired the Consensus Building Institute of Boston to work with representatives of industry, environmental organizations and state government, all appointed by the governor, to develop by consensus guidelines to be followed in preparing the required regulations. I participated in this exercise.

After two years of many meetings, our committee reached consensus, all of us including the governor signing off on a detailed memorandum of understanding that paved the way for Secretary Tulou to prepare regulations that should be free from legal challenges by either industry or environmentalists. His regulations, approved by our committee, were submitted as required by the Coastal Zone Act to the Coastal Zone Industrial Control Board on June 1, 1998. Following several public workshops and a hearing, the Coastal Zone Industrial Control Board approved the regulations in November 1998. All regulations were now legally binding twenty-seven years after they had been mandated in the CZA. Governor Carper's decision to pursue a consensus-building approach was the key to success.

Will the people of Delaware ultimately prevail in protecting their coast? I believe so. Despite unrelenting efforts by opponents, our experience in Delaware shows that it can be done. The law has withstood all attacks, and its effective administration will be enhanced by the mandated regulations.

An oil-company executive once said he was sure of eventual victory which he defined as gutting or somehow circumventing the CZA. "The oil companies will be around much longer than Peterson," he was quoted as saying.

He missed an important point. There are many other citizen activists besides Peterson who care about the quality of life in Delaware. Pressure from thousands of voters has saved the CZA despite efforts by the chemical industry, oil and coal interests, state and federal government, and Delaware Chamber of Commerce to undermine it. From the large number of citizens who invariably rally to defend the Act, from the 90 percent of Delawareans who want to protect their coast from the industrial activity that has destroyed so many other coasts, will come leaders who will be around long after the world runs out of oil by the middle of the next century, and long after the oil industry takes it place in history.

The oil company spokesman missed another point. The CZA is not the final step in the process of protecting our coast. By banning heavy industry and regulating other industrial development, the CZA serves as a holding action. It has held now for twenty-seven years. In the meantime, all of the land the oil companies once owned has been acquired by the state or by private conservation groups operating in the public interest. These lands will be permanently maintained as open space, as wildlife habitat, as places for public recreation. No amount of political pressure from big business, no amount of campaign contributions or other financial incentives to elected and appointed officials will ever change that.

In 1985, the critical 1,750 acres at Big Stone Beach, where the consortium of oil companies had planned major building activity, were acquired by Delaware Wild Lands. More recently that same group acquired an adjoining 900 acres, giving them control of the coastline that the oil companies, William Gaither, Kermit Justice, and the Delaware River and Bay Authority, among many others, have had designs on.

The heroes of the movement to protect our coastal zone and other natural areas include people like Ted Harvey, who headed Delaware Wild Lands for many years. Ted is memorialized formally in the Harvey Conservation Area near Big Stone Beach and informally up and down the coast, in the many places that will remain perpetually protected thanks to him and his colleagues, among them his son, Rusty, who has continued the quiet, unrelenting campaign to insure the *lasting* preservation of our coast.

Another hero is William Daniels, owner of 383 acres on Delaware Bay that was surrounded by the open land that Shell purchased as its refinery site. Despite repeated generous offers from Shell, Mr. Daniels refused to sell.

One day when I was governor, I dropped by unexpectedly to meet Mr. Daniels and to thank him for his resolve. I was driven up to his house in the governor's black limousine. As I stepped out of the car, Mr. Daniels came out of his front door, rushed over to me and ordered me off his land.

"Get the hell out of here," he yelled. As I walked toward him, he realized who I was. His anger turned to embarrassment.

He apologized and said he thought I was "one of those Shell guys." Then a friendly smile came over his weathered face. He threw his arms around me and exclaimed, "Welcome, Governor, welcome!"

I thanked him for his support of the CZA, and for resisting the overtures from the oil company. Proudly he showed me around his property, which bordered the river. He showed me the old piers where ships came to dock early in the century, bringing picnickers to escape from the heat and clamor of Philadelphia for a day in the country. They were here to enjoy Delaware's beautiful bay. It was still unspoiled, and if Mr. Daniels and I and most other Delawareans had our way, it would remain so.

When I left, he promised he would never sell out. As we drove away, my driver pointed out the bumper sticker on a car in Mr. Daniels' driveway. It said, "To Hell with Shell."

This story has two endings, one sad and one happy. The sad ending is what happened after Mr. Daniels' death a few years later. His two sons quarreled over the disposition of the property. One wanted it to be publicly owned and protected. The other had different ideas. The latter son ambushed and killed his brother, was convicted of murder, and incarcerated nearby at Smyrna. The happy ending is that the people of Delaware, through their state government, were able to buy Mr. Daniels' land a decade later.

How often we hear the advocates of business-as-usual call the arguments of environmentalists "emotional," as if there is something wrong with feeling passionate about the need to protect the Earth. At the beginning of the coastal zone fight, Shell tried to dismiss our cause because it was based on emotionalism. More recently, in a paper presented at a symposium on the CZA, oil and chemical industry representatives stated that "the CZA of 1971 was an emotional response to the fear of loss."

You bet it was! The word emotion comes from the Latin *movere*, to move. Who can not be moved by the destruction of our natural heritage, or by successful efforts to save some of it?

Loving a place, such as a wild and beautiful ocean coast or bay is what motivates people to work for its protection. While our side lacks one of the most powerful motivators of all—the profit motive—we have the ability to move people in other, equally compelling ways. Our love for our coast proved to be one such way.

Of course we need to be as factual and as scientific as we can, and of course we must refute the arguments of developers about job creation, tax benefits, national security, and competitiveness with data and statistics of our own. For example, environmental regulations have created many more jobs than they have lost, and many business leaders now claim such regulations have been good for the bottom line.

Another necessity in working to save the Delaware coast, and anything else of value that stands in the way of what our society has traditionally regarded as progress, is to propose better ways of doing things. As our opponents like to point out, as if it were somehow a failing, the Coastal Zone Act is a *prohibitory* law. Indeed it is. It prohibits destructive uses. That is what makes this CZA one of the best environmental protection laws ever devised.

But the CZA also encourages many other uses. Advocates of the act have spent at least as much time proposing as they have opposing.

To the oil companies who claimed they had to build a new refinery on Delaware Bay to produce more gasoline to fill the tanks of more automobiles, the people of Delaware responded with a better idea. "Don't build a new plant on virgin lands," they said. "Expand production at existing sites."

To the Delmarva Power and Light Company [now Conectiv], which unsuccessfully tried to get the law changed so it could build a coal-fired facility in the coastal zone at some future date, those of us who treasure unspoiled beaches and wild marshes called on Delmarva to work with the state to pursue the soft-energy path by wasting less electricity and developing environmentally benign solar energy, thus avoiding the need for more fossil fuel or nuclear plants.

When the State Chamber of Commerce complained about what was prohibited on the coast, we emphasized what was allowed. When our opponents talked about jobs lost by banning heavy industry, we talked about the jobs to be gained by protecting the coast for tourism and recreation. When opponents talked about Delaware's "bad image" with businesses that might otherwise move to our state, we talked about preserving a quality of life that attracts new businesses and research facilities.

We were not saying "no way" to the use and development of Delaware's coast. We were—and still are—saying that there is a better way.

Often a news reporter has asked me: "Oil refineries, steel mills, paper mills, supertankers all have to go somewhere. If not here, where would you put them?"

Well, let's talk about oil refineries as just one example. There is no need to put a new refinery anywhere on the bay. We can use what we already have by careful expansion. At DuPont, we had the assignment of increasing the capacity of some major plants. And this is what oil refineries on the Delaware River did when they were blocked from building along our undeveloped coast. We have already allocated a certain amount of space to the operation of refineries; the challenge now is to use that space more effectively.

We also need to give higher priority to safeguarding our natural areas and their plant and animal life. People all over the world need to draw lines around choice natural areas and say they are off limits for certain incompatible operations.

The Coastal Zone Act has made the choice between conservation and wasteful consumption. It addresses some fundamental questions about which way this country should go.

Do we really need to import more and more crude oil to meet

the energy needs of an expanding population? Or can we find ways to reduce the energy our society needs by insulating our homes more effectively and building cars that will go sixty miles on a gallon of gas? Do we really need to turn Delaware Bay into the nation's largest oil port?

It seems fair to ask, twenty-seven years after its passage, if the CZA has done what it was created to do. I think it has. When the act became law, more than 80 percent of Delaware's shoreline and adjacent land south of the Chesapeake and Delaware Canal was used for recreation, wildlife preserves, parks, farms and woodlands. Today that is still the case, and more of the coast enjoys *lasting* protection, thanks to the work of Delaware Wild Lands and many others.

Can CZA do the job alone?

Of course not. Delaware shares its river and bay with three other states—New Jersey, Pennsylvania, and New York. Unless those states also enact strong protective measures, Delaware Bay can be damaged in any number of ways.

The CZA does not deal with the exploding residential subdivision and commercial development that continues to wreak ecological havoc on coastlines from Newfoundland to Key West. Additional controls are clearly needed.

Nevertheless we have come a long way. Delaware has established a national model and maintained its coast as a national treasure.

Today one can find hanging on the wall in many Delaware homes (as it does in mine) a poster of a beautiful scene along Delaware's coast. Beneath the picture is the statement, "We have faced a challenge and made a choice. If uncontrolled industrial growth means great loss of our natural resources, then the price is too high and we don't want it."

18

Rejuvenating the Wilmington Riverfront

On May 30, 1992, I took my large umbrella and walked in a modest rain the few blocks from my home to the Soldiers and Sailors Monument on Delaware Avenue to observe Wilmington's annual Memorial Day commemoration. There stood State Senator Robert Marshall, rain dripping from his chin.

"Stand under my umbrella, Senator," I said. He jumped at the invitation.

"Thanks, Governor," he responded. Then, showing little concern for the on-going speeches, the senator immediately got down to business. Saying he had been wanting to talk to me, he asked how we could stop the International Petroleum Corporation from starting up its plant on the Christina River.

"We're too late, Bob. I visited them a week ago. Their plant is completely finished and they have all the necessary permits. If we had had the foresight and were properly diligent a year or so ago, we could have stopped them."

International Petroleum's plant was ready to start distilling and reclaiming used motor oil. This served a good environmental cause, recycling used oil rather than dumping it down sewers or on the ground. But the plant could have been built elsewhere.

Like me, Senator Marshall was interested in cleaning up the abandoned industrial sites along the Christina River rather than adding new industry. Rusting derricks, dilapidated buildings and extensive dumps lined the river as monuments to its industrial heyday. Over 700 ships, for example, were built there during World War II. Earlier it had been a major center for building railway cars.

Now we talked about what we could do to keep other new plants from being built there, as Delaware had done in the coastal zone.

I suggested he ask Governor Castle to appoint a task force to develop a plan for the future of the river and get his fellow senators to support his request. Senator Marshall did so, and on June 24, 1992, only twenty-five days after our meeting in the rain, the Delaware Senate unanimously endorsed Resolution No. 62, calling on Governor Michael Castle "to appoint a blue ribbon task force to make recommendations concerning the future of the Brandy-wine and Christina Rivers."

These two rivers, one on the north and one on the south, wrap the heart of Wilmington before they join and flow together into the Delaware River and Bay. The Swedes landed near the mouth of the Christina River in 1638 and established the first permanent settlement of Europeans in the Delaware area. The rapidly flow-ing Brandywine supplied early industrial plants along its banks with water power. A paper mill was built there in 1787, and other commercial mills followed, including the E. I. duPont de Nemours powder mills at Hagley in 1802. Thanks to the vision and generos-ity of William P. Bancroft, a highly successful mill owner in the late 1800s, the natural integrity of much of the Brandywine as it passes through Wilmington was preserved or restored, creating what is now called Brandywine Park. The lower part of the Bran-dywine, however, like the Christina, had been industrialized and subsequently abandoned.

In October 1992, Governor Castle appointed the task force re-quested by Senator Marshall and named Dr. E. Arthur Trabant, president emeritus of the University of Delaware, and me as co-chairmen. The task force included the mayor of Wilmington, James H. Sills, Jr.; New Castle County Executive Dennis E. Green-house; State Senators Robert I. Marshall and Andrew G. Knox; Secretary of the Department of Natural Resources and Environ-mental Control Edwin "Toby" Clark; and forty other representa-tives of governments, businesses, environmental organizations and neighborhood groups. An additional fifty advisors were en-listed. William J. Cohen was assigned as executive assistant.

Shortly after our appointment, Dr. Trabant and I met with Joseph Carbonell and James Nelson in their offices along the Christina River. Over the years these two prominent architects had developed separate plans for rejuvenating the riverfront. We asked them to enlist the pro bono services of the Delaware Society of Architects in developing a common vision for the waterfront. They agreed to do so, and over the next year, fourteen architec-tural firms worked closely with the task force worked to create an exciting vision of what the Wilmington waterfront could become.

Hundreds of community leaders and neighborhood residents were consulted during the project.

On October 11, 1994, the task force presented its *Vision For The Rivers* to 350 community leaders at the Delaware Theatre Company. After showing a video of the history of the waterfront, Jim Nelson masterfully presented the architects' plan by projecting on a huge screen an artist's conception of what the river could become. Among other things, the plan called for dredging a huge dump to create a new inner harbor, building a walkway the length of the riverfront, constructing a convention center, a sports arena, marinas, entertainment facilities, restaurants, hotels and parks. It also included establishing a major tourist attraction around the site of the Swedes' landing in 1638 and dedicating 285 acres as an urban wildlife refuge.

As chairman of the meeting, I handed our report to Governor Thomas Carper and encouraged him to get out front of the project and bring substantial state resources to bear to make it happen. He responded enthusiastically, recognizing our "creative proposal as having statewide importance." He pledged his support and agreed to appoint a transition team to develop a detailed plan for implementing the vision.

One by one, Mayor James Sills, County Executive Dennis Greenhouse, U.S. Representative and former Governor Michael Castle, U.S. Senator William Roth, and U.S. Senator Joseph Biden's representative, Michael McCabe, came to the podium to express strong support for the project. Although the news media and many citizen leaders praised the proposal, some skeptics belittled it as another pipe dream.

On January 18, 1995, Governor Carper appointed the forty-six member Brandywine and Christina Rivers Transition Team, naming DuPont Vice President Peter Morrow and me as cochairmen. During the next five months, with the aid of fifty-four technical, business, engineering and financial advisers, the team developed a plan for implementing the thirty-eight specific projects identified in the *Vision For The Rivers*. The plan called for the legislature to establish the Delaware Riverfront Development Corporation and to appropriate $25 million for fulfilling important infrastructure needs, such as improving access to the riverfront, providing bulkheading and boardwalks along the river, and acquiring critical properties.

In order to impress the legislature with the merits of our proposal, I arranged for Jim Nelson and me to appear on successive days before official sessions of Delaware's House of Representatives and Senate, using our highly effective big screen presentation. Both houses received our message positively.

On June 30, 1995, the legislature established the Delaware Riverfront Development Corporation and appropriated $10 million for its use. The governor, the mayor of Wilmington, the county executive, four leaders of the legislature and eight others, including me, were designated as board members. Peter Morrow became chairman.

On March 11, 1996, Michael S. Purzycki, a prominent lawyer and former government official, was appointed executive director. Delaware's ambitious and exciting effort to rejuvenate the Wilmington waterfront was underway. Thanks to the superb work of our executive director and his deputy, Michael Hare, much has been accomplished in only two and a half years.

Governor Carper, true to his word, has been out front on this program, coupling the power and prestige of his office with a boundless enthusiasm for making the Wilmington waterfront a major Delaware attraction. And Mayor Sills has joined him in an effective partnership.

Several major projects were completed on the riverfront in 1998. A full-size replica of the *Kalmar Nyckel II,* the ship that brought the Swedes to Wilmington, was built and commissioned by the Kalmar Nyckel Foundation and started plying the eastern seaboard as Delaware's goodwill ambassador and as a symbol of Wilmington's rejuvenated riverfront. The ship will be important to the promotion of what we expect will become a major tourist attraction, the place where the Swedes landed and established the first colony of Europeans in Delaware. The Kalmar Nyckel Foundation was assisted in this project by a grant and a loan totaling $2.7 million from the Riverfront Development Corporation.

Wilmington's Riverfront Park was dedicated, providing an inviting gateway to the Christina River, and the first sections of the eventual 1.5 mile-long riverwalk were completed. The new Riverfront Arts Center opened with a spectacular exhibit of the wealth of Nicholas and Alexandra on loan from Russia's celebrated Hermitage Museum. Amtrak established its Consolidated National Operations Center on the riverfront in a building renovated and expanded by the Riverfront Development Corporation for lease to Amtrak. New streets and parking areas were completed to improve access to the area.

Early in 1999 a new concept of retail marketing will be introduced when the nation's first outlet center designed just for up-scale catalog companies opens. And a 285-acre urban wildlife refuge will be dedicated. Plans for building a large movie theater, a civic arena and a marina are being championed by Mayor Sills.

When thousands of people start coming to the riverfront, skeptics will stop their naysaying, and it will be time to move to the next stage—building the inner harbor, the jewel in the city's vision of its waterfront. Then Wilmington will be able to join San Antonio and Baltimore as outstanding examples of how enlightened communities can use a natural asset.

19

Reducing the Crime Rate by Attacking the Causes

FOR THIRTY-FIVE YEARS I HAVE BEEN WORKING TO HELP SOLVE America's serious crime problem: in the Three S Citizens' Campaign, as governor, as chairman of the National Commission on Criminal Justice Standards and Goals, and as a citizen lobbyist on the national scene. The crime rate has escalated over that time, except for occasional temporary downturns. Only time will tell whether or not the current downturn, at this time of a booming economy, will last.

I believe the major long-term growth in crime occurred because America has never worked hard at preventing crime—at getting to the causes of crime. Instead, we have concerned ourselves with symptoms. Individuals break the law, the police apprehend them, the jails hold them, the courts sentence them, the prisons warehouse them, and a handful of probation and parole officers try to keep track of the huge army of offenders released to the community. This is the present criminal justice system. Its expenses escalate, but little is spent on preventing people from entering the system. The most cost-effective approach to this alarming national problem is virtually ignored. Instead, we are on a prison-building spree.

This is no measure of the diligence of our political leaders in protecting us from criminals; it is a measure of their failure to come to grips with a major national problem. It is also an example of government's irrational behavior. In the name of crime prevention, nonviolent offenders are packed into enormously expensive prisons, in essence entering them in "colleges of criminal knowledge" from which they graduate better trained by their classmates for a life of crime.

While many parents plan, save, and borrow to send their teenagers off to college at a cost of $10,000 to $40,000 per year (less for those who can live at home), realizing that such training is vital to their children's future livelihood and happiness, other parents stand helplessly by while their teenagers are sent off to prison at a cost of $35,000 to $50,000 per year of taxpayer dollars to acquire criminal skills and antisocial attitudes that are permanent handicaps to their future happiness and productivity. According to an article in *The New York Times*, September 28, 1997, California and Florida now spend more to incarcerate people than to educate their college age population.

The news media daily regales us with reports of criminal violence and provides us with the most brutal examples they can find. Violence sells, as the most popular movies show. Fear of the citizenry understandably increases. Politicians respond with get tough measures focused too often on nonviolent offenders, including mandatory imprisonment for first offenders.

The United States leads the world in putting people in prison. According to the Bureau of Statistics of the U.S. Department of Justice, in 1996, 427 out of every 100,000 Americans were housed in state and federal prisons. This compares with 40 in The Netherlands, 45 in Japan, 81 in France and 97 in England. Our prison population has doubled in the past ten years and is growing at the fastest rate in the world.

The rate of imprisonment for blacks is seven times that for whites. Of black men between ages 18 and 35, 57 percent in Baltimore and 42 percent in the District of Columbia are in prison or on probation or parole. In spite of huge prison construction programs, overcrowding persists. We cannot build new prisons fast enough. In some prisons, cells built for one inmate now house two or three. New York State built 27 prisons in seven years (1983–90) and still cannot keep up with the demand. In 1997, little Delaware was carrying out its largest prison construction in state history, a $128 million project. It already has 23 percent more of its citizenry incarcerated than the nation's average. Projections of the growing prison population in Delaware indicate there will be a shortage of beds when the current construction is completed. Some legislators are calling for still more construction.

James Brooke described in *The New York Times* (November 2, 1997) how prisons have become a welcome growth industry in some parts of America. Fremont County, Colorado, for example, with a population of only 40,000 has embraced thirteen federal and state prisons. Once depressed, it is now a thriving community proud of its prison industry.

David J. Rothman, reviewing four books on crime in the February 17, 1994, issue of the *New York Times Review of Books* concluded: "The least controversial observation one can make about American criminal justice today is that it is remarkably ineffective, absurdly expensive, grossly inhumane and riddled with discrimination. The Clinton Administration, Congress and many state legislatures, claiming they are responding to the public's fear of crime, are determined to promote and strengthen the very policies that make the criminal justice system so bad."

In the name of protecting America from crime, we allow and even encourage millions of Americans to buy handguns, a custom that facilitates the killing of over 16,000 people annually. Meanwhile, other countries avoid such carnage by outlawing the manufacture, sale, and possession of these weapons.

We lock up young people and cripple them with the lifelong handicap of a prison record for possessing the drug marijuana. At the same time, we subsidize the production of tobacco, another habit-forming drug, and permit huge American corporations to manufacture, advertise, and sell cigarettes known to kill nearly half a million Americans every year.

We demonstrate conclusively in tests that recidivism can be dramatically reduced—that is, far fewer released prisoners will return to prison as repeat offenders—if we provide inmates with education, job training, or rehabilitation from drug or alcohol use, or a combination of these programs. Then what do we do? Instead of expanding such programs we reduce or eliminate them. Why? To stop coddling prisoners.

We contend, properly so, that getting a legitimate job and receiving a decent wage is fundamental, in terms of both sustenance and self-esteem, to being a law-abiding citizen. Then we deny the poorest, most disadvantaged person a decent job. This is probably the greatest injustice in our society. How can a person take care of himself and his family without a job? And if he cannot find an adequate legal job, an illegal job can be an attractive alternative. No wonder the highest crime rates are found in our poorest neighborhoods.

In these inner-city ghettoes, a severe national crisis of hopelessness, despair and hatred is brewing that could very well lead to a rebellion. Even back in the 1960s, when I worked as a volunteer in predominantly black neighborhoods in Wilmington, Delaware, I was dismayed by the obstacles that conscientious, loving parents faced in trying to bring up a healthy, educated, economically sustainable family. In the intervening thirty years, the situation in America's inner cities has markedly deteriorated. Many inner-city leaders and young people with leadership potential have moved to safer and more prosperous areas. Drug dealers have expanded their activities. The criminal justice system has branded ever more young, male, nonviolent offenders with a prison sentence. Nearly every inner-city family has at least one male member, relative, or neighbor in prison or on probation and parole.

While evidence mounts that the first few years of a child's life largely determine that child's destiny, most children of the ghetto are now born to a single overburdened mother, often a teenager, and often addicted to drugs or alcohol.

Adam Walinsky, writing in the July 1995, edition of *Atlantic Monthly* discussed "The Crisis of Public Order." He pointed out that one out of twenty-one black men can expect to be murdered. That is a death rate double that of American servicemen in World War II. In ten years of war in Vietnam, 58,000 Americans were killed. "Over an equal period," Walinsky noted, "we have had almost the exact equivalent of two Vietnam wars right here at home."

Although he emphasized the need "to reform welfare, minimize illegitimacy, change the schools, strengthen employment opportunities and end racism," he gave priority to stopping the killing in inner cities, where most of the killing in our country occurs. In 1993, Walinsky revealed, each police officer in the U.S. had 11.5 times as many violent crimes to deal with as his predecessor had in 1960. Add 500,000 new police officers to protect inner-city neighborhoods, he advised, "not to imprison more of our fellow citizens but to liberate them—to protect public space that now serves as the playground and possession of the violent."

He compared the $30 billion a year this would cost the country to the $270 billion we spent for defense against foreign enemies who killed fewer than one hundred Americans in all of 1994.

Since crime has escalated right along with criminal justice expenditures, is it time we question their relationship? Could it be that our criminal justice system is, in fact, a major cause of crime?

Could it be that, once an offender gets into that system, he is doomed to a life of crime?

Here is something else to consider. When an offender is locked up, it can be assumed that, unless he is in for life, he will be coming back into the community. And when there are twice as many people in prison, the number coming back into the community is roughly doubled. When there are ten times as many in prison, there will eventually be ten times as many being fed back into the community. Now consider this: most of what an inmate learns in prison comes from fellow inmates. When he leaves prison, he can usually find friendship and support from his fellow alumni from the College of Criminal Knowledge.

Government is the criminal-justice system. It creates the laws. It funds or does not fund the programs. Most importantly, it sets the policy—most often a get tough policy—a lock 'em up and throw away the key policy. This policy has never been more popular with politicians and voters than it is today.

Pretending not to know what to do about the growing crime problem, our political leaders call for more prisons, longer sentences, and harsher treatment of inmates. Why? Because experience has taught them that "getting tough on prisoners" appeals to their constituents. Thus it helps to solve their top-priority problem: getting reelected. At the same time, not wanting to be accused of coddling prisoners, they eliminate the few existing crime prevention programs.

Meanwhile, behavioral workers and scientists continue to show, in small-scale demonstration projects, how to prevent crime and how to salvage human beings who have become offenders. But we refuse to fund their programs on a larger and more meaningful scale. Consequently crime goes up, while funds for preventing crime go down.

Can we solve the crime problem? Yes, but first we must mount a huge effort to reduce its causes and forego our love affair with prisons and punishment. We know what the causes are. We have identified practical ways of dealing with them. What we need now is national leadership committed to solving the problem, leadership that can convince the American people to spend the many billions of dollars required to implement solutions. National leadership that gives top priority to getting reelected and runs on the platform "reduce taxes, cut costs and lock up the bastards," will never solve the crime problem.

America has two choices: continue the way we are going, which will lead to anarchy and rebellion in our inner cities followed by the disintegration of American society and a police state, or invest enough in attacking the causes of crime to insure everyone a safe and decent life.

Any rational analysis of the choices must come down on the side of the second choice, investing in attacking the causes. But where will the money come from when our federal government is already mandated to cut expenditures? Clearly this is a political problem. It stems primarily from the ideology of such leaders as Presidents Reagan and Bush and certain congressional leaders who believe that cutting taxes is sacred. Our super-wealthy country, with its huge and growing economy, can easily support increases in taxes, especially when its soul is at stake, as surely it is right now.

When our nation struggled in the Great Depression, President Franklin D. Roosevelt had the vision and courage to make major changes in our society that called for huge expenditures. And it worked. When Hitlerism and Tojoism threatened our way of life, Roosevelt led the nation to expend dollars to successfully battle them. Our crime problem is another national crisis.

Not only can we afford to invest in solving this problem; we *must* invest, tax, and pay as we go to do so. It will take enlightened national leadership plus several million people throughout all 435 congressional districts to push through such a program.

When we carried out our successful Three S Citizens Campaign in Delaware (in the early 1960s) to Salvage People, Shrink the Crime Rate, and Save Dollars, 6,000 citizens rallied behind it. That was one percent of Delaware's population. One percent of our nation's population would be 2.6 million. With such a citizen army in the field, the current get-tough retribution policy of many politicians could be changed to one of prevention. I believe that—as happened in Delaware—the churches, synagogues, and service clubs of the country would join the battle. And what better motto to involve such groups than "do unto others as you would have them do unto you."

Prisons should be for violent offenders only, and they should be funded and staffed to provide extensive educational and recreational activities, job training, and treatment for drug addiction and alcoholism. A good model would be the first six years (1989–95) of the McKean Federal Correctional Institution in Bradford, Pennsylvania, probably the most successful medium-security prison in the country. In those six years it had no homicides, no escapes, no sexual assaults, no suicides, and only three assaults on staff members. Its warden, Dennis Luther, was given major credit for this. He based his approach on his study of business management.

Robert Worth, in his article, "A Model Prison" in the November 1995, *Atlantic Monthly*, reported that Dennis Luther explained his remarkable success this way: "If you want people to behave responsibly, and treat you with respect, then you treat other people that way."

Unfortunately the McKean Institution's success led to bitter attacks by traditional prison administrators and get tough politicians. Luther is now gone, as is much of the funding for educational and treatment programs.

The National Rifle Association, whose resistance to gun control is surely one of the major causes of violent crime in America, needs to be brought under control. If millions of citizens lobby legislators to eliminate the causes of crime, we can overwhelm the NRA in Washington and all the state capitals. Then the manufacture, sale, and possession of handguns, assault weapons and machine guns can be outlawed.

The nationwide, anticrime, citizen army can also have a negative impact on the entertainment industry's bottom line, especially TV, where a preoccupation with violence nourishes the culture of violence in America. The simplest way to do this is by boycotting the guilty advertisers' products and the film industry's productions.

Max Frankel, writing in the July 1997 *New York Times Magazine* asked, "Which is the bigger crime—that pathetic murder or our report of it?" He was highly critical of local TV stations all over America, because they are hooked on feeding mayhem to their listeners. He should have included local newspapers, the network news, and the movies. They are also hooked.

The reason for this is that the owners of these entertainment media know through polls that over 70 percent of their viewers or readers are highly interested in crime stories—the more violent the better. So, to increase their businesses, they compete to outdo each other.

Frankel, for example, related how Carol Marin, anchor at

WMAQ in Chicago, quit her job because of "frustration with the quality of the news she was required to read." Her resignation evoked so much audience protest that her coanchor had to quit. Frankel pointed out that "television anchors everywhere jumped on this story with obvious sympathy and envy." But they did not quit themselves. They continue to read what is fed them.

A 1997 report by the Center for Media and Public Affairs showed that network news (NBC, CBS and ABC) between 1993 and 1996 increased the number of their murder stories by 721 percent, while the nation's crime rate went down. Yet crime stories jumped to first place on the evening news. It is not surprising that polls show Americans consider crime our most important problem. They are just feeding back what the news media tells them. It would be better if the news media told the people the real problem—the conditions in our poor neighborhoods that lead to crime.

It would also be immensely helpful if Peter Jennings, Dan Rather, and Tom Brokaw were to cooperate in telling their bosses that they would no longer participate in glorifying mayhem on their newscasts. These men have the power and the influence to turn their bosses around. The question is, "Do they have the guts to do so?"

Another important action toward reducing the crime rate is to stop imprisoning nonviolent offenders. Instead they should be sentenced to treatment and counselling in the community. The large number suffering from drug addiction and/or alcoholism should be treated as medical patients and sentenced to hospital-like treatment centers. The good news for such patients is the development of some effective new medicines. For example, Revia,® a nonaddictive drug produced by DuPont/Merck, has worked miracles with heroin addicts and has recently been approved by the Food and Drug Administration for treating alcoholics. It removes the craving for both. The pharmaceutical industry is expanding its research in this area, hoping to find a similar drug for cocaine and crack users. Additional research should be subsidized generously.

Courts should be specialized and limited in their jurisdiction. Only courts specializing in violent offenses should be allowed to send offenders to prison. States have moved in this direction with the establishment of drug courts—for adults in 48 states and for

juveniles in 30 states. If first time juvenile non-violent drug offenders, for example, successfully complete treatment and counseling programs, the police charges against them are dropped.

Youth Courts in general should be equipped with educational,
vocational and athletic facilities, and substance abuse treatment
programs so as to return youthful offenders to the mainstream
as soon as possible.

Criminal codes need major revision to remove the mandatory
and harsh sentencing now called for, thereby giving judges and
court administration officers the discretion they need to tailor the
treatment required to further rehabilitation. House arrest using
the electronic leash and tightly supervised community-service
sentences should be markedly extended for nonviolent offenders.

Moreover, an aggressive campaign is needed to help teenagers
avoid pregnancies. The current effort to teach that "Virgin is not
a dirty word" is commendable, but it is hard to believe it can
compete successfully with the biological urge to have sex. Instead,
the knowledge and means of avoiding pregnancy must be made
available to teenagers in order to stop the current debilitating
culture of teenagers having babies. It is not only a major hardship
for the young mothers; it is a particularly serious crime against
the babies who are born into an almost impossible-to-succeed-in
environment. Avoiding unwanted pregnancies is also the best way
to combat the problem of abortion. High birthrates since 1985,
especially in inner-city neighborhoods, are predicted to cause an
epidemic of youth crime over the next twenty years. A campaign
to avoid additional unwanted pregnancies could help head off
this epidemic, as it reduces the growing competition among youth
for a decent livelihood.

Adam Walinsky, as noted earlier, has called for an increase of
policemen to protect inner-city neighborhoods from crime. His
plea deserves our serious attention. As Walinsky says, "We need
a larger police force not to imprison more of our fellow citizens,
but to liberate them."

Millions of conscientious families who inhabit our inner cities
are appalled by the crime around them and are desperately striving to earn a decent living and raise happy, successful children.
They can be an important part of the army we need to free those
communities from excessive crime. They need our help, as we

need theirs. Friendly neighborhood police officers can help them take back their neighborhoods.

Over the past twenty-five years there have been several downturns in the frequency of violent crime in America, but each time it shortly resumed its upward climb. Since 1995, we have been experiencing a significant decline throughout much of the nation, and a major decline in New York City. This calls for intense study to learn why it is happening so more resources can be allocated countrywide with confidence to programs that appear to be working.

There were 980 murders in New York City in 1996, down from a peak of 2,245 in 1990. Four out of five victims were murdered by relatives, neighbors, friends or other acquaintances.

Police believe that the drop in the number of handguns on New York City streets is a major cause of the reduced murder rate. This decrease stems from tougher gun control legislation and a new strategy applied by an augmented police force, which cracks down on "quality of life" offenses like drinking beer in public, jumping fares in subways, and urinating in public. When caught, many such offenders are arrested for weapons possession. This, in turn, has led to people stashing their weapons rather than carrying them. In addition, state and federal handgun control laws have markedly reduced the smuggling of guns into the city for resale on the streets.

New York City's experience strengthens the argument for increasing community policing and for a nationwide effort to legislate much tougher gun-control measures. As further support for this view, consider fact that the United Kingdom has as high an overall crime rate as the United States but only a fraction as many homicides. It is commonly believed that this is due to the extremely low rate of handgun possession in the United Kingdom.

Some people credit the locking up of twice as many people in 1996 as in 1986 for the reduced crime rate. Doing so may have helped temporarily, but eventually it will lead to twice as many offenders annually returning to the community from prison— from the College of Criminal Knowledge—and adding to the crime rate.

The reduction in crime since 1994 has almost certainly resulted in part from our booming economy. Unemployment has fallen below 4.8 percent. The Bureau of Labor Statistics reports that new jobs are being created at a record rate, outpacing the growth in the working age population. People in low-level jobs are moving up to fill the better jobs becoming available. This provides opportunities for the unemployed. All over America "Help Wanted" signs are appearing on numerous retail establishments, especially fast food restaurants. Employers desperate to find help are now reaching out to people they previously ignored, including people with criminal records.

Moreover, the White House has pointed out that the rapidly growing number of entry level jobs has contributed to the dramatic 20 percent drop (over the past four years) in the number of people on welfare nationwide. Clearly our current prospering economy is reaching the lower economic strata of our society. A downturn in our economy, however, could rapidly reverse this trend. What we need is a means of insuring everyone a job in good times and bad.

We have the knowledge and the means to solve our crime problem and thus build a stronger, more productive America. The question is, do we have the compassion, the generosity, and the determination to do so? I believe we do. These have long been American characteristics. We now need to find the leadership to articulate the mission and to carry the torch.

Preventing Crime with Jobs

To me, the single most important means of preventing crime is to make sure every young person has a decent job. Over the years I developed a proposal for doing this which I called the Job Security Act. Shortly after Jimmy Carter was elected president, I wrote to him recommending that he make the Job Security Act a means of fulfilling several of his campaign promises, including reducing unemployment and reducing crime.

Carter and I first met in 1970 when he, as a newly elected governor, attended a bipartisan training session for new governors held every two years by selected incumbent governors. I was on the faculty that year and was soon impressed by Carter's compassion for the underprivileged, a trait he has demonstrated repeatedly over the years.

When he was elected president, I thought his strong convictions might lead him to push the Job Security Act in spite of the major political risk it would entail. Since the proposal called for a new tax, it would be highly controversial. Thus to gain the necessary support of the Congress, it would be advantageous to push for its passage early on—as far away from the next election as possible.

I suggested to the president-elect that the Job Security Act provided a means for him and the Congress, in one momentous act, to eliminate unemployment in the United States and to do so with little if any impact on inflation. In addition to abolishing the grave injustice of denying millions of citizens a job, the act would substantially reduce crime, eliminate the controversial dole aspects of our welfare system, eliminate the cost of unemployment compensation, and put millions of people to work on critical tasks crying out for our attention.

Passage of the Job Security Act would create the Job Security Agency which would provide work at 75 percent of the prevailing wage for anyone in the United States who could not otherwise obtain a job. It would be financed by a new tax—a Job Security Insurance Premium—to be paid by all American workers and all employers, a portion by each as is the case with Social Security. The Job Security Agency would train its employees on the job and motivate, counsel, and help them to move into the private work force when jobs became available there. No able-bodied person would be on the dole. Each would be guaranteed a job and thus an income instead. The security assistance programs for those who are handicapped—the blind, the disabled, the aged— would be continued. Nearly everyone is willing to help support such disadvantaged people.

In addition, no unemployment compensation would be required or administered by government. Management and labor would, however, be free through their normal negotiating processes to establish privately administered unemployment insurance. The income of those in the Job Security Agency would be taxed like other income.

President-elect Carter called me to commend me for the recommendation. He said he would have his staff look into it. They did, calling me several times. But the task of mounting such an ambitious undertaking at the start of a new administration, with so little notice, proved daunting.

Back in 1976, there were about 95 million people working in the United States and about nine million unemployed. I calculate that the Job Security Insurance Premium necessary in order to provide a job for all those employed (at 75 percent of the prevailing wage) would have been 7.5 percent that year. At 1998's much lower unemployment rate (4.7 percent) the tax would be approximately 3.9 percent.

This tax would be split in some appropriate fashion between employer and employee. Since most employers pay into a compulsory unemployment compensation program, which under my proposal would gradually be phased out, it would seem appropriate to allocate a greater share of the Job Security Insurance Premium to the employer. Today, that might be 2.3 percent to the employer and 1.6 percent to the employee.

In addition, some funding would be required to provide the capital investment needed for the Job Security Agency. This could come from the several billion dollars saved each year by eliminating the welfare system. Over the long run there would be an even greater dollar saving through the reduction of crime.

If our country were successful in building jobs in the regular work force, then the number of jobs required in the Job Security Force would decrease and so would the Job Security Premium. Thus would we remove one of the worst injustices of our society. Today, when our system fails to create enough jobs, the disadvantaged and least competent suffer most. When a recession or depression comes, those who lose their jobs pay a disproportionate penalty for the failure of the system. The rest of us keep on working and living much as before. However, under a Job Security Act, no one would be out of work. As the Job Security Force builds, so would the Job Security Premiums, insuring that all of us were participating more equitably in paying the costs of recession.

Currently, our competitive economic system makes certain that the least qualified among us will remain among the unemployed. Conscientious as they might be, hard as they might try, that is where they will be. It does no good to call them lazy, to blame their parents. As long as there are fewer jobs than people who need jobs, there will be unemployed. The solution is to see that everyone has a job.

Federal and state governments are reforming welfare simply by cutting off the payments after a given time. "Let those on welfare find a job," they say. But where are they going to find a job? A better and more practical solution would be to provide a job first and then cut off the welfare.

At the end of 1997, the recent federal and state laws eliminating welfare after a specified period were beginning to have an impact. Lines at soup kitchens were increasing. At the same time, a booming economy lowered the unemployment rate to 4.7 percent, the lowest in twenty-four years.

Our legislators talk about providing jobs for those removed from welfare but appropriate only minimal funds toward that end. They claim the private sector, especially the already overburdened social service organizations, should provide jobs. In the midst of our booming economy, business *is* reaching down to the disadvantaged to recruit employees. But what will happen when the economy turns around or enters a recession and business lays off millions? Once again the poor will be without jobs or welfare. Who will be to blame then for the even greater destitution that will plague America's poor neighborhoods?

The focus must be on providing a job for everyone. Millions of jobs are crying for attention. Anyone who has had experience in preparing a budget, whether in business, government or academia, knows that the main problem is being unable to fund all the jobs one would like to fill.

Given a little encouragement, the management profession could readily define enough jobs so that everyone could have one. Many of our public institutions, such as schools, hospitals, nursing homes, day care centers, prisons, parks, and playgrounds are greatly understaffed. Our streets, streams, parks, seashores, highways, and mass transit systems need much better maintenance. Major public works such as housing projects could be launched. Currently employed people could move up, leaving their less demanding jobs to the newly employed.

A good example of what public works jobs can accomplish was provided by President Franklin D. Roosevelt's Works Progress Administration which he started during the Great Depression in 1935. In its eight-year existence, the WPA constructed 40,000 buildings and repaired 85,000. It also built 18,000 playgrounds, 8,000 parks, 651,000 miles of roads, 124,000 bridges, and advanced slum clearance and rural electrification.

Much remains to be done in our country to provide for the justice, equality and pursuit of happiness our Founding Fathers envisioned. Providing a job opportunity for everyone would be a giant step toward fulfilling these goals.

VI
Battling in Washington

20

Becoming Chairman of the President's Council on Environmental Quality

AT THE END OF THE 1960S, AMERICA LAUNCHED AN ENVIRONMENTAL revolution. Alerted by Rachel Carson's *Silent Spring* and Aldo Leopold's *Sand County Almanac,* shocked by a burning river, unswimmable lakes and streams, vanishing species, polluted air, disappearing vistas, and all manner of environmental threats to human health, Americans decided to act. In a flurry of bipartisan activity, Congress passed a series of far-reaching environmental laws to protect our environment. These laws created the Environmental Protection Agency (EPA) and the Council on Environmental Quality (CEQ) and established a national environmental policy. President Nixon signed the bills into law.

The first Earth Day was held in 1970, and huge crowds all over the country demonstrated their support for cleaning up and protecting the environment. Recognizing the global nature of the environmental problem, the United States and other nations encouraged the United Nations to sponsor a world conference in Stockholm in 1972. There the United Nations Environment Program was established.

Delaware played a part in that revolution by passing the landmark Coastal Zone Act. Delaware also brought the first case ever filed under our nation's new Clean Air Act all the way to the U.S. Supreme Court, forcing Delmarva Power & Light Company to reduce the amount of sulfur dioxide it was pouring into the air from its Delaware City power plant. We consolidated the fourteen separate agencies dealing with environmental issues into one department under a secretary in the governor's cabinet, the Department of Natural Resources and Environmental Control (DNREC), the most encompassing environmental issues department in America. And we initiated, in cooperation with the Hercules Company, a major research effort to develop processes for converting solid waste to marketable products.

During my gubernatorial term, I became increasingly concerned about humankind's threat to the environment and eager to apply what I was learning in Delaware to protect air, land, water, and wildlife on a national and global level. After I lost my bid for reelection in 1972, the Republican governors, hearing that William Ruckelshaus was leaving as administrator of the Environmental Protection Agency, unanimously resolved to ask President Nixon to appoint me to that position. But Ruckelshaus decided not to leave, so there was no opening.

Almost a month later, I was offered the job as administrator of the Law Enforcement Assistance Administration, the agency with which I had worked closely while I was chairman of the National Commission on Criminal Justice Standards and Goals. At the same time, the two U.S. Senators from Delaware, John Williams and J. Caleb Boggs, obtained President Nixon's agreement to appoint me ambassador to Sweden. And, after interviews with students, faculty, and trustees, I was offered the presidency of the University of Connecticut.

Then Governor Nelson Rockefeller called, asking me to come to New York to see him before I accepted any job. Calling me the most innovative governor he had ever met, he asked me to help him carry out a major study of critical global issues. I accepted his offer, concluding it was the most promising way to enter the global environmental arena. The day after I left the governor's office in Dover I was at work in New York City with Rockefeller on this new venture. With a stellar staff and access to the best thinkers and doers in America, we launched our study of *Critical Choices for Americans.*

During this time Lillian and I lived in a pleasant home on the 200-acre Rockefeller estate at Pocantico Hills. What a different world it was for us! Nelson and Happy lived above us in Kykuit, the fabulous home that his grandfather and father had built. They treated us as honored guests, inviting us repeatedly for private dinners at Kykuit and twice for fabulous parties. We spent late evenings discussing our project and Nelson's probable run for the presidency in 1976.

They also allowed us to use The Playhouse that John D. Rocke-

feller, Jr. had built for his five sons and one daughter. It contained
a fantastic swimming pool, tennis, basketball, and squash courts,
exercise equipment, a bowling alley with automatic pinsetter,
locker rooms, and a well-stocked soda fountain. Lillian and I used
the facilities frequently at night—all by ourselves. At such times,
I could not help but contrast The Playhouse with the primitive
field and track facilities we neighborhood boys built for ourselves
in Portage when I was eleven years old. And I often wondered
what the oil baron on whose estate we now lived would have
thought of the father of Delaware's Coastal Zone Act being there.

Occasionally I rode home from Manhattan with Nelson in the
Rockefeller helicopter. On one such evening David Rockefeller
was aboard. The two brothers had an argument that was different
from any my brothers and I ever had.

The previous Saturday David had held his annual outing at
Pocantico Hills for the heads of major banks. While they were
playing golf, Nelson was relocating the famous sculptures he had
collected and positioned around the estate. He used the helicopter
to move them. David was unhappy that, as his guests prepared to
tee off, a large bronze by Henry Moore—as just one example—
had come flying over the fairway. Nelson argued that positioning
a sculpture was almost as much an art as being a sculptor. He said
he had been planning for some time to move his treasures that
Saturday and did not know of David's plans. When David complained that he did not appreciate what Nelson had done, Nelson,
with that trademark twinkle in his eye, countered, "Yes, but Henry
Moore would."

The goal of our study, *Critical Choices for Americans*, was to tap
the most innovative minds to develop by 1976—the start of our
Republic's third century—a plan for coping with the fundamental
state, national, and international problems. In launching the
study, Governor Rockefeller stated in a February 8, 1973, interview with the *Los Angeles Times*, "The challenges and opportunities
of today's world seem to have outrun both the concepts and the
institutions available to manage them. What is called for is a new
look at the needs of society and at the ways these needs can most
effectively be dealt with."

During this period in 1973, with plenty of time to think, I
drafted a manuscript called, "Up the Ladder—A Declaration of
Interdependence," which described how all of us are connected

to each other, to other forms of life, and to the air, water, and soil. It presented ideas for using energy more efficiently, developing renewable forms of energy, and recovering and recycling materials. It emphasized that we were headed for tragedy if we did not reduce the rate of population growth, resource depletion, and environmental degradation. When I reread it recently, I realized how negligent I was in not trying to publish it twenty years ago.

Through this work I met Professor Jay Forrester of the Massachusetts Institute of Technology and his graduate students Dennis and Donella Meadows. They had just produced the book, *Limits to Growth*, of which several million copies were subsequently sold around the world. The authors compellingly argued that the world could not sustain the exponential increase in the number of human beings, consumption of resources, and quantity of waste. *Limits* caused quite a stir, particularly among economists and businessmen whose basic philosophy called for ever more growth.

I also got to know Lester Brown who had begun to do some highly important work. He had just launched his Worldwatch Institute, which every year since then has published the *State of the World*. His revelations, well documented with vital statistics, increased my resolve to do what I could to help change the world's direction.

Laurance Rockefeller, Nelson's brother and a nationally respected conservationist who also lived on the Pocantico Hills estate, encouraged me to emphasize in *Critical Choices* the need to safeguard our natural resources. Laurance was reputed to be his brother's environmental conscience, though he was anything but a knee-jerk environmentalist. In fact, when I first met him, he criticized me for "going too far" with passage of the Delaware Coastal Zone Act. Some of his friends in the oil industry had condemned me for it. I told him I had not done anything different from what he had done. "You bought 60 percent of St. John in the Virgin Islands and gave it to the people of the United States as a national park. I couldn't buy the Delaware Coast, so I persuaded the people of Delaware that we needed legislation to protect it. We both did what we could to save a national treasure for future generations."

He replied, "By gosh, you're right." Over time he became a very generous supporter of mine.

Meeting these people, thinking and writing about environmental and other global problems, made me eager to help find solutions. When I heard that Russ Train was resigning as chairman of the President's Council on Environmental Quality to become head of the Environmental Protection Agency, I decided to go after his job.

CEQ had been established through the National Environmental Policy Act (NEPA), a law which defined our policy as follows:

> The Congress, recognizing the profound impact of man's activities on the interrelations of all components of the natural environment, and the critical importance of restoring and maintaining environmental quality to the overall welfare and development of man, declares that it is the continuing policy of the federal government to create and maintain conditions under which man and nature can exist in productive harmony.

That policy was tailor-made for my interests and commitment. The chairman of CEQ reported to the president and was also responsible for preparing an annual environmental report from the president to the Congress. But when I told Nelson Rockefeller what I intended to do, he tried to talk me out of it. He pointed out how Henry Kissinger, then Nixon's widely acclaimed Secretary of State, had headed an earlier study for Rockefeller. "Look what happened to him," he said. Then he asked why I could not continue to work for him "like creative people worked for the Medicis."

My first reaction was, "How conceited can he be?" But upon reflection I decided it was not a matter of conceit. Nelson Rockefeller was a major patron of the arts, a four-term governor of New York State, savvy and influential in national and international affairs, and a perpetual student. He saw himself and his friends in a larger-than-life way. He was highly intelligent and knowledgeable, wealthy and powerful, and an even greater force in combination with his four brothers and many influential friends. Nevertheless, I had to follow my own star. When Nelson realized I was determined to do so, he agreed to help me get the CEQ job.

Shortly thereafter I was told by the White House Personnel Office that the president would announce my appointment in a few days. Nothing happened for two weeks. Then a friend at the White House called to tell me my appointment had run into trouble. I asked Governor Rockefeller to call his friend, General Alexander Haig, who had recently replaced Robert Haldeman as the president's chief of staff. Rockefeller did so and reported that a group of oil-company executives had gone to see the president to talk him out of appointing me. The long arm of the oil industry was continuing to haunt me. Clearly they had been outraged by my actions as governor when I blocked their plans to build refineries along the Delaware coast.

Then General Haig called and asked me to come to the White House. When I arrived he asked, "Do you know the president thinks that all of you environmentalists are kooks?" "Yes," I said, "Three key people in the Nixon Administration have told me that—Elliot Richardson, Russell Train, and William Ruckelshaus."

General Haig continued, "Then why do you want the job?"

"Because protecting the environment is one of the most important missions in the world, and I want to change the president's mind."

My answer seemed to please the general who told me he was going out on the presidential yacht that evening with "the Old Man." He promised, "I'll talk to him about it."

This was the same Richard Nixon who signed more significant environmental protections into law than any other president before or since. He must have done so because he considered it politically expedient, however, for according to White House tapes, he told Lee Iacocca, Henry Ford, Jr. and John Ehrlichman at a meeting in his office two years earlier on April 27, 1971: "Environmentalists are a group of people that aren't really one damn bit interested in safety or clean air. What they are interested in is destroying the system. They're enemies of the system . . . The great life is to have it like when the Indians were here."

The next morning Haig called me to tell me I had the job.

Why did he go to bat for me? I do not know. Could it be because he was a futurist and did have some concern for the environment? Or that he was no admirer of George Bush who had tried to scuttle my nomination? Or, as was most likely, was it because his friend Nelson Rockefeller asked him to do so?

Next I had to be confirmed by the Senate. Over three days of hearings, October 30 and November 2 and 5, 1973, several Republican senators on the Committee on Interior and Insular Affairs grilled me over my position on the Coastal Zone Act. One of them questioned me about a provision in DuPont's pension plan that permitted the company to cancel its payments to a retiree who did something to the detriment of the company. "That would be a club over your head, if you became chairman of CEQ, to keep you in line with DuPont's interests," he claimed.

"Oh, no," I said. "I have a letter from DuPont in my safe deposit box. I requested and received it before I ran for governor; it exempts me from that provision. I would be glad to give you a copy." That satisfied him.

The chairman of the committee, Democrat Henry (Scoop) Jackson, who was the "father" of the National Environmental Policy Act that created CEQ, strongly supported me. Seeing me in the hall during a break in the hearing, Senator Jackson advised me to not let my Republican friends on the committee upset me. He assured me the Democrats would support me. Punching me in the chest, this tough Norwegian said, "You're a tough Swede. You can take it."

Earlier I had met with most of the fourteen members of the committee, six of whom were former governors. Two of them, Paul J. Fannin of Arizona and Clifford P. Hansen of Wyoming, the two most senior Republicans on the committee, told me that because of pressure from their strong supporters in the oil industry, they would have to give me a rough time. But in the end, they said, they would vote for me because, "we governors have to stick together."

The vote for confirmation was unanimous. In a ceremony in the Roosevelt room in the White House I was sworn in as chairman of the President's Council on Environmental Quality on November 30, 1973, less than ten months after I left the governor's office in Delaware. The president was in the Oval Office twenty yards away, but did not come to the swearing in ceremony. In the midst of his Watergate problem, President Nixon had other, more pressing matters on his mind.

At last I had the job I wanted. It seemed I was now in a position where I could have some real impact on saving—and restoring—environmental quality on a national and even international scale.

The next three years would be among the most rewarding of my life.

Peterson sworn in as chairman of the Council on Environmental Quality by Judge Walter Stapleton in presence of Lillian Peterson, Melvin Laird representing the President, Peterson's son Glen and granddaughter Karin, November 13, 1973. White House Photo.

21
CEQ in Action

THOSE WERE EXHILARATING DAYS WHEN I FIRST ARRIVED AT MY CEQ offices located in an attractive townhouse in Lafayette Square across from the White House. Here I was the president's minister for environmental affairs, directing an effort to help advance our nation's environmental policy, "to create and maintain conditions under which man and nature can exist in productive harmony."

I was ably assisted by the other two members of the Council, Beatrice Willard and John Busterud. Our CEQ team under the leadership of Staff Director Steve Jellinek was superb. They understood the workings of both the Executive Branch and Congress and had many friends among the staff there as well as in most national nongovernment environmental organizations. They were deeply committed to the National Environmental Policy Act and highly motivated to honor its policies and goals, such as furthering the environmental impact statement (EIS) process. They were highly intelligent, good communicators, remarkably industrious and did not seem to care that their salaries were much lower than those they could have earned elsewhere. They were a choice group of people about half my age, who were "turned on," as I had been, by the opportunity to work on the frontier of the blossoming environmental movement. We hit it off beautifully.

They apparently thought so, too. Twenty years later, three members of that early CEQ group told 500 environmental leaders at a dinner meeting in Washington of the golden years when CEQ made much happen in spite of strong opposition from business and the Nixon-Ford administrations.

I did lose one member of my staff, CEQ's counsel, Tim Atkison, at the very start of my chairmanship. He called me one Sunday at Rehoboth Beach, Delaware, where I was spending the weekend, to tell me he was resigning. He was upset by the Saturday Night Massacre, when Attorney General Elliot Richardson and his deputy both resigned rather than do as they were ordered by President Nixon, that is, to fire Watergate Prosecutor Archibald Cox.

Tim told me, "I refuse to have anything more to do with the Nixon Administration."

He had previously prepared the required report of my financial holdings for the Senate hearings on my confirmation. After I gave Tim the required data, he came back to say, "It took me only a few minutes to fill out your report. My God, Governor, you don't own anything. It took me days to fill out the report for Russ Train's confirmation hearings." I still recall how humiliated I felt at the time. After all, Lillian and I owned a home in Rehoboth Beach, one car, and several thousand dollars worth of stock.

Two of my colleagues and I continued to work together during many of the intervening years: Dr. Lee Talbot, director of scientific and international affairs, and Senior Economist Dr. Edwin (Toby) Clark. They have contributed much to my understanding of the natural world and what needs to be done to protect it. Lee, for example, consulted for many countries around the world and became an internationally renowned ecologist serving, among other posts, as director general of the International Union for the Conservation of Nature. He opened doors for me to many of the world's leading naturalists.

Those early years were not free of discord, however. The antagonism of the oil people had followed me to Washington. On one of my early visits to the White House I ran into George Bush, who was then chairman of the National Republican Party. I said, "I'm Russ Peterson, former governor of Delaware and the new chairman of CEQ."

He said, "I know."

When I asked if we might get together to discuss environmental issues, he responded that he was too busy and walked away. Several weeks later on a similar occasion he was even more abrupt and unfriendly.

When I told several of my colleagues back at the office about my experience, they wondered why I was surprised at his behavior. "Don't you know?" one of them asked me. "It was Bush who took the oil company executives to talk to the president about nixing your appointment."

George Bush's career had been primarily in the oil business, as the records in Delaware's Division of Corporations show in detail. The CZA had blocked one of his companies, Zapata Norness, from building islands in Delaware Bay for transshipping oil and coal. No wonder he did not like me.

When I came to CEQ, the nation was in an energy crisis. The oil-producing nations of the Middle East had pushed oil prices up fourfold. President Nixon had launched Project Independence to make the United States independent of oil imports. The president created the Federal Energy Office to coordinate this effort and appointed William E. Simon, a friend of the oil industry, to head it. (Simon shortly thereafter became secretary of the treasury.) I called Simon to sell him on my Half and Half Plan, to get half of our future energy needs from conservation and improved efficiency and half from additional sources.

I will never forget how angry I was when he responded, "Governor, do me a favor. Help me get that Delaware Coastal Zone Act repealed."

I said, "Hell, no. It's more important than ever."

As I recall, Simon then said, "Guv, next time you are in Washington, stop in to see me."

"I *am* in Washington," I replied. "I'm chairman of CEQ."

"Guess I'd better talk with the present governor, then," he said.

Whether he did so, I never learned. But this conversation occurred at the time when the oil companies and their business cohorts were mounting a concerted campaign in Delaware to nullify the act.

Our CEQ assignment kept us regularly in confrontation with leaders and agencies in and out of government who were opposed to the environmental movement. This was well exemplified by our important assignment to oversee the environmental impact statement (EIS) process.

The National Environmental Policy Act (NEPA) required all federal agencies, before undertaking any project that would have a significant impact on the environment, to describe the impact and prepare and define alternate procedures which might have a lower impact. This was a major irritant to cabinet secretaries and the heads of agencies. Most were not environmentalists; most saw no need for an EIS. Their staffs were busy on "important things," and they had no one available to work on impact statements. With persuasion and help from CEQ, which had no authority to order them, the agencies reluctantly began to prepare EISs. Most were inadequate. After being taken to court by nongovernment environmental organizations, the agencies were ordered to rewrite them.

Shortly after I became chairman of CEQ, a story about the huge and wasteful effort required to prepare an EIS circulated around Washington. Reportedly the Department of the Interior had prepared a fifty-four-pound EIS. I went to see Secretary of the Interior Tom Kleppe about this. He called in the three lawyers on his staff who had prepared the EIS; each of them carried several sections of it. The secretary put them on a scale on his desk. Sure enough, they weighed fifty-four pounds.

Earlier my staff had briefed me on the then current practice that had developed among the agencies to assign their lawyers the job of writing the EISs to cover every imaginable environmental impact a new project might make, so as to be sure the courts found their statements adequate. The result was voluminous, but largely worthless statements.

I told Secretary Kleppe that if I were in his job and my staff brought me a fifty-four pound EIS I would tell them, "Get the hell out of here and don't come back until you have a concise, meaningful report covering what the National Environmental Policy Act calls for." Then I told the lawyers that their assignment under NEPA was not to snow the courts under an avalanche of words, but to minimize the impact of their department's actions on the environment.

The secretary sputtered a little, and the lawyers tried to explain what they had done. I was unimpressed. I offered the secretary our help in advising his staff how to write an EIS. A few days later he called, thanked me, and asked for our help. We were happy to provide it.

Some weeks later William Simon, who had just become secretary of the treasury, came to my office. He, too, was upset by the need to prepare EISs. I sensed he had been sent by the White House staff. When he suggested that he and I work together to change the EIS requirement, I told him I could not do that. It was my responsibility under NEPA to support the EIS process and, even if I could change it, I would not, because I strongly believed in its importance. A short time later my staff informed me that Secretary Simon had invited the other cabinet secretaries to a meeting to discuss what they could do about environmental impact statements.

Because he had not invited me, I called Secretary Simon's office and said, "Bill, I am calling a meeting for tomorrow with a number of cabinet secretaries. I hope you can come. I want to discuss what should be done about interest rates."

"What did you say?" he asked. I repeated my message.

After a brief silence, I said, "I hope you got the point of my call. I don't like your calling a meeting to discuss the EIS without inviting me."

"I'll send you an invitation," he said. But he called off his meeting instead.

At about the same time, the French ambassador to the United States invited Lillian and me to dinner to meet the leaders of France's nuclear-energy program. I sat on the ambassador's right and Dixie Lee Ray, then chairman of the United States Atomic Energy Agency, sat on my right. After a superb dinner served magnificently, as the French know so well how to do, the ambassador stated that his friends from France were interested in our environmental impact statement process. He asked me to explain it. Before I could say a word, Dixie Lee Ray proclaimed loudly that the EIS was one of the worst things the U.S. government ever promulgated. She went on and on, telling the French nuclear leaders to have no part of it.

I do not know whether or not the French ambassador knew she would react this way. He maintained a pleasant smile throughout her lengthy diatribe, and made no attempt to interrupt her, although he had called upon me to make the opening remarks. And the chairman of the French delegation nodded approvingly during Dr. Ray's condemnatory comments.

At that time and for years thereafter, the French were very cocky about their nuclear energy program. They led all of the nations of the world in the percentage of electricity coming from nuclear power plants—80 percent in 1993 compared to 20 percent in the U.S. They did not need any outsider, especially one from the United States, telling them they needed to reanalyze their program and envision what long-range negative impacts they might be making on the environment. Their activities were well protected from public scrutiny and France, unlike the United States, had few citizen activists and environmental organizations to critique their actions.

When Chairman Ray (that is what she wanted to be called, not Chair or Chairlady) finished, I thanked the Ambassador for inviting Lillian and me and for the opportunity to meet with the leaders of the French nuclear program.

Then I said,

> Let me summarize my view of our environmental impact statement process. It is exactly the opposite of Chairman Ray's view. I believe adoption of the EIS process will, in the long run, be recognized as a major advance in helping an agency or a nation to steer its way more satisfactorily into the future. In the past humans have carried out many developments that have had devastating impacts on the environment with little concern for or pre-evaluation of such impacts. The result has been a rapidly deteriorating environment. It is time that government agencies be required to at least weigh the impact on the environment of their decisions before they make them and to consider less environmentally detrimental alternative ways to further their objectives. In your field, nuclear energy, with its super hazardous materials and long lived hazardous wastes, it is especially important that your decisions be enlightened by pre-analysis of their environmental impacts.

Chairman Ray frowned. We had been over this ground before. One day in her office she lectured me on the safety of nuclear energy, interspersing her remarks with cuddly embraces of the two dogs who were her constant companions.

Now she brought up the safety issue again, but this time she was joined by her French compatriots. "Nuclear energy is safe," they arrogantly explained to me in a number of ways. "Don't bother us with the facts," was their implication.

In less than twenty years, the French nuclear-energy business was in deep trouble. From the beginning, it has been run exclusively by a national company, Électricité de France (E&F) whose reactors are plagued with serious technical problems. In addition, the French economy is feeling the impact of the national obligation to pay E&F's huge operating debt, and citizens are outraged about the accumulating mountains of radioactive waste. Not until 1995 did the National Assembly conduct its first investigation of the nuclear industry. Other French industries are now rebelling against being tied to nuclear power. They want to do what industry elsewhere is doing: co-generate some of their own electricity and move to alternate sources such as wind energy. Clearly France would have benefited if its government had forced E&F to prepare environmental impact statements years ago.

Now, in 1998, there are no firm plans to fund any more nuclear reactors in France, the rest of Western Europe, North America, and Japan. Only some developing countries in Asia, especially China, remain bullish on nuclear power. But the high cost of this source of energy makes it doubtful they will complete their plans.

For many years, the expression "nuclear energy is safe," was a mantra of the nuclear energy movement. It was an expression of the movement's faith. They thought they did not need an environmental impact statement. The irony of that mantra was on my mind when we members of President Carter's National Commission to Investigate the Accident at Three Mile Island inspected the idle nuclear reactor adjacent to the one that had recently undergone partial meltdown, the worst nuclear-plant accident ever experienced in the United States. Clothed in several layers of protective gear and wearing heavy boots taped around our ankles, gloves taped around our wrists, and hoods with protective glasses which necessitated hearing our guide's radio messages through earphones, we entered the reactor building. We were told to "step briskly through this area; there is more radiation here," as we passed down one corridor. While we waited outside the containment structure which surrounds the nuclear reactor, our guide explained that its walls were three feet thick and were reinforced with two-inch-diameter steel rods so as to contain the radioactive products that might be released by certain accidents in the reactor vessel itself. While I listened, I could not help but notice a neatly lettered sign behind him, "NUCLEAR ENERGY IS SAFE."

It is interesting to note that at the height of the excitement over the accident at Three Mile Island, when much of the country was panic-stricken, the Nuclear Regulatory Commission's top technical experts, after extensive consultation, ordered evacuation of the area around Three Mile Island. But Governor Thornburgh of Pennsylvania, with little technical basis for his action, vetoed the evacuation order. Fortunately for the thousands of Pennsylvanians who lived in the threatened area, Governor Thornburgh's intuition proved more accurate than the calculated judgement of the responsible experts. Later they admitted that the chemical reaction they postulated was occurring within the damaged reactor and was producing an explosive mixture of hydrogen and oxygen could not have taken place under the conditions that existed.

They were all flying blind.

As to Chairman Dixie Lee Ray, her fearless dedication to the safety of nuclear energy played a role in her being removed from the chairmanship of the Atomic Energy Agency. After more people questioned her objectivity, she was appointed assistant secretary of state with responsibility for our country's international programs on science, environment, population, and other matters. She invited me to her swearing-in ceremony in the elaborate reception area on the seventh floor of the State Department. The rooms were decorated with priceless carpeting, furnishings, paintings, and other historic treasures collected from past presidencies. Dr. Dixie Lee Ray arrived with her two dogs who roamed around the reception area. When Secretary of State Henry Kissinger, who was to swear in Dr. Ray arrived, he exclaimed loudly, "Who let those damn dogs in here?" An aide said, "They are Dixie Lee's." The secretary knew better than to challenge Dixie Lee publicly on such a matter.

Assistant Secretary of State Dixie Lee Ray went on to become governor of the state of Washington and the bane of environmentalists there.

The tremendous cost of the contempt of the nuclear energy and nuclear weapons establishments for environmental considerations such as the EIS became increasingly apparent during the 1980s and early 1990s. One can understand how, during World War II when the free world was threatened by Hitler, Tojo, and their cotyrants, the creators and builders of our nuclear weapons had little time to consider the long-term environmental problems they were creating. But during the second half of the century, our management of our nuclear enterprises has been horrendous. Gradually, however, the people, with increasing commitment to the environment and knowledge of the nature and size of the nuclear problem, got Congress to act and, with the aid of such tools as the EIS, we have made considerable progress.

We now know that it will cost the United States hundreds of billions of dollars to clean up our nuclear-weapons facilities. The Hanford Works, for example, now employs more people to clean up the site than were employed there to operate it during its peak production days. Their jobs and the costs associated with those jobs are assured for at least a decade.

Today our nuclear energy plants continue to store on-site increasing amounts of highly radioactive waste awaiting the day when our nation establishes a means of disposing of it. How we will eventually dispose of the many aging nuclear power plants is also uncertain. The nuclear-energy fiasco clearly illustrates the great need for society to weigh the long-term potential impacts of its decisions before they are undertaken. Fortunately, today, on the advent of the twenty-first century, many countries are practicing such foresight.

22

Protecting the Ozone Layer Amidst Scientific Uncertainty

IN JUNE 1974, PROFESSOR FRANK S. ROWLAND AND DR. MARIA J. MOL-ina, of the University of California at Irvine, postulated in the British publication *Nature* that chlorofluorocarbons (CFCs) in aerosol sprays and refrigerants could, upon release to the atmosphere, slowly diffuse into the stratosphere, undergoing chemical reactions there that would deplete the ozone layer. Since the ozone layer is an important shield that protects life on Earth from intense ultraviolet radiation, they concluded that releasing of CFCs into the atmosphere might be an environmental threat. Although little scientific evidence was then available to substantiate that hypothesis, the stakes were so high that immediate research and analysis were in order.

Appraisal of the problem clearly fell into the Council on Environmental Quality's area of responsibility. I asked Dr. Guyford Stever, chairman of the Federal Council for Science and Technology and head of the National Science Foundation to meet with me. By January 1975, we had created the Federal Interagency Task Force on Inadvertent Modification of the Stratosphere (IMOS). Dr. Stever and I were the cochairs. Representatives were drawn from fifteen federal agencies. After a five-month intensive study the task force issued its report, "Fluorocarbons and the Environment," concluding that continued release of chlorofluorocarbons, especially Freon 11 and Freon 12, was a "legitimate cause for concern justifying further research and evaluation—fast."

Our report noted that chlorofluorocarbons are remarkably stable molecules that can exist for years in the lower atmosphere. However, over a number of years, some molecules diffuse into the stratosphere where, under intense ultraviolet radiation, they break down to release chlorine atoms that enter into a chain reaction with ozone molecules and convert them to ordinary oxygen. The depleted ozone layer would allow more UV radiation to reach the ground, "probably causing increased incidence of skin cancer and changes in physiological, biochemical, anatomical and growth characteristics of some plant and animal species."

The task force recommended that, if a National Academy of Sciences study due to be completed in 1976 backed the task force's findings that widespread use of CFCs like Freon 11 and Freon 12 posed "a legitimate cause of concern," then their use in all aerosol sprays should be banned by 1978, and research should be undertaken to find alternatives to these CFCs for use in refrigeration and air conditioning.

At the press conference announcing our findings I observed that, "It is difficult to perceive that when you are spraying an antiperspirant under your arm in the privacy of your bathroom, you are endangering the health of everyone in the world."

This was quoted widely. It drove home the worldwide nature of the problem, implying that using spray-on deodorant was a selfish luxury which endangered the health of people everywhere, and intimating that individuals had a responsibility and opportunity to do something about it. Dr. Stever and I, in response to a question, stated that our families were stopping all personal use of aerosol sprays.

The National Academy of Sciences report came out September 1, 1976. Its detailed scientific assessment was remarkably consistent with the IMOS report. It reinforced the possibility of ozone reduction and found little new evidence to justify lowering our fear of such depletion. But it found no conclusive scientific proof that ozone depletion was actually occurring.

This raised the question, "What do we do now?"

On September 17, 1976, I had the opportunity to try to answer that question when I spoke at an international conference on "The Stratosphere and Related Problems" sponsored by the National Aeronautics and Space Administration (NASA) at Utah State University.

I asked these questions: "What kind of action, if any, is appropriate in the face of scientific uncertainty? Do we bar fluorocarbons on the assumption that ozone reduction *is* occurring, and that the health effects of such reduction are so serious as to require immediate action? Do we take some less drastic step, such as limiting the production and use of fluorocarbons, while we pursue definitive research? Do we defer judgement awaiting further study? Or do we do nothing, recognizing that a substantial industry is at stake here, and that we have no conclusive scientific *proof* for banning fluorocarbons?"

The answers to these questions are applicable to other chemicals as well. The problem of determining prudent public policy in the face of scientific doubt recurs again and again as some chemicals developed for specific purposes prove to have—or threaten to have—unanticipated side effects.

Coping with this problem has become more difficult as the number of new chemicals has escalated. It is especially difficult when we are dealing with risks whose effects may occur years and even decades after exposure to the cause, as is the case with the fluorocarbon-ozone issue.

I believe firmly that we cannot give chemicals the same rights that we humans enjoy under the Constitution. Chemicals are not innocent until proven guilty. This should not, however, be construed to mean a chemical is guilty or hazardous until proven safe. In fact, absolute safety can seldom, if ever, be demonstrated conclusively. However, the burden of proof should be placed on the manufacturer to demonstrate that in the face of possible risk—which may not be scientifically proven—the likely benefits of marketing his product outweigh the anticipated risk.

Inherent in virtually every environmental or public-health policy decision are two components: scientific judgment and social-value judgment. No individuals are better qualified to make scientific judgments than scientists. But scientists are no more qualified than anyone else in making social-value judgments.

Both types of judgment are plagued by uncertainties and seldom will any finite amount of study totally eliminate them. Obviously, study to reduce the uncertainties is required, but the reasonable amount of time that can be allotted to this task is dependent upon the magnitude of the risk involved.

That is why my speech at Utah State emphasized that the magnitude of the potential risk from the cumulative impact of releasing ever more fluorocarbons to the atmosphere was huge—a worldwide environmental health hazard that might last for many generations into the future. In view of this, it was my social-value judgment that federal regulatory agencies should commence developing rules to restrict discharges of CFCs like Freon 11 and

12 into the atmosphere, that industry should start voluntarily phasing-out such CFCs in favor of environmentally acceptable substitutes, that consumers should stop using all aerosol sprays involving these fluorocarbons, and that manufacturers should stop selling them voluntarily.

My speech was widely covered by the news media. Fluorocarbon manufacturers were incensed by such advice coming from the principal environmental advisor to the president (and a Ph.D. scientist at that), when there was so little scientific information to support the proposition that fluorocarbons would deplete the ozone layer.

This was especially true in Wilmington, Delaware, the home of DuPont, the principal producer of the highly profitable fluoro-carbons. DuPont leadership had previously become disenchanted with me when, in 1971, I fathered Delaware's Coastal Zone Act. And in 1974, when I was chairman of CEQ, I returned to Delaware to lead a successful effort to block a major, orchestrated effort involving DuPont's top management to repeal the CZA. DuPont management had been convinced they would succeed because they were allied with the then governor, most unions, the State Chamber of Commerce, thirteen international oil companies, the U.S. Department of Commerce, and a majority of the members of both houses of the state legislature who had signed on to repeal legislation. So when the people of Delaware, responding to environmentalists' call for help, convinced these legislators to change their minds, DuPont was quite embarrassed. The company does not like to get out front on controversial public issues. To have done so—and then lost—was especially irritating.

My outspoken opposition to nuclear energy had also exacerbated my problem with DuPont. After all, DuPont had built and operated the huge Hanford Works and Savannah River Works for making plutonium, and they knew "nuclear energy was safe."

"What's your background, Peterson, to qualify you to judge nuclear energy?" my DuPont friends asked.

So, when in 1976 I challenged DuPont's major, highly profitable fluorocarbon business, I stepped right on the toes of pre-sensitized DuPonters.

In each of the cases I have described, it was not my intent to attack either DuPont or its leadership. I was just doing my job—working to protect the long-term health of the local and global environments, letting the chips fall where they might.

By 1977, scientific and governmental units around the world were taking the postulated threat to the ozone layer seriously. The United Nations Environment Program (UNEP), under Dr. Mostafa Tolba, established the Coordinating Committee on the Ozone Layer to produce annual science reviews. In March 1978, the U.S. banned the use of CFCs in nonessential aerosols. Other nations followed.

Scientists developed ever more support for the theory that CFCs could seriously deplete the ozone layer, resulting in millions more cases of skin cancer around the world. In 1985 British meteorologists reported that an ozone hole—a 40 percent depletion—opens up every October over Antarctica. This was confirmed by data collected by NASA's Nimbus 7 satellite. The following year NASA identified surprisingly large quantities of chlorine-containing molecules—including chlorine dioxide, a product postulated to result from the reaction of CFCs with ozone—in the stratosphere over Antarctica.

Now governments accelerated their efforts to ban CFCs. But CFC industry representatives, including Dr. Elwood P. Blanchard, a vice president of DuPont, testified in 1986 at a Congressional hearing that there is no imminent threat to the ozone layer and human health and urged that care be taken not to damage the economy with precipitate action to ban CFCs. Nevertheless, at this juncture, DuPont revved up its research on replacements for its CFCs. To the dismay of environmentalists everywhere, DuPont also admitted at that time that it had ceased earlier research on this objective in 1981. That coincided with the advent of the Reagan presidency's promise to provide business with major relief from environmental regulations.

A series of world meetings under UNEP's auspices and extensively aided by the U.S. government led to a final round of negotiations by the world communities in Montreal in September 1987. The "Protocol on Substances That Deplete the Ozone Layer" was quickly ratified by the requisite number of nations and entered into force on January 1, 1989. It established a timetable for phasing out CFC production.

Ten months earlier, on March 4, 1988, DuPont's chairman, Richard Heckert, had written a combative letter to three U.S. senators who criticized DuPont for continuing to make CFCs. Heckert stated, "At the moment scientific evidence does not point to the need for dramatic CFC emission reductions."

Eleven days later, on March 15, 1988, a National Aeronautics and Space Administration panel of scientists, including Mack McFarland from DuPont, held a news conference in Washington to announce that their extensive study of all the known scientific data showed that the ozone layer was definitely thinning, not only over Antarctica in its springtime, but in other areas as well, and indicated that CFCs might be responsible.

On March 24, just nine days after that, the same Dr. Heckert announced that DuPont would get out of the CFC business entirely. In the 1970s the company had taken out full-page advertisements in many major newspapers, saying DuPont would get out of the CFC business if scientific data showed the chemical posed a threat to public health. Now DuPont decided *that* time had arrived.

The New York Times reported that on the day DuPont management made its decision, Joseph P. Glas, director of DuPont's Freon Products Division went home and told his wife and children what the company had decided to do. "They said, 'Dad, that's fantastic,'" he recalled. "I knew I was doing something that's important, and it felt good."

Only fourteen years had elapsed since Rowland and Molina *theorized* that CFCs might be a threat to the ozone layer. Only eighteen years had passed since the establishment of the first significant national and international laws and institutions to protect the environment. Successfully coping in such a short time with a monumental global environmental problem, in spite of eight years of President Reagan's campaign against environmental regulations, is grand testimony to the need for and effectiveness of the fledgling environmental movement.

During the past ten years, the world scientific community has carried out ever more extensive studies of the ozone depletion problem through field observations, laboratory experiments, and computer modeling. In 1995, over 300 scientists from forty nations attended a week-long International Conference on Ozone in the Lower Stratosphere in Halkidiki, Greece. They concluded that the record ozone loss in the Arctic polar regions the previous winter resulted from the same chlorine catalyzed chemistry that causes the major losses in Antarctica. The record ozone depletion rates in February and March were as high as those in the Antarctic ozone hole. They appeared to be related to the record low stratospheric temperatures experienced in the winter of 1994–95 in the Arctic—low temperatures approaching those regularly experienced in the Antarctic.

The conference also confirmed the gradual ozone thinning trend over the mid-latitude regions of Europe, North America, and Asia where most of the world's people live. The United Nations Environment Program has concluded that ozone levels in these regions has been falling 4 percent per decade since 1979. The World Meteorological Organization, which monitors stratospheric ozone concentrations, reported that in the spring of 1996 ozone concentrations over a huge part of the northern hemisphere were 20 percent below normal—a record low. Intensive research continues to elucidate the actual mechanisms involved.

Meanwhile down at the other end of the world in Punta Arenas, Chile, at the tip of South America where people live under the Antarctic ozone hole from late August to early December, there is growing concern about the threat to their health. Most people apply sunscreen and wear dark glasses before they venture outside. They blame excessive solar radiation for a variety of exposed skin disorders and eye problems and for the increasing blindness of sheep, salmon, and rabbits.

A professor of electrical engineering at the University of Magallanes in Punta Arenas has taken on the task of warning people to shield themselves from the sun. *The New York Times* quoted him on March 3, 1995, as saying, "It is much too early in the process to say for certain that the problems these people are experiencing are due to ozone depletion. But what we do know is that such high levels of radiation are dangerous and destroy. We are facing a worldwide emergency that is starting in Antarctica and spreading north and something must be done."

Professor Magas is a voice of reason to many and an irresponsible ecofreak to others. The latter depiction comes from government and travel agents who see their main business—tourism—threatened by the publicity on the high radiation reaching Punta Arenas. This is the typical confrontation that occurs worldwide between environmentalists concerned about the future and those who see their current income threatened by environmental concerns and regulations.

I say to Professor Magas, "Stay in there!"

I know firsthand, though, how distressing attacks on "ecofreaks" can be. My conflict with DuPont over the fluorocarbon issue, coupled with earlier environmental confrontations about other issues, clearly harmed my relations with the Delaware community. When Lillian and I visited Delaware from our home in Washington in the late 1970s, we felt like personae non grata among many old DuPont friends and Republican leaders, although we were welcomed by many new friends. One reporter wrote, "Former Governor Peterson now has almost no friends in Delaware among either Democrats or Republicans."

At a cocktail party at the home of a senior DuPont executive, I was confronted by a former friend who had worked under me when I headed the start-up of the first Dacron plant, a talented engineer whom I admired, Jim Piet. He said to me, "Russ, what has happened to you? We have been reminiscing here tonight about how you used to be such a competent, reasonable leader. Now you adopt the most outrageous positions."

I said, "Jim, I haven't changed. You don't have all the facts. I wish you still worked with me. You would be strongly in my corner."

The problem persisted. In 1988 the Republican secretary of state of Delaware, Michael Harkins, who had been a strong supporter in my two gubernatorial campaigns, came to my home to get my approval of some legislation he was pushing and which I had blocked four years before. He said, "Governor, I'm probably the only friend you have left in Delaware." Lillian said, "And that's why you came to get his approval!"

In 1992, recently retired DuPont CEO, Richard Heckert, speaking to a meeting of retired chemists including me, commended several of them for the important community work they had done after retirement. During the question-and-answer period, I raised my hand to ask a question. I have never forgotten what it felt like when he said, "I see you there, Russ. I knew you were here. I *deliberately* didn't include you among the retirees who have made an important contribution."

Dick Heckert enjoyed belittling the environmental regulation of chemicals by telling how we are exposed to more carcinogens in our food than from the stacks and drains of chemical plants. When Heckert retired, Ed Woolard succeeded him. Woolard understood the environmental predicament and displayed strong leadership, not only in DuPont but around the industrial world, in advancing programs to protect the environment. He earned the respect of most environmentalists.

During the sixteen years (1977–93) of Republicans Pierre du-Pont and Michael Castle's gubernatorial terms, I was never invited

President Carter welcoming Peterson for weekend discussion of energy issues. Camp David, 1979. White House Photo.

to the governor's office—not once. On the other hand, I have been in Democratic Governor Tom Carper's office many times. I surmise that the Republicans did not want to associate with me because their major power base, the business community, was too outraged with me.

I had a similar experience on the national level. During the twelve years that Republicans Ronald Reagan and George Bush, both antienvironmentalists, were in the White House, I was invited there twice, both in President Reagan's first term, both times for confrontational meetings with the president's subordinates. During President Carter's four years I was there once a month on the average, always on positive substantive matters and usually with the president personally involved. Compared to all the leaders in the White House or the State House in Delaware during the past 22 years, Carter was by far the most environmentally conscious and committed. Although we came from different political parties, we were able to work together and have become increasingly good friends, as he has publicly stated.

What do I conclude from these experiences? First of all, one

must be true to oneself. If one wishes, as I do, to practice good-
ness, to advance justice, and to solve problems that threaten the
long-term quality of life locally or globally, then one must be prepared for and willing to accept the "slings and arrows" that will
be thrown. If one chooses to get out front in the environmental
revolution as I have done, then one must expect to battle resistance
to change. I learned early that I would have to forego the comfort
of "going along to get along." It was worth it, for I have gained
the most coveted award of all—great job satisfaction.

23

Countering the Big Lie
that Environmental Regulations Cost Jobs

FROM THE DAWN OF THE ENVIRONMENTAL MOVEMENT, BUSINESS HAS claimed environmental regulations would lead to a loss of jobs and profits. This belief was never true, but it became the linchpin in their all-out attack on environmentalism. Today it is still the cry of many businessmen who battle to block the world community's effort to face the threat of global warming.

When I became chairman of the President's Council on Environmental Quality (CEQ) in late 1973, I set out to show that environmental regulations actually stimulated the economy. Although I was convinced that they did, my assignment was daunting, because the belief that environmental regulations cost jobs and reduced earnings had become a strong ideology. With business leaders and their right-wing allies in elected office proclaiming that environmental protection was bad for the economy, millions of employees and constituents adopted this blind faith. Together they formed a potent antienvironmental force.

Let me provide an example: when Americans realized they deserved to breathe clean air and knew they could not buy clean air in the marketplace, they demanded it from their elected officials. When Congress considered regulations to insure cleaner air, business launched a major attack, claiming that regulations would destroy jobs. Congress passed the Clean Air Act anyway. Among other things, this act required that automobile manufacturers reduce the pollutants in auto exhaust. Auto companies screamed that to do so would result in the loss of tens of thousands of jobs. But when governmental regulations forced them to install catalytic convertors on all new cars in order to reduce hazardous emissions, tens of thousands of jobs were created. These jobs resulted from a major expansion of facilities for producing the required platinum catalysts, from the several new plants which were built to manufacture the aluminum oxide substrate on which the catalyst is placed, and from the manufacture of stainless-steel containers which house the convertor. Additional employees were necessary in auto assembly plants to attach the catalytic convertors and in auto service businesses to maintain them.

When environmental regulations were considered for increasing auto fuel efficiency, getting more miles per gallon of gasoline and thus fewer air pollutants per mile, the auto companies were right back with more job blackmail. But when these companies markedly increased fuel efficiency in order to meet government regulations, there was no evidence of job loss or reduced earnings. On the contrary, the regulations forced U.S. auto companies to develop cars that were able to stem the accelerating growth in sales of fuel-efficient imports from Japan and Europe.

Most businesses, and business organizations such as the National Association of Manufacturers, have been particularly critical of regulations to insure cleaner air. It strikes me as paradoxical that they can argue that manufacturing and selling catalytic converters that produce clean air is not productive, but manufacturing and selling air conditioners that produce cool air is. Is clean air less desirable than cool air? And what of the new business opportunities each provides?

An early study of the relationship between environmental costs and jobs carried out by two Wall Street analysts for CEQ showed that the $15.7 billion spent for pollution control by private industry and federal, state, and local governments in 1975 opened up over one million jobs. At the same time the Environmental Protection Agency reported that its ongoing tabulation of jobs lost because of environmental regulations totalled not more than 15,700 during the five years from 1971 to 1975.

Not all those jobs were lost either. Then—as now—when an obsolescent plant was shut down because it was befouling the community, some of its jobs were transferred to more efficient, more environmentally sound facilities. The resulting, increased number of jobs was not the only benefit of the expenditure on pollution control. Many businesses who sold pollution-control equipment also reported increased earnings. Of even greater importance was the benefit of reduced pollution. CEQ cited eight studies which estimated that between $6.5 and $38.6 *billion* could be saved annually in health and other costs by eliminating air and water pollution.

Subsequent studies have confirmed the good return resulting from investing in pollution control. A popular slogan in the chemical industry is "Pollution Prevention Pays." Today environmental regulations are widely credited with having a major positive impact on economic growth—and with having created a major growth industry.

Then why do champions of economic growth continue to fight environmental regulations? Because they do not like government telling them what to do.

I argued twenty years ago and continue to insist today that the conflict between business and environmental regulations can be traced back both to our own fierce sense of freedom as a people and to classical, free enterprise theory, as expressed in the book, *The Wealth of Nations*, by Adam Smith. Smith wrote in a time when all foreign trade and much domestic commerce were strictly regulated by the central government.

Take away governmental restraints, he said, and you will free the powerful force of private initiative. And it does not even matter, Smith argued, if a man intends only his own selfish profit rather than the good of the entire society for, "By directing [his] industry in such a manner as its produce may be of the greatest value, he is . . . led by an invisible hand to promote an end which was no part of his intention. . . . By pursuing his own interest, he frequently promotes that of the society more effectually than when he really intends to promote it."

Smith's book was enormously influential. It liberated the force of private initiative which spurred immense growth in the West. Private initiative remains the prime mover of human activity today. However, as population increased and both the pace and scale of man's activities—magnified by technology—expanded their impact on our common lives, the deficiencies of Adam Smith's invisible hand theory revealed themselves. Private enterprise often did benefit the public good by creating jobs, valuable new products, and profits for further expansion of industry. But private enterprise could also conflict with the public good by polluting the air, water, and land, wiping out plant and animal species, destroying great natural vistas, and exploiting child laborers.

The young conservatives who populated the pro-business Reagan White House sporting Adam Smith neckties and shouting for freedom for business and opposition to government environmental regulations, apparently never read Adam Smith's book. If they had, they would have known that Smith wrote that some functions *had to be reserved to the government.* Clearly, environmental regulations fall into this category. One of Adam Smith's current admirers, conservative economist Nobel Laureate Milton Friedman, told me he agreed with that when we were taping a program for his 1980 television series, *Freedom of Choice.* If we want the freedoms to breathe clear air and to drink clean water, we will have to depend on government to assure them.

In a speech I wrote for the 1975 National Audubon Society convention and which was published in *Audubon,* July 1975, I discussed Adam Smith's invisible hand. I talked about how provocative it is that the words "economics" and "ecology" come from the same Greek root: oikos, meaning house. Ecology means the study of the house and economics means the management of the house. Ecology views the house—our Earth—as a trove of natural resources to be managed as a single interrelated system of which man is a member, not the master. Economics says we should use the resources of our house to make it a better place to live. Ecology replies that we must be careful, for whatever we do to our house we do to ourselves. And as ecologists and all the rest of us are finding out, the interconnections between man and nature are often hidden, surprising, and highly sensitive—and many of them have quantifiable economic consequences.

The lesson of ecology is not that man must halt all efforts to improve his lot and return to the cave; the lesson, rather, is that he must learn to estimate *all* the costs in terms of both depletion of nature *and* financial outlay before he undertakes an environmentally damaging project. Economics has given us the concept of the *invisible hand,* a useful, productive concept. But ecology reminds us that there is also an *invisible foot* and that while one is capable of directing us, the other is capable of kicking us. The invisible foot has already demonstrated its power many times—and its potential for greater, even irreversible damage grows daily with the increasing pace and scale of man's activities.

Most conservation, nature, and wildlife organizations draw their sustenance from that simple yet profound admiration for the wonder, variety, and beauty given us by nature. It is important that these groups recognize that arguments rooted in that sense of wonder are not strong enough by themselves in a time when economic developments that threaten our environment are multiplying and when each such development is supported by powerful economic arguments and interests. Environmentalists must be able to demonstrate to their critics that their concern for the environment is at least as practical as their critics' concern for the economy.

Through conferences, many speeches, and press releases in the mid 1970s, we at CEQ helped to convince many in the news media of the validity of the environmentalists' case. The news media in turn, through objective reporting and the influence of their editorials, did much to counter the business claim that environmental protection was harmful to the economy. Two *New York Times* editorials, for example, strongly supported CEQ's findings that environmental controls aided the economy (December 12, 1975, and October 10, 1976).

As the critics of environmental regulations in business and government continued their attacks in the mid-1970s, I called an Environmental Industry Conference at the Mayflower Hotel in Washington, D.C., on December 9–10, 1975. Representatives from over 300 American companies manufacturing and selling pollution abatement equipment and/or services attended. In some cases, where the head of a large company was publicly chastising environmental regulations, one or more of his divisions was busy capitalizing on such regulations and, in so doing, providing jobs and profits. The conference was a huge success. Participants were enthusiastic about having their fledgling businesses recognized and exchanging information in their field.

In my keynote speech, I pointed out that the demand for clean air and clean water was well established—not as a fad, but as a permanent requirement of our way of life. I emphasized that our laboratories and factories were responding, producing the ideas, the processes, and the products necessary to satisfy that demand and, in so doing, were creating new jobs and new investment opportunities.

I felt at home with this group—the same kind of people I had worked with at DuPont for twenty-six years—people excited about developing new ventures to satisfy a societal need and earning good return on their companies' investments.

I presented the results of the 1975 CEQ study that profiled the pollution control industry and analyzed with many examples the benefits as well as the costs associated with environmental invest-ments. This was a forceful rebuttal to the thesis that we must choose either a healthy economy or a healthy environment; on the contrary, it showed that economic health and environmental health are interdependent.

This study showed that the $15.7 billion being spent in 1975 on pollution control by all governmental and private entities would not only contribute to the quality of life by cleaning up the environment but would also produce over one million jobs. At my recommendation, the participants established an Environmental Industry Council and a National Environmental Industry Awards Program. Under the leadership of Frank Sebastian of Envirotech and David Klipstein of Research-Cottrell, they did both. For most of the next ten years, until I retired from full-time leadership roles in the environmental movement, I was invited to participate in their annual meetings.

When Ronald Reagan became president in 1981 and launched his all-out attack on environmental regulations, the pollution con-trol industry suffered a setback. Many companies decided they would no longer be regulated and stopped buying pollution-abatement equipment and services. When Congress blocked the president's antiregulation program, the environmental control in-dustry resumed its growth curve, acquiring $70 billion of business in 1985, according to Management Information Services, Inc. (MISI) of Washington, D.C. As *Atlantic Monthly* reported in Octo-ber 1990, James Easterly of MISI said in 1985, "Here was every-body bitching and moaning about the cost of cleaning up the environment while PAC [the pollution abatement and control in-dustry] was raking in seventy billion dollars a year. That's bigger than IBM and getting up to General Motors."

Since then the industry has continued to grow. In addition to thriving in the usual economic sense of increased sales, earnings, and jobs, this industry is also thriving by protecting our air, water, soil, plants, and animals, thus improving the quality of our lives.

In 1995 the Institute for Southern Studies completed a study of the economic and environmental health of the United States. It showed that the states with the best environmental records also offer the best job opportunities and best climate for long-term economic development. The study concluded that the argument that strong environmental standards threaten economic development has little merit. The institute's research director, Bob Hall, wrote, "The choice is not jobs or the environment. It is both."

Stephen Meyer of the Massachusetts Institute of Technology, who studied twenty years of economic performance, reported the same conclusion in *National Wildlife*, June/July 1995. There he wrote, "States with stronger environmental standards tended to have the higher growth in their gross state products, total employment, construction employment, and labor productivity than states that ranked lower environmentally."

In November 1997 Kathleen McGinty, CEQ chairman, cohosted the National Marketplace for the Environment, a large conference for buyers and sellers of environmental technologies. She told the conference that the market for such technologies was now "a cornerstone of our economy. There are more than 100,000 environmental technology firms, providing 1.3 million high-wage jobs, and generating $180 billion in annual revenues. That is larger than aerospace, computers and textiles."

Although environmental industry leaders present praised the Clinton Administration for its support, they expressed concern about the decrease from the preceding five years in growth of their industry and its profit margins. They pointed out that many potential customers do not see an adequate incentive to buy technology to protect the environment. Lax enforcement, lowered risk of penalties and expectations that regulatory reform will reduce cleanup requirements were cited as causes. Consequently, the powerful environmental industry plans to join environmentalists in lobbying the current antienvironment Congress to provide the necessary incentives.

As I noted at the beginning of this chapter, freedom of enterprise will not insure our freedom to breathe clean air, drink safe water or enjoy nature's wonders. Such freedoms require government actions such as tax incentives, regulations, fines and emission taxes. We, the people, must demand such actions.

A large number of business leaders now recognize that environmental regulations do not cost jobs and profits. They believe, however, that industry could do a better job of protecting the environment if government regulations allowed industry more flexibility in how it does so. Many environmentalists now agree, as I do.

With the big lie that environmental regulations cost jobs pretty much behind us, the confrontation between business and environmental leaders has subsided. Many business leaders around the world are now accepting responsibility for protecting the environment and are focusing more of their substantial resources on this objective. This important development gives me hope for the future.

24

Head-on Collision with Captains of Industry

In October 1974, president Ford announced his whip inflation Now (WIN) program to overcome the double digit inflation
(12–14 percent) that plagued his administration. To obtain suggestions for resolving this problem, his staff organized conferences with many leaders, including captains of industry in various
regions of the country. It was popular among key people in the
Ford administration (but not with the president himself) and
among business leaders and business associations to blame environmental regulations for the high inflation rather than the fourfold increase in oil prices that the Middle Eastern oil-producing
nations had promulgated earlier.

We in CEQ concluded that environmental regulations could
have only a minor impact on inflation. However, due to the markedly different views of business and the White House, we hired
three different institutions to study the relationship: Chase
Econometrics Associates, Inc., The Brookings Institute, and Data
Resources, Inc. All of them decided that the maximum impact
had to be less than 0.5 percent.

Vice President Nelson Rockefeller presided over some of the
regional meetings. As chairman of CEQ, I was invited to three as
sort of an in-house rebel. Witness after witness from the business
community would proclaim that environmental regulations were
a principal cause of the problem. Then I would get up to challenge them, using information supplied by Chase Econometrics
and the other two agencies.

The president also called for a summit meeting over which he
would preside on Saturday, September 27, 1975, in Washington.
Selected witnesses from the regional meetings would appear.

About 3:30 p.m. on the day before the meeting, Secretary of

Commerce Fred Dent called me to ask if I would be coming to dinner in his office that evening, after which participants from a business and industry panel would rehearse their presentations for the next day. Surprised, I told him, "No, nobody invited me."

He asked, "Didn't the White House call you?"

"No."

He told me he wanted me to say what I had been saying around the country. "You will have four minutes," he said.

I scribbled a few notes and went to the secretary's huge office. The last time I had been there I was governor of Delaware and then Secretary Maurice H. Stans told me I was being "disloyal to the country" in trying to pass the Delaware Coastal Zone Act.

When I arrived, the other participants were drinking sherry. They had come in earlier for a separate meeting with the secretary. When I saw Irving Shapiro, CEO of DuPont, I asked, "Irv, where did you get your sherry?"

"The secretary passed it out," he replied. Just then, a white-coated waiter walked by.

"Would you please bring me some sherry?" I asked. He nodded, then walked away. Later I asked the secretary directly, "How does someone get a drink around here?"

His response was, "We are ready to sit down to eat now."

I felt like a persona non grata as we walked into the dining room. There were six other participants besides Secretary Dent and me: Congressman Gary Brown from Michigan and the CEOs of five of the largest corporations in America—Irv Shapiro, Richard Gerstenberg of General Motors, John DeButts of AT&T, Reginald Jones of General Electric, and Arthur Wood of Sears.

I sat between Gerstenberg and Jones at dinner. After dinner Secretary Dent announced that it was time to rehearse what we planned to say at the meeting. He said everyone would have four minutes, except me. I got two.

I crossed off some of my notes. No one asked any questions or made any comments after the others spoke from their notes. After all, they were captains of industry. Each referred to the serious impact of environmental regulations on their respective industries.

I was the last to speak. As I had done in the regional meetings, I emphasized that the maximum impact environmental regulations could have was less than 0.5 percent. Immediately Congressman Brown told me that if I was going to speak for the panel I would have to say what they wanted me to say. That was the last straw. "To hell with that," I responded. "If you want something different said, get some one else to say it. If I appear at the summit meeting, I will say what I know is true."

Irv Shapiro then told me that I was creating the impression that I was the most antibusiness man in government. This was the same Irv Shapiro who had earlier been involved in the unsuccessful attempt to repeal Delaware's Coastal Zone Act. What a contrast to the mid-1960s when I had headed a corporate research division in DuPont responsible for helping to get DuPont into new business ventures, and Irv was the lawyer assigned to help us. He was easy to work with, because he helped us find ways to launch a new venture instead of, like most lawyers, telling us why we could not do so.

I remember responding to Shapiro along these lines:

> I believe I do a lot of good for business and the free enterprise system. I speak on many campuses around the country and invariably I am asked about my potential conflict of having worked for the DuPont Company and now heading CEQ. I tell them of my wonderful twenty-six years with the DuPont Company, my respect for the free enterprise system, and my conviction that a healthy economy and a healthy environment reinforce each other.
>
> I say to you here tonight that what is truly bad for business is the outrageous contention of you captains of industry and your lieutenants that environmental regulations are a principal cause of today's high inflation when you have no data to support such an assertion. We in CEQ have tried repeatedly to get from you, your economists, and others your data to support your position. It has not been forthcoming. That's because you don't have any. I have the data in depth to support my position.

There was a long moment of silence. Then Secretary Dent thanked us for coming and said he would see us in the morning.

When we adjourned, Reg Jones of General Electric, who had been very friendly to me during dinner, asked how I could tolerate the tremendous pressure of key people like him beating on me.

I replied, "It's easy when you have done your homework and are convinced you're right."

The next day, Saturday, I appeared at the summit meeting and gave my two-minute statement. Three reporters surrounded me after the session, wanting to know how I could take positions diametrically opposed to the administration and still survive. I told them I was "just doing my job" and walked away. President Ford had left before my appearance so he could be with his wife while she was having breast surgery.

When I arrived at my office on Monday morning, my secretary excitedly reported that the president himself had called and wanted me in the Oval Office immediately. On the short walk over to the White House from my office on Lafayette Square, I figured I was about to be fired. It was a wonderful fall day. The flowers on Lafayette Square and in front of the White House were beautiful. The guards were as friendly as ever. I entered the White House wondering if I were making my last such visit.

I was promptly ushered into the Oval Office and sat down across the desk from the president. After the president's ubiquitous photographer left, we were alone. I expressed my concern for Mrs. Ford, and he explained she was doing well. Then the president told me he was sorry he had to leave before my talk and asked me to tell him what I had said.

After I had given the president my summit meeting message, he pointed out that I was giving the macroeconomic picture. He asked if certain individual environmental regulations caused more than the 0.5 percent increase in inflation. There was no question in my mind that his aides had prepared these questions for him to ask. From where I was sitting, I could even see several pieces of paper on his desk with my name on them. I speculated that they were from his chief of staff who was no friend of environmentalists.

"Oh, yes," I replied. "Some have a greater impact and some even cause deflation. Just as when you say the overall rate of inflation in the country is 12 percent, some things are having several times that impact and others much less than the 12 percent. The *average* overall impact is 12 percent. The *average* impact from environmental regulations is less than 0.5 percent."

He appeared to be satisfied, thanked me for coming, walked me to the door, and in a friendly gesture placed his hand on my shoulder as I left. I believe the president had seen that my point was a valid one and that his staff and cabinet had not given him the total picture. When I returned from the White House, my staff was anxiously waiting. They were relieved that I had not

Peterson summoned by President Ford to explain his controversial position on environmental regulations. September 29, 1975. White House Photo.

been taken to the woodshed, just to the Oval Office for a friendly, constructive chat.

I heard no more from the president, the White House, the secretary of commerce, or any of the five captains of industry on this issue. But the fact that I *was* right was obvious several months later. In testimony before the Joint Economic Committee of the Congress, the Office of Management and the Budget, the Congressional Budget Office, and the General Accounting Office all supported CEQ's position. And in his campaign for election in 1976, I cannot recall the president ever blaming environmental regulations for high inflation.

25

Conflict in the Cabinet Room:
Should a Government Executive Tell the
President He Is Wrong?

ALTHOUGH I WAS NOT A MEMBER OF PRESIDENT FORD'S CABINET, I was invited to some Cabinet meetings when environmental matters were being considered. One day we were discussing the desire of conservative western Republican senators, who were supported by conservative members of President Ford's White House staff, to convince the president to issue an executive order that would nullify President Nixon's earlier Executive Order prohibiting the use of the poison 1080 on public lands. The poison, which was inserted in carcasses of dead sheep or other animals, had been placed there to kill coyotes that allegedly were killing large numbers of sheep grazing on such land. Ranchers who owned the sheep paid a ridiculously small fee for using public land and then seriously overgrazed it. Even a United States senator participated in this profitable venture.

Investigation by environmentalists had shown that very few sheep were killed by coyotes and that only a small percentage of coyotes actually preyed on sheep. Furthermore, the 1080-laced carcasses killed many other animals, including eagles. Even some ranchers opposed the use of this poison, as Lillian and I had recently learned while picnicking with twelve of them. They were evenly divided—six for killing coyotes and six opposed. The latter group insisted that packs of town dogs were the main killers and agreed that only a few coyotes preyed on sheep.

The U.S. Fish and Wildlife Service had demonstrated that an effective way to kill only those few coyotes that were sheep predators was to place collars containing sodium cyanide on a few sheep deliberately staked around the outside of the flock. Since coyotes killed by biting the sheep in the neck, their teeth would pierce the collar and they would die rapidly. I had seen a video of this procedure and it was quite persuasive.

At the cabinet meeting, President Ford said he was upset by the damage the coyotes were causing so he was going to sign the executive order.

I said, "Mr. President, you are wrong." Then I explained to him that only a few coyotes were killing sheep and that they could be controlled by the cyanide collar technique, whereas the use of 1080 would kill many other animals indiscriminately.

He listened attentively to my statement and asked several questions. Then he thanked me, but made no decision at that time.

After the meeting Vice President Nelson Rockefeller called me aside outside the Cabinet Room and told me I should not have told the president he was wrong.

"But he was wrong," I replied.

"I know, but you shouldn't tell him so."

Convinced that I was right, I told the vice president that I was being paid to advise the president, and if I had not spoken out at the meeting, I would not have had another chance to speak to him on the matter. Yet I also knew that most people are afraid to tell the boss directly that he is wrong. That was true in DuPont and it was true in my office when I was governor. But in the case of the president of the United States, it is true many times over.

About three weeks after the cabinet meeting, I saw the president during an evening entertainment in the White House to which Lillian and I were invited. He thanked me for speaking out on the 1080 issue, saying, "You were right." And he did not sign that executive order.

Years later I still think about that cabinet meeting. Should I have accepted it as a fait accompli? Or should I have challenged it as I did?

If I had not done so, he almost certainly would have signed it. I would almost certainly not have been able to get a private appointment with him in time to stop the signing. His staff would have seen to that.

I could have used more diplomatic language, but telling him he was wrong clearly got his attention.

From that point on, coyotes, eagles, and a wide variety of other wildlife continued to be protected from indiscriminate poisoning by federal employees on public lands—lands owned by all Americans.

Certainly questioning the president in the Cabinet Room had been a risk worth taking.

Today, in 1998, I look back with respect for President Ford. My direct contacts with him during the three years I reported to him were quite satisfying. Previously I had served with him on Governor Nelson Rockefeller's Commission on Critical Choices for Americans, where Ford displayed a strong interest in such global concerns as the environment, population growth, and energy use.

In my first one-on-one meeting with him (on September 30, 1974, in the White House when I was chairman of CEQ), I had been pleasantly surprised by his knowledge of and concern about environmental issues. He told me that he had always considered himself an environmentalist. What a contrast this was to President Nixon who clearly did not like environmentalists and who never found time to meet with me about CEQ matters.

President Ford made me feel like a friend. Once he even told me he considered me his adviser on "all matters dealing with the human environment including global issues." When I asked him what his position was on the growing campaign of conservatives to fight environmental regulations, he replied that he did not like it. He expressed his belief in the need for laws to control pollution. This was one of many examples of his moderate views. He was no hard-shell conservative.

When I got up to leave after about thirty minutes (I had been signed up for fifteen minutes) he asked me not to leave. He then asked me about my Half and Half Energy Plan. This was a key idea of mine for dealing with the energy crisis at that time. It called for filling half of our growing need for energy by using it more efficiently and half from additional sources. He asked a number of pertinent questions and then requested that I present the plan to William Seidman, executive director of the President's Economic Policy Board.

I did so. Seidman was interested and said he would discuss it with others. But with only a few months left in the Ford Administration, there was no time for a new initiative.

26

New Directions:
A National Lobbying Group on World
Issues

In LATE 1976 I RECEIVED A CALL FROM ROBERT MCNAMARA, PRESI-
dent of the World Bank and former secretary of defense under
presidents Kennedy and Johnson, inviting me to lunch with him
in his office. He told me that sixty people, many of whom had
held key positions in the Kennedy and Johnson administrations,
were forming a new national organization to be called New Directions. He said they wanted me, a moderate progressive Republican, to be the founding president. The group included Margaret
Mead, John Gardner, Norman Cousins, Father Ted Hesburgh,
Paul Warnke, Harry McPherson, James Grant, and Douglas Dillon. New Directions would be a lobbying group patterned after
Common Cause, but would work on world issues such as the environment, world population, the threat of nuclear weapons and
global poverty. Theirs was an agenda which fit my interests very
well.

This group had projected that New Directions could grow to
300,000 members within three years, which at $25 per year dues
would give New Directions the substantial annual income of $7.5
million. With such finances it could be potent indeed.

At this time I was wondering what I would do in 1977. If President Ford lost the upcoming 1976 election, as then appeared
probable, I would almost certainly be out as chairman of CEQ. If
he won, it appeared his team would be even more conservative
than in his first term and would be more difficult for me to
work with.

After visiting separately with the four members of the nascent
organization's planning commission, Father Ted Hesburgh, presi-

Margaret Mead and Father Ted Hesburgh as they launch New Directions with Peterson (in background) as president. Washington, D.C., October 13, 1976. Courtesy of the author.

dent of Notre Dame; Margaret Mead, the world-renowned anthropologist; Norman Cousins, publisher of the *Saturday Review;* and John Gardner, secretary for Health, Education and Welfare and founder of Common Cause, I was excited about the prospects for New Directions. I decided to accept their offer to become its president even though they had only $5,000 in the bank, $25,000 worth of bills, and no telephones or typewriters in their recently rented office.

On September 1, 1976, I went to the White House to see President Ford; we met alone in the Oval Office. I told him about New Directions, how I had been approached by Robert McNamara to take the presidency of this organization, and that I had decided to accept. I thanked him for the opportunity to be chairman of CEQ and described how rewarding that assignment had been.

The president was very friendly. He thanked me for "doing a good job at CEQ"—for standing up for the environment against considerable opposition from others in the administration. His

compliment pleased me, as did his recognition of the opposition
I experienced. Earlier I had surmised that he was much more
interested in and appreciative of what I was doing than many of
the people around him. His parting words reinforced that view.
He thought New Directions could be an effective organization.
"One tailor-made for you," he said.

He walked out of the Oval Office with me, and I wished him
well in the upcoming election. Suddenly he appeared depressed.
"That damn Reagan is going to make me lose the election," he
stated. I believe the president was right. Ronald Reagan had opposed his nomination and was still bad-mouthing him. Reagan's
negative impact could well have made the difference in the close
election that followed.

In 1976, President Ford was defeated, and Jimmy Carter became president. Carter was a great supporter of all of New Directions causes, especially environmental protection and energy
development. Ironically, the fact that the new president, in contrast to his predecessors, gave high visibility to the causes New
Directions espoused became one of our problems. The incentive
to join a citizens group to lobby government on these causes was
suddenly and markedly reduced.

My prime initial assignment was to raise money to get the fledgling organization started. Douglas Dillon, Wall Street financier
and secretary of the treasury in the Kennedy and Johnson administrations, had promised to give $10,000 and sponsor a fund-
raising luncheon in Manhattan. When I went to see him, he was
friendly and enthusiastic about the potential of New Directions.

We picked a date for his luncheon, to be held in the River
House on the East River. He listed a number of wealthy people
he would invite. I asked if he would mind if I asked Laurance
Rockefeller to co-sponsor the luncheon, and he replied, "No, that
would be fine." Then I asked if I could tell Laurance that Douglas
Dillon would be giving $10,000. His response was, "Tell him I will
give $25,000."

I went to see Laurance Rockefeller in his office on the fifty-
sixth floor of Rockefeller Center. He agreed to cosponsor the
luncheon and expressed surprise that Dillon—who was then
chairman of New York City's famed Metropolitan Museum, and
one of its generous benefactors—had pledged $25,000. Laurance
said, "I'll match his gift for a starter."

Laurance also suggested several people to invite and then said,

"Russ, let me give you some advice. Don't be self-conscious when asking for money for a good cause. I do it all the time and have taught myself that I am not asking for a favor. I'm offering prospective donors an opportunity to invest in something important."

That was great advice. I put it to work all over the world during the next eighteen years as I comfortably gave many people "the opportunity to invest in an important cause." It really works. If you only fund raise for things you deeply believe in and display your enthusiasm for the cause as you offer prospective donors the opportunity to participate, they will, on most occasions, give you their support.

The Dillon-Rockefeller luncheon was a great success. I gave the sales pitch, preferably called the opportunity pitch, and the two hosts strongly reinforced it and announced their gifts. We raised $135,000, and I got to know several very wealthy people who supported my causes over the years.

For the next year I travelled constantly all over America, giving speeches, holding press conferences, and meeting with editorial boards, but primarily raising money in living rooms, clubs, and hotel suites. I raised $700,000 in hard money—a tax deduction was not permitted, since we were a lobbying organization.

What a wonderful group of people I met—knowledgeable about world affairs, interested in the future quality of life everywhere; concerned about world poverty, excessive population growth and environmental degradation; opposed to the excessive buildup of nuclear weapons, and rarely complaining about taxes or environmental regulations. Clearly my staff and members around the country had shepherded me to people who shared New Directions' interests and mine.

Back home in Washington, New Directions' small six-member staff was augmented with volunteers who worked long hours to lobby Congress, back up my fund raising, produce news and promotional pieces, and most of all launch a massive direct-mail campaign to build membership.

We were located only one block from Common Cause. With the blessing of chairman, John Gardner, and direct involvement of his staff, we made good use of Common Cause's extensive and successful direct-mail membership-building experience. We used the same two San Francisco writers Common Cause employed. We spent much of our resources on this effort, but never did find a mail piece that returned in membership dues the cost of the mailing. While Common Cause rapidly built a membership of over 300,000 with its initial campaign during antiwar rioting to get the U.S. out of Vietnam and sustained it later with its Watergate-era campaign for improved ethics in government, we signed up only 14,000 members that first year.

Clearly, future-oriented world programs attracted many fewer people willing to invest $25 in membership in an organization dealing with these programs than did current high-profile domestic programs. And as stated earlier, President Carter's coming to office at the same time New Directions was founded and speaking out for the same issues no doubt reduced the incentive to support New Directions' lobbying program.

Maximizing our effort to build membership continuously put us in a financial bind. Meeting our monthly payroll was difficult, although we always made it. This made life particularly difficult for my wife and family finance manager, Lillian, since as president I put myself last in line to be paid.

I had gambled financially when I took this job, betting on our success in building a large membership. Now at 59 years of age I had too little security for my family: I had only a minor pension from my twenty-six years with DuPont and none from my four years as governor, one year with Nelson Rockefeller and three years with the White House team. New Directions could afford neither a pension plan nor health insurance. But fortunately, in my subsequent careers, we were able to build reasonable security for the two of us from a National Audubon Society pension, my social security pension, and Lillian's shrewd investment of our small capital.

During New Directions' first year, we organized citizens nationwide to lobby their U.S. senators to ratify the Panama Canal Treaty, which we were convinced was important to the security of the western hemisphere. When it was ratified, we were given credit by the Senate leadership for turning around a number of senators on whose votes the ratification depended. President Carter also thanked us.

We participated in the successful effort to gain congressional support for President Carter's initiative to launch America's first major effort to push solar energy and more efficient energy use, the so-called soft-energy path. We considered this vital to fulfilling the world's long-term energy needs and to safeguarding the global environment. And we weighed in heavily but unsuccessfully in efforts to reduce the production of plutonium, large stockpiles of which already threatened world security.

But we were sorely disappointed by the small membership of 14,000 we built in our first year, far short of the 100,000 that Bob McNamara, John Gardner, and the other New Directions founders had projected. What is more, we had no ideas that we had not already tried for increasing the effectiveness of our direct-mail effort to build membership. We knew our principal donors, who invested start-up money in New Directions on faith that there were many more Americans waiting to be signed up in our important cause, were not likely to continue such donations for long. So, when I received a bid for a more promising job, I accepted.

New Directions membership never exceeded the 14,000 reached that first year. Over the next six years it gradually fell off until the organization was dissolved in the early 1980s. Now in the 1990s it appears that too many Americans continue to have too little interest in global affairs. Certainly this is true of the U.S. Congress which is moving to reduce markedly our commitment to foreign aid, to stabilizing world population, protecting the global environment, and funding the United Nations.

27

Depoliticizing the Congressional Office of Technology Assessment

NEAR THE END OF 1977 I RECEIVED A CALL FROM DEMOCRATIC SENAtor Ted Kennedy asking me to meet with him and Republican Senator Clifford Case of New Jersey. They offered me the job of Director of the Office of Technology Assessment (OTA) of the U.S. Congress.

What a wonderful opportunity! I would be paid for exercising foresight and common sense. Officially, the job description for OTA was to advise members of Congress on "the long term impact, domestically and globally, of technical applications on economic, environmental, social and political factors." In other words, OTA's role was to assess the likely positive and negative results of new developments such as exploiting nuclear energy, building mammoth dams, spraying pesticides, or building supersonic jets. It involved anticipating problems so they could be avoided or solved early on. Directing OTA would tie me to the scientific, technical, environmental, and business communities in which I had previously worked. It would allow me to approach problems holistically, rather than one piece at a time. It would probably permit me to have more impact on Congress than through my job at New Directions. The two senators strongly emphasized that last point.

I told them I was leaving that day for a trip to India and Sri Lanka with the Overseas Development Council and would give them an answer on my return. There was barely time to tell Lillian about the surprise job offer. I was confident she would be in favor of such a move, for she had been concerned about the disproportionate amount of time I had to spend raising funds for New Directions, leaving little time to work on the issues. At OTA there would be no fund raising. Moreover, I would be assured that my monthly salary would be paid on time, and I would be included in a pension plan and have health insurance.

A few days later in a village outside New Delhi, the attaché at the U.S. Embassy arrived with a cable from Senator Kennedy who was chairman of OTA's board. In it he congratulated me on being elected unanimously by OTA's board (six senators and six representatives, half Democrats and half Republicans). When Kennedy and Case had offered me the job, I thought they had the authority to do so. But they did not have the official approval of the board at that time. I learned later from two board members that the actual vote was ten to two.

The press reported promptly that I had been elected unanimously as director of OTA. This was news to my bosses, the board members of New Directions. I had not even told them of the job offer. Hurriedly, I cabled them to say that I had not accepted the new job, but would discuss the offer with them when I returned home. Then I phoned Lillian to explain the details of the offer. She was thrilled.

The next message awaiting me, after I arrived back at Dulles Airport, was from Dr. Philip Handler, president of the National Academy of Sciences. He invited me to meet with leaders of major technical organizations who wanted to convince me to accept the OTA offer. But I should *not* take the job, they warned me as soon as we sat down together, until the board of that congressional advisory body agreed to give me the authority to hire and fire staff members. They felt that OTA had the potential to become a valuable institution, but currently was hamstrung by politics. What particular problem would be studied, and how the study itself turned out, was determined in some cases by the political needs of some elected officials who sat on its board. Consequently OTA had low credibility in both Congress and the scientific community.

I received similar advice from OTA's prestigious advisory board headed by Dr. Jerry Wiesner, then president of MIT.

Scientific organizations had been responsible for proposing and formulating the legislation to establish OTA. It originally called for a board consisting of a chairman and a majority of members appointed from the community at large, with two senators and two representatives appointed by Congress. When the bill reached the floor of the House, it was amended at the last minute to provide for a board composed entirely of members of Congress.

Dr. Margaret Mead, representing the New Directions board, invited me to lunch in her club in New York City and encouraged me to stay where I was. As a leader in the scientific community, she knew of the problems at OTA. But she also acknowledged that OTA, once freed from political pressures, could become an important force. As we parted, she said, "Russ, I will love you no matter what your decision." I believe she meant it. One of the special pleasures of my New Directions job was getting to know and work with Margaret Mead.

I told Kennedy and Case I would take the job, with two conditions; OTA must give me the authority to hire and fire. They must also give up the practice of each of the twelve board members having one OTA staff person working part-time for him. They agreed. I accepted and was sworn in. Then I met with each board member. Ten of the twelve supported the change, but Ted Stevens (Republican from Alaska) and Ernest Hollings (Democrat from South Carolina), both leading members of the Senate Appropriations Committee, were adamantly opposed.

One OTA staffer, William Davis, was assigned to Stevens. Davis was in charge of an OTA study of Alaskan lands that should be protected as national parks, wilderness, wildlife refuges or national forests. Stevens, who devoted much of his career to promoting short-term exploitation of Alaska's natural resources, had publicly called for limiting such designation to 25 million acres. Representative Morris Udall (Democrat from Arizona), senior member of the OTA board from the House, was in favor of protecting 125 million acres. Certainly any OTA report prepared by Senator Stevens' man would have little credibility.

I remember that when I told Stevens this in the minority whip's office in the basement of the U.S. Capitol, his face reddened and his lips quivered. He ordered me to stop questioning his integrity and berated me. He even went so far as to threaten to cut my budget in half. I told him I would rather have half the budget and a credible organization than twice the budget and no credibility.

I also recall an almost identical experience in Senator Hollings's office, including the threat to cut my budget in half. I responded as with Stevens, but at least he and I shook hands when we parted. Hollings would not even go that far. "I don't want to give you the wrong impression," he said, keeping his hand, fist firmly clenched, by his side.

Next I met with Kennedy and Case. They now told me they

Senator Ted Kennedy swearing in Peterson as director of the Office of Technology Assessment of the U.S. Congress. Lillian Peterson holding Bible. U.S. Capitol: January 23, 1978. U.S. Senate Photo.

could not keep their commitment to me because of senatorial privilege. I asked them what the term meant, and they told me that with two senior senators opposed, they just could not go against them. I replied that I was resigning and would hold a press conference to explain what was happening in OTA. After repeated attempts to convince me to change my mind, Kennedy said he would use some of his chips with Stevens to gain his support. The Massachusetts senator had apparently supported the Alaskan senator on some issues of importance and now would ask Stevens to return the favor.

At the next board meeting where Hollings repeatedly lambasted me, the board voted eleven to one to give me what I had asked for. Only Hollings voted "no." Each of the twelve board members, except Hollings and Stevens, privately thanked me for what I had done. So did Jerry Wiesner and other members of the advisory committee. Shortly thereafter Philip Handler of the National Academy of Science asked me to come to see him. When

I arrived the heads of the National Academy of Engineering and the Institute of Medicine and several members of their staffs were also present. He said, "On behalf of the entire scientific and technical community, I thank you."

Of special importance to me was the fact that most OTA staff members were pleased. They were highly competent individuals who had been embarrassed and frustrated by OTA's reputation for putting political expediency ahead of scientific objectivity. With my new authority I removed a few staff members, and thenceforth prohibited any staff from working for any member of Congress. OTA has been depoliticized ever since. Thanks to effective leadership by Dr. John Gibbons, who succeeded me in 1979, OTA developed an outstanding reputation.

This was evident at the celebration of OTA's twentieth anniversary I attended in 1993. Praise for the organization from governmental, scientific, and industrial leadership was generous indeed. I was pleased to hear from John Gibbons, Ted Kennedy, long-time board member Congressman George Brown, Jerry Wiesner, and several OTA staffers that if we had not removed the organization from politics in 1978, "it wouldn't have been worth a damn." Jack Gibbons's leadership ability was also recognized by President Clinton in 1993 when he appointed Gibbons science adviser to the president.

It was challenging and fun to be director of OTA. Once the place was depoliticized, the talented staff worked together smoothly and effectively, advising Congress on the long-term impact of the most important issues facing our nation and the world—energy development and use, population growth, environmental degradation, nuclear proliferation, telecommunications, applied genetics, global food production, and other matters affecting the lives of our children and those who come after them. In retrospect, my standing up to Senators Stevens and Hollings, and then to Senators Kennedy and Case, had been risks worth taking. OTA was markedly stronger, and I personally gained much job satisfaction.

It has been reported that I left OTA after 15 months because of the conflicts I had with these senators. That is not true. I had strong support from nine of the twelve board members and all of the advisory board, including the two alternating board chairmen, Senator Kennedy and Congressman Morris Udall.

I left because of the strong appeal of an offer made to me repeatedly during my stay at OTA to become president of National Audubon Society, a job I had dreamed of for years. The presidency of Audubon proved to be every bit as satisfying for both Lillian and me as we had anticipated. And OTA, under new leadership, was relieved from any lingering antagonism I had stirred up by forcing major changes in the organization.

As I reflect on my OTA experience, I recognize that I was attracted to the job of advising Congress on the long-term impact of new technology on humans and the total environment. But doing this convincingly meant that a serious problem had to be solved first. So I set out single-mindedly to solve that problem. To get it done I was willing to sacrifice my job, knowing the job would have been a waste of time if politics instead of science continued to drive the enterprise. It called for confrontation, for standing firm, for threatening to go public. But the odds were with me, key board members were my allies, and most of the others believed in what I wanted to do.

In other words, it really was a risk worth taking.

28

Remembrances of Washington

O<small>N MAY 15, 1973, NELSON ROCKEFELLER AND I WENT TO THE WHITE</small>
House to see President Nixon. Nelson had arranged to have the
president designate the committee he and I had put together to
study critical global issues as a national commission. That morning we had met with the Republican and Democratic leaders of
Congress, all of whom agreed to serve on the commission. Among
them was Representative Gerald Ford, soon to become vice
president.

While waiting in the Cabinet Room to see the president, Nelson
made some disparaging remarks about him. I said, "Nelson, you
had better be quiet. This room may be bugged." Neither of us
realized that our remarks *were* being recorded on the soon-to-be-
famous White House tapes.

When we entered the Oval Office, the president was pacing up
and down, cursing Martha Mitchell, Attorney General Mitchell's
wife, who made a habit of calling reporters late at night to run
down the president. I had been with President Nixon on several
occasions when I was governor, but never heard him use a foul
four-letter word. That afternoon they were streaming out of his
mouth. Then I noticed his eyes. At first I thought he was winking
at me, but then I decided it was a nervous twitch.

After we sat down by the fireplace and after the White House
photographer left, Nelson explained the status of our study
group and our interest in its being designated The National Commission on Critical Choices for Americans. By now the president
appeared calm. He asked good questions about our study and
seemed pleased in proclaiming our group a national commission.

We then went to the White House Press Room, where Nelson
announced our mission to the assembled press. Two years later,
and after Governor Rockefeller had become vice president, the

President Nixon approves Rockefeller's request that the Commission on Critical Choices for Americans be designated a national commission. The Oval Office, May 14, 1973. White House Photo.

commission published fourteen books covering its comprehensive study of the major national and global issues facing America.

* * *

In the summer of 1973, I received a call from the attorney general of the United States, Elliot Richardson, asking me to come to his office in the Department of Justice. When I arrived, his deputy, William Ruckelshaus, was with him. They wanted me to take the job of director of the Immigration and Naturalization Service. Several agencies had recently been consolidated into this service. My experience during the previous three years as chairman of the National Commission on Criminal Justice Standards and Goals, where I worked closely with the Department of Justice, very likely accounted for my being recommended for this job.

Richardson said, "This is a very important job. It needs someone tough like you, who has had experience in management."

Ruckelshaus added, "It can be a good stepping stone for advancement."

I admired both of these men and disliked being uncooperative. However, I was determined at this time to become head of the President's Council on Environmental Quality (CEQ). I told them so.

"That's a nothing job," Richardson said.

Ruckelshaus, who had just resigned as administrator of the Environmental Protection Agency, where he had reported directly to the president, confirmed Richardson's appraisal. However, my mind and heart were set on getting into the environmental movement. I turned them down.

A few weeks later, during the so-called Saturday Night Massacre, both Richardson and Ruckelshaus resigned rather than fire the Watergate prosecutor, Archibald Cox, as the president had ordered.

* * *

"This is Agnew. I need to talk to a friend. How about coming over to my office to see me?"

"Where are you?" I asked.

"In the town house right next to you."

"I'll be there," I responded.

The vice president had recently resigned under pressure from the Department of Justice for the financial illegalities he allegedly committed while he was governor of Maryland and U.S. vice president. He was using a town house on Lafayette Square, provided him by the government, while he wound up his affairs. My office as chairman of CEQ was in an adjacent town house. On the way over to see him, I recalled that he and I had worked together well when President Nixon, in his first term, assigned Agnew to be the administration's principal contact for governors. The vice president almost invariably came through when I, as governor, asked for help.

We had had a number of public confrontations as well. Once, at a governors' conference in Sun Valley, I called on him in an executive session to stop his extreme attack on the news media, because it was hurting all Republican officeholders. This supposedly secret confrontation ended up on the evening news.

At another governors' conference he urged all of us to push an aggressive law-and-order program. I interrupted him to say, "Mr. Vice President, law and order with justice."

A number of my colleagues applauded. The vice president yelled, "Hell no. Law and order, period," for which he received much greater applause.

That day, when I arrived at his temporary office, Agnew greeted me like a long-lost pal. He explained that he was innocent and was being treated unfairly. I refrained from passing judgment, and we reminisced about how well we had worked together when I was a governor. It was sad to see this beaten man and to realize how far those in power can fall when they violate the public trust in a democracy that practices law and order with justice.

＊　＊　＊

One day in 1976, when I was attending a cabinet meeting, Nobel Laureate Secretary of State Henry Kissinger arrived late. Rather than sit in his assigned seat next to the president, he sat down next to me near the end of the table. After I made a comment, the secretary leaned over and asked, "Who are you?"

"I'm Russ Peterson."

"What do you do?"

"I'm chairman of CEQ."

"What's CEQ?"

After I briefly explained, I reminded him that he and I had met a number of times with Nelson Rockefeller. "I remember well the lengthy conversation you and I had at that party Nelson threw at Pocantico Hills for you and Nancy after your marriage," I said.

"Oh, yes. You are the former governor of Delaware."

That was quite a disillusionment. Up until that moment I had felt pretty important attending a cabinet meeting, especially when the world-renowned Henry Kissinger sat next to me.

Yet he did not even recall who I was. Even more serious, he did not know what CEQ was. What a tremendous letdown!

At that point, I had been head of CEQ for three years, reporting directly to the president. We had been deeply involved with Kissinger's Department of State on what we thought were critical *international* issues like saving the Earth and stabilizing human population growth. I had received two letters bearing his signature and appointing me vice chairman of the U.S. delegations to two world conferences sponsored by the United Nations, one on population in Bucharest in 1974 and one on human settlements in Vancouver in 1976. Yet Kissinger said he did not know that CEQ or I existed.

I left that meeting more aware than ever of the great task faced by environmentalists in enlightening the leaders of the United States and the world about the threats to our global environment and hence to the quality of life of all people everywhere.

* * *

In 1975 Vice President Nelson Rockefeller called me in my office on Lafayette Square and asked if I was free to come to see him. I immediately walked across Pennsylvania Avenue to his office in the Old Executive Office Building adjacent to the White House.

When I arrived, I said, "It's good to be with you, Mr. Vice President."

He frowned and said, "I called you because I need to talk to a friend."

He was unusually agitated, pacing up and down his office. He told me to sit down.

"I can't sit down when the Vice President of the United States is standing," I responded.

With Vice President Nelson Rockefeller, Executive Office Building, 1976. White House Photo.

"Damn it, sit down," he said. "You are here as a friend, and don't call me Mr. Vice President." I sat down.

Then he continued, "President Ford told me that if I accepted this job he would give me some authority and responsibility to get things done. All I do is take orders from a bunch of kids in the White House."

It is more the rule than the exception that presidents give enormous authority to relatively young people who have helped them gain office, people who have not earned that power and are poorly equipped to administer it. President Ford's staff was no exception.

Nelson Rockefeller—a highly experienced leader, much more qualified than anyone else in the White House—was hog-tied and humiliated by such a system. (Years later at a 1986 symposium at the University of California-San Diego, Dick Cheney, President Ford's chief of staff admitted that he had been "the sand in the gears" of many of Rockefeller's policy initiatives.) I advised Nelson to go directly to the president and demand a meaningful assignment. I sensed, since he rarely, if ever, had a boss, he did not know how to do that. After our meeting, Nelson did talk to President Ford and was assigned the key responsibility for Ford's Whip Inflation Now project.

In my opinion Nelson would have made a great president, but was thwarted by a sustained attack by the leaders of the right-wing Republicans, mainly westerners, who saw Rockefeller as the main threat to Goldwater and Reagan. They succeeded among Republican delegates to national conventions in labeling Rockefeller erroneously as a dangerous liberal. His long track record shows he was a moderate conservative.

When President Ford ran for election in 1976 to become president in his own right, Ronald Reagan, supported by the far-right Republicans, challenged him for the nomination. Ford and his advisers feared Reagan would win the nomination if Ford kept Rockefeller as his vice president. So Ford chose conservative Robert Dole, won the nomination, and with Reagan still fighting him, lost the election.

I believe if he had stuck with Rockefeller, a proven potent campaigner with strong appeal to moderate Republicans and Democrats, he would have won. And Rockefeller might have gone on to eventually reach his life-long ambition of becoming president of the United States.

* * *

Each quarter during his presidency, Jimmy Carter and/or his aides met with national environmental leaders in the White House. Clearly he was the most dedicated and effective environmental leader who has ever occupied that office. At each meeting we usually forgot to thank him for what his administration had already done to protect the environment, because we were so eager to push for the next improvements.

As the time approached for the 1980 election, I asked national environmental leaders to agree to personally endorse President Carter for reelection. At our next meeting with the president in the Cabinet room, twenty-five of us were present, and at least five of us were Republicans.

At this time the president was being harassed on many fronts—Iran was still holding Americans hostage, the Middle East had quadrupled the price of oil, causing inflation to skyrocket, and the Republicans were castigating Carter at every turn. The president

President Carter responding to announcement just made by Peterson (on Carter's right) that all of the assembled CEOs of national environmental organizations would, on a personal basis, endorse him for reelection. The Cabinet Room, 1980. White House Photo.

probably thought, "What are those environmentalists going to beat on me for this time?"

I sat on the president's right and spoke for the group.

"Mr. President, we want you to know how pleased we are with what you have done for the environment. Accordingly, everyone of us around this table has pledged personally to support you for reelection."

The president almost broke down. He was obviously surprised and then highly pleased. We reminisced about our accomplishments and then got on with our agenda for the future.

Although we tried to make it clear to the news media that we had endorsed Carter personally, many people concluded from the news that our *organizations* had endorsed him. Each of us got in some trouble with his or her organization. Two almost got fired. At the next board meeting of the National Audubon Society, I found myself surrounded by five conservative Republican members of my board. They warned me that I was jeopardizing Audubon's financial support. I said, "I don't think so. We don't get more

than $1,000 from any of our conservative board members, while
some other members give from $25,000 to $100,000 per year.
They have all thanked me for what I did."

At our national convention of over 1,000 members I explained
what I had done and received a standing ovation.

Despite our efforts, environmentalist Jimmy Carter lost the
election and Ronald Reagan, the most antienvironmentalist to
ever hold the presidency, moved in. He then launched his campaign to try to undo the environmental regulations and destroy
the institutions established through the bipartisan efforts of Congress and the White House. Not until twelve years later, when
Bill Clinton became president, did the White House once again
become a champion of the environment, thanks in major measure
to Vice President Al Gore.

*   *   *

President Reagan assigned James Watt, secretary of the Interior, and Anne Gorsuch, administrator of the Environmental Protection Agency, to lead his anti-environment crusade. James Watt
had headed a western legal institute that was funded by some
wealthy members of Ronald Reagan's so-called Kitchen Cabinet.
This group of lawyers worked to protect the interests of western
businessmen and ranchers. Administrator Gorsuch also came
from the West and had a record of strongly opposing environmental protection measures. Now she had the job of managing
the principal agency responsible for protecting America's
environment.

These two, through administrative measures, managed over a
few months to markedly downgrade the effectiveness of their
agencies. EPA had always been greatly understaffed in light of
the Herculean assignments Congress had given it. Now Anne
Gorsuch made deep cuts in its staff. Other key staff members
resigned in disgust. Among other things, James Watt moved to
make it easier for westerners to exploit the nation's public lands.
Fortunately, their attempts to get legislation passed in Congress
went nowhere, because strong bipartisan support for the environment still existed there.

We national environmental leaders coordinated our efforts to
inform the American people about these changes. Among other
things, we produced a large volume documenting what the

Reagan administration had done and was trying to do to weaken environmental protection regulations and institutions. When we released it to the press in San Francisco, it triggered numerous news stories and editorials all over the country. This helped strengthen congressional resolve to oppose what the Reagan Administration was trying to do.

During this time, as president of the National Audubon Society, I made many speeches around the country. I labelled James Watt, "A fox in the chicken coop." This led to his inviting me to his office. (On several previous occasions I had tried to see him, but with no success.)

I had been in the Secretary of the Interior's huge office many times before, especially during the tenure of Cecil Andrus, President Carter's appointee. The last time I was there to help Secretary Andrus plan the strategy for gaining congressional support for passage of the legislation that subsequently set aside over 100 million acres of federal lands in Alaska as national parks, wildlife refuges, wilderness areas and national forests. But under Watt, the pendulum had swung in another direction.

Secretary Watt welcomed me in a very friendly manner and motioned me to a seat beside him. After a few pleasantries, he told me he wanted me to change my mind.

"President Reagan and I are both pretty good environmentalists," he said.

He explained how they both loved the wide-open spaces in the West, the flowers, the trees, and wild animals.

I replied, "That's good, but if you succeed in doing what you are trying to do, our grandchildren will not have the same opportunity." Then I ticked off the most environmentally threatening actions they were trying to implement.

He asked me to join him in another part of his office where he showed me a huge photograph of a fox. "You see," he said, "we do have a fox in this office." He was clearly pleased with that.

A few weeks later Secretary Watt talked to over 1,000 businessmen in New York City. In his speech he identified me as the principal culprit in the environmentalists' campaign to label him and the president as anti-environmentalists. I was pleased to be so honored, but his claim was far from the truth. Hundreds of us participated in leading that important mission.

The secretary went on to tell his audience that in spite of my role, the Celanese Corporation had given Audubon $800,000.

The CEO of Celanese was present in the audience and was deeply embarrassed in front of so many of his business friends. He subsequently ordered his subordinates to forego any more support for the travelling exhibit "The Audubon Ark" that Celanese had sponsored and that two Audubon employees took to shopping centers all over America, teaching the importance of saving endangered species.

Shortly after this, James Watt and Anne Gorsuch resigned. They had become an increasing liability for the Reagan Administration. They were replaced by two more moderate people: William Clark, advisor to the president, became secretary of the Interior and William Ruckelshaus, the first administrator of EPA, returned to his old post.

* * *

Many politicians and members of the news media, when wishing to belittle our government in Washington, refer to the "inside the beltway crowd," as though that group is out of touch with the real world. I contend that the inside the beltway group, relative to all other entities in our country, is not only the most representative of America, but also the best in tune with America. That group is made up of elected officials and their staffs and families from every congressional district in our country as well as previous officials and staff members from all over America who have chosen to live in Washington. These elected officials are wrestling with and studying all the issues of America, not just those of Alaska, the Bronx, Miami, or Houston—not just those of farmers, businessmen, unions, environmentalists or news media. Furthermore, they are in touch daily with their constituents, and they must return home frequently to report and campaign for reelection. Washington is also full of lobbyists who represent the people and their interests back home—small and big businessmen, poor and rich people, teachers, laborers, men, women, and children.

The next time you hear someone belittling the "inside the beltway crowd," remember they are talking about a representative sample of America.

VII

Non-Governmental Environmentalism: We-The-People and Planet Earth

29

Realizing a Dream: Becoming President of the National Audubon Society

WHILE HEAD OF THE COUNCIL ON ENVIRONMENTAL QUALITY IN Washington, I got to know Dr. Elvis Stahr, president of the National Audubon Society. He stood out among the leaders of the many environmental organizations with whom I met regularly. He had been a Rhodes Scholar, dean of the law school at the University of Kentucky, president of West Virginia University and of Indiana University, and Secretary of the Army. He built Audubon into a stronger and more activist organization.

At the time, I thought it would be great to be president of Audubon. Its deep commitment to protecting bird life fit well with my own well-established, intense interest in birding. I recalled the excitement of my first birding trip with my two sons Peter and Glen (then ages eleven and fifteen) in the Florida Everglades. An Audubon naturalist showed us sixty species of birds we didn't know existed and pointed out the site where Guy Bradley, Audubon's first warden assigned to protect Florida's herons and egrets, was murdered. Bradley was killed by hunters who did not like Audubon's interfering with their business of slaughtering these birds to collect their plumes to sell to the millinery trade for decorating ladies' hats.

Audubon's nationwide network of wildlife sanctuaries intrigued me. So did its grassroots organizations in all fifty states. Both appealed to my long-term interest in mobilizing citizens to act on critical issues. So, in 1975, when Elvis Stahr invited me to be the principal speaker at National Audubon Society's convention in New Orleans, I jumped at the opportunity. I spoke on "The Invisible Foot: Ecology's Appendix to Adam Smith." This was one of the earliest discussions of the interdependence of a healthy economy and a healthy environment. It emphasized the mutual need and opportunity for business and environmental leaders to work together to accomplish their long-term objectives. The speech hit such a responsive chord with the Audubon Board that they ordered it published in full in *Audubon*—the only speech ever to be printed in their prestigious publication. And they subsequently awarded me the Audubon Medal.

It is not surprising then that in 1976, near the end of President Ford's term when I was considering what my next job might be, I decided to look into the possibility of becoming president of National Audubon. I went to *Who's Who In America* and found that Elvis Stahr and I were the same age and that he was blessed with twenty honorary doctorates and many other prestigious awards. I immediately crossed off that possibility.

Then, two years later, when I had been head of the Office of Technology Assessment of Congress for only three months, I received a call from the chairman of Audubon's executive committee, Thomas W. Keesee, Jr. offering me the presidency of Audubon. I told him that, if he had called three months earlier, I would have jumped at the opportunity, but I could not leave OTA at that time. Three months later he tried again, and after another three months he sent a head-hunting firm to see me. Still the answer was "no." After one year at OTA, I was asked once again. This time I agreed to meet confidentially in Texas with Audubon's search committee.

They told me they had been impressed with my record as an environmental activist and by my speeches and articles calling for a comprehensive, integrated, global approach (multidisciplinary, multinational, public, and private) to protecting the environment. They wanted me to make Audubon into a potent activist organization following the approach I had recommended. They described Audubon's 350,000 membership and how this could become an effective lobbying force.

They were also very frank about Audubon's current condition: a one-million dollar deficit with larger future deficits threatening, serious staff in-fighting, and the board running the organization. They wanted a tough executive who would take the job away from the board. Moreover, they offered a salary, health insurance, and pension plan that promised the best financial security my family had enjoyed since I left DuPont.

I considered my friends at OTA. Was it right for me to leave at that time? We had depoliticized OTA. We had a good staff, had gained the respect of our advisory board and the technical community and were now working on the broad priority projects that its enabling legislation called for. OTA no longer needed me. In fact, I thought it would be better off without the continued unpleasantness of board members Stevens and Hollings toward me. I also concluded that if I remained at OTA, it would be difficult—if not impossible—to be the kind of leader on critical issues that I wanted to be while reporting as an adviser to a bipartisan committee of powerful politicians. Furthermore, Audubon offered the opportunity to blend my hobby of nature study and birding with a job where I could associate with respected, professional naturalists. I accepted the job and found I had made the right decision for OTA, Audubon, and me.

Audubon had major problems, but that was why I was hired. The problems stemmed primarily from a lack of funds and lack of an organization qualified and specifically assigned to raise funds.

The board had been insisting that Elvis Stahr cut costs and that Frances Breed, the only person assigned to fund raising, be more attentive to key donors. But since she had a multitude of other assignments, she could not. Seeing this, I recruited four experienced development people who put me, the board, and some of the staff to work raising funds. The result was a 19 percent per year growth in revenue during my six years as president.

Fund raising was fun. Travelling all over America, meeting individually with hundreds of affluent and prestigious people in their homes or offices and offering them the opportunity to invest in Audubon's cause, I met many kindred souls. No one was unpleasant. Some gave as much as $100,000. Most gave in the $5,000 to $25,000 range. Today I continue to enjoy the friendship of many of these donors, and my Audubon years have driven home to me how fundamentally important it is to a nonprofit organization that its CEO be deeply involved in fund raising.

With our increased funds, we operated in the black and raised our staff's pitiful salaries, more than doubling them in many cases. We recruited new talent and launched a major effort toward fulfilling each of the five missions that comprised The Audubon Cause: conserve plants and animals, foster the wise use of land and water, promote rational strategies for energy development

Press Conference (U.S. Capitol) with Senator William Cohen opposing construction of Dickey-Lincoln Dam in Maine. May 1979. U.S. Senate Photo.

and use, protect life from pollution and radiation, and seek solutions for global problems involving the interaction of population, resources, and the environment. We expanded Audubon to 550,000 members, 520 chapters, offices in the capitals of ten of the largest states, a potent Washington, D.C., office, and 72 wildlife sanctuaries.

We also strengthened our scientific and environmental policy research and developed and promoted the Audubon Energy Plan for the U.S. It called for programs and regulations that would promote the more efficient use of energy and the development of renewable forms of energy. A major effort was instituted to support national and international programs to stabilize world population. Audubon provided the initiative and sustained leadership and support for several alliances of national environmental and population organizations, including the Group of Ten and the Global Tomorrow Coalition. I chaired the latter for its first six years.

We also established an international program to permit Audubon to play a role in United Nations conferences and programs

World Congress, International Council for Bird Preservation. Sir Peter Scott (left), S. Dillon Ripley (center), Russ Peterson, the new president. Lower left, former president Jean Delacour; lower right, Lillian Peterson at Great Banquet Hall, Kings College, Cambridge University, England, August 1982. Courtesy of the author.

on the environment, in the World Conservation Union (WCU) and the International Council for Bird Preservation (ICBP). I personally served as vice president of WCU and president of ICBP. These two challenging assignments allowed me to work closely with leading environmentalists and natural scientists from every region of the world.

I must thank my friend Howard P. Brokaw, a former DuPont colleague and a long-term birding companion, for getting me elected president of ICBP. When I headed the Council on Environmental Quality, Howard joined us as a volunteer and worked with leading wildlife scientists in the United States to produce an important book, *Wildlife in America*. This led to his becoming treasurer of ICBP, then a half-century old but tiny organization. We played key roles in building ICBP into a potent worldwide operation. Today Howard is chairman of American Bird Conservancy and a continuing long-term board member of National Audubon.

Helping Youth Discover the Wonders of Nature

Shortly after I became president of the National Audubon Society in 1979, Roger Tory Peterson, one of the world's most celebrated naturalists and early in his career a staff member of National Audubon, came to my office to wish me well. Dr. Peterson, through his field guides, motivated millions of people to observe and enjoy animal and plant life, thereby making them more environmentally aware. He told me how his own career as a naturalist began when he joined a Junior Audubon Club, and how many other prominent naturalists had similar experiences. In the intervening years Audubon had abandoned this program. Dr. Peterson wanted me to restart it and I resolved to do so.

He and I became good friends and worked together on projects

With Roger Tory Peterson, father of Peterson Nature Guides. Harbor Island, Maine, June 1980. Courtesy of the author.

to save birds and other wildlife. He was an inspiration to millions of people around the world, and he received numerous international and national awards, including the Presidential Medal of Freedom.

In 1982, after two unsuccessful attempts to launch an effective Junior Audubon program under people recruited from outside, I assigned the job to Marshal Case, one of our own environmental educators. His program, named Audubon Adventures, involved recruiting teachers around the country as volunteers. Each one led an Audubon Adventure Club of 30 fourth, fifth and sixth graders—a good age for teaching youngsters about the wonders of nature and about being stewards of the earth. Every month during the school year, participating teachers received a lesson plan for involving the group in hands-on experiences with nature, and students received a news letter describing that month's program.

These students also received membership cards. On the back of the card was printed the Declaration of Interdependence, a message I wrote in 1973:

> We the people of planet earth
> With respect for the dignity of each human life,
> With concern for future generations,
> With growing appreciation of our relationship to our environment,
> With recognition of limits to our resources,
> And with need for adequate food, air, water, shelter, health, protection, justice and self-fulfillment,
> Hereby declare our interdependence;
> And resolve to work together in peace
> And in harmony with our environment
> To enhance the quality of life everywhere.

By 1997, there were over 7 million Audubon Adventure Club Alumni. That is over 2.5 percent of the U.S. population. In addition, 660,000 students were enrolled, many from low income, inner city neighborhoods, and Audubon chapters were enthusiastic sponsors. Many chapters assisted the teachers in taking Audubon Adventurers on birding and nature study trips. Chapters in Los Angeles now sponsor 1,000 Spanish-speaking Audubon Adventures Clubs and 1,000 English-speaking clubs. They are also starting a new program called *Audubon Yes* to involve teenagers in high schools and colleges. Out of the ranks of Audubon Adventurers will emerge many leaders—competent naturalists and dedicated advocates for the environment. If one of them becomes a Roger Tory Peterson, how profitable the program will have been.

Roger Tory Peterson died on July 28, 1996. The last time I saw him, he remarked how pleased he was with Audubon Adventures. He is greatly missed.

Organizing Audubon Activists in All Congressional Districts

In 1981, when I became increasingly concerned about the devastating impact of the antienvironmental Reagan administration, I decided Audubon had to use its clout to combat this assault. Accordingly, I wrote a letter to each of our approximately 500,000 members asking for their support. The letter said, "The Reagan Administration is trying to undo all that Audubon has fought for over several decades. It is time to take off the gloves and fight. We are going to organize a Citizens' Mobilization Effort toward this end. Please sign up and send what you can to help finance this program."

We received over 37,000 responses with checks totalling almost $1 million, far beyond the record response of $84,000 received from previous solicitations of our members. We used the funds to establish a computerized file of Audubon activists, organized by congressional district. This proved to be an excellent device for promptly mobilizing them to communicate with their elected officials on issues of major concern to Audubon. Before that time, if we wanted to mobilize them, we had to send a letter to each of our 500,000 members, an expensive and thus infrequent approach. Now if we wished to influence a given representative, we could call up on our computer the names and addresses of the activists in a specific congressional district and mail only to them. Or if we wanted to contact only those members of a given congressional committee who were opposed to our position on a given issue, we could mobilize activists who lived in their districts.

It is important to recognize that elected officials pay little attention, if any, to letters coming from nonconstituents. Thus, Audubon members living in California would be wasting their time and money trying to influence a congressman from Maryland. This fact was driven home to me earlier when, as director of the Office of Technology Assessment of the U.S. Congress, I visited the offices of many members of Congress and learned how they tabulate the communications they receive. If a letter or telegram or telephone call comes from a constituent, it receives attention. If from a nonconstituent, it is essentially ignored. Moreover, when mobilizing an organization's own members, the first step is to identify those who are willing to be activists. The next step is to mobilize them, because most members have no desire or intention to become activists. Other organizations have followed this approach. It is clearly an effective and economical way to influence decision makers.

Over the years, Audubon has developed a multifaceted method of bringing its considerable information and influence to bear effectively on Congress and state legislatures so they will support legislation designating open spaces as refuges, parks and wilderness areas; strengthen air and water quality protection; and promote family planning and more efficient energy use. It worked tirelessly to block the Reagan administration's efforts to undo previously established environmental protection measures.

I was personally involved in much of this activity, speaking all over the country, working with the news media and testifying before congressional and state legislative committees. A few members of the Audubon board and others complained that I was hurting Audubon by being so outspoken. However, an extensive poll of our members showed that 97 percent of those who had an opinion thought Audubon was being properly outspoken or should be more outspoken, while only three percent thought we were being too outspoken.

My six years with Audubon were among the happiest and most satisfying in my life, for I worked closely with a competent staff, a strong, highly supportive board, and thousands of dedicated, Audubon leaders and activists from every corner of America. We collaborated with kindred souls from organizations at home and abroad and made things happen on some of the biggest quality of life issues of our age—issues of special import to future generations. In this work we were strongly supported by successive chairmen of Audubon's board—Thomas W. Keesee, Jr. and Donal C. O'Brien, Jr. I claim these two effective leaders and partners as good friends to this day.

Mary Joy Breton and Richard Beamish were especially important contributors to my personal efforts. Audubon's vice president Breton, who managed my office, brought her high industry and strong commitment to the environmental cause to bear in supporting my management of our national organization. Previously she had served as my secretary when I was governor and when I headed New Directions and the Office of Technology Assessment. Her book, *Women Pioneers for the Environment*, published by Northeastern University Press, reflects her continuing interest in the environment. Dick Beamish managed public relations, contributed to my editorials and speeches, and travelled with me around the country as we delivered our Audubon message to the community. He was an important consultant to me as I drafted this book. His newspaper, *The Adirondack Explorer*, began publication in July 1998.

30

Motivating People Through Television: A Partnership with Ted Turner

EARLY IN MY CAREER AT NATIONAL AUDUBON, I DECIDED THAT IF WE were to contribute in a major way to educating people and motivating them to become advocates for the environment, we needed to use television. Our prime means of communicating our message was through our bimonthly publication, *Audubon.* We were very proud of our magazine and its talented editor, Les Line, and of the many journalism awards *Audubon* had won. But the magazine reached only 500,000 homes. I knew we could reach millions through television.

However, my initial attempts to get us into television were unsuccessful: Audubon's publications department resisted, and the foundations that generously supported Audubon's other programs showed no interest. Then we hired a talented consultant, Tom Belford, who helped to educate us about what would be required to get National Audubon into television. Because Chris Palmer, a highly effective member of our Washington, D.C., staff showed a strong interest in our proposed use of television, I played a hunch and put him in charge of the effort. He prepared a proposal for an initial program which we estimated would cost $250,000 to produce. With the aid of board members, we obtained entry to the private offices of CEOs of major corporations to solicit funding. We were rewarded with delightful lunches but no money.

Then Chris said, "Why don't we ask Ted Turner for help?"

When we arrived at Ted Turner's office in Atlanta, he was pacing around his desk waving a copy of a speech I had given in London. It dealt with interconnected global problems and our need to deal with them. He told me it was the best description he had seen of the problems he considered to be the most serious in the world. Then he said, "I want you to give this speech again. I'll send a crew to tape it and we will air it on WTBS." I agreed.

Barbara Pyle, a free lance producer of documentaries on environmental issues who worked for Turner, had given the copy of my speech to Ted. She had been a photographer for *Time* magazine and had met Ted while photographing the America's Cup races that Ted won in 1977. Barbara's parents had founded the first Audubon chapter in Oklahoma and she quite naturally had become a strong environmentalist. Over the years she became internationally renowned, and in 1997 she received the prestigious World Environment Award from the United Nations. I had the good fortune to present the laudation for Barbara when she received this award from Secretary General Kofi Annan at a ceremony at the United Nations in New York.

With discussion of the speech behind us, Chris and I explained our plans and told Turner we needed $250,000 to produce the first program. "I hope you can help us," I said.

"I'll give you half of it," he responded, just like that.

I replied, "Mr. Turner, we don't have any other money. Why don't you give us all of it?"

He said, "O.K., I will." With these three words, the world of conservation got a new tool: television.

After our meeting Ted sent a crew to tape me giving an edited version of the London speech. I stood in front of a huge photo of Yosemite National Park at a Fate of the Earth Conference at the Cathedral of St. John the Divine in New York City. Turner Broadcasting Company ran the fifty-minute program three times on WTBS. That was really the start of the highly successful *World of Audubon* series on Turner Television. It was also the start of a strong friendship between Ted and me. We share a deep concern about environmental degradation, population growth, poverty, and the threat of nuclear weapons, and we are committed to trying to do something about them. We both speak freely about what is on our minds and respect each other for it.

Chris Palmer rapidly became an expert in producing and promoting television programming—as well as highly respected by the professionals in Turner Broadcasting, PBS, and other institutions who taught him.

Audubon programs were enhanced by some of our most celebrated movie stars who narrated them for no more than the satisfaction of supporting a cause they believed in. I was impressed

1997 United Nations Sasakawa Environment Prize. (L to R) Peterson, UN Secretary General Kofi Annan, Jane Fonda, Award Recipient Barbara Pyle, Reizo Utagawa of Nippon Foundation, Ted Turner, Under-Secretary General Elizabeth Dowdeswell, November 12, 1997. United Nations Photo.

when I called a number of them, including Robert Redford, Paul Newman, and Cliff Robertson, to ask for their help *pro bono* and they promptly and warmly said yes.

The *World of Audubon* programs demonstrated television's great power of taking viewers to the far corners of the earth to observe and enjoy the wonder, beauty, and variety of nature more comprehensively than if they were there in person. They also show how such television programs can present to an audience the frequent conflicts between those who want to protect the natural environment and those who want to exploit it. Sometimes these programs convinced viewers to take a stand.

Two good examples of the *World of Audubon*'s impact on critical environmental issues are its programs *Rage Over Trees* and *The New Range Wars*. The former, narrated by Paul Newman, dealt with the excessive cutting by logging companies of old growth forests in the Pacific Northwest. Such cutting destroyed wildlife habitat and threatened to drive some species to extinction. It also wiped out some of the last stands of century-old, awe-inspiring trees. Environmentalists all over America were impressed by this program and demanded action to control the cutting, especially when it occurred in national forests—forests owned by all Americans. The logging companies fought back, saying their companies would be forced out of business by controls on their cutting and that thousands of jobs would be lost—the blackmail that exploiters of the environment frequently use when environmental regulations threaten their economically attractive but destructive practices.

Nine corporations were funding the *World of Audubon,* principally Stroh Brewing Company when, in 1989, *Rage Over Trees* was aired. After loggers boycotted their products, all nine of them withdrew sponsorship. Ironically, Mr. Stroh, the head of Stroh Brewing Company, sat on Audubon's board at the time.

The New Range Wars appeared in 1991. Narrated by Peter Coyote, it dealt with the problem of ranchers grazing excessive numbers of cattle for a pittance on federal lands and, in the process, destroying the land's ability to produce natural grasses. After Audubon transformed an issue in a quiet ranching area into a national issue, the ranchers organized a nationwide boycott of the sponsor, General Electric. Shortly thereafter, G.E. withdrew its sponsorship. And four members of Audubon's board, upset by Audubon's strong adversary role, resigned. This put Audubon in a bind; there were no financial resources to replace the G.E. support.

Then Ted Turner stepped in to cover production costs of the *World of Audubon,* putting himself and his money on the line. He is now one of the largest, if not the largest owner of ranch land in our West. His holdings are almost as large as Rhode Island. In August 1995, my wife-to-be, June, and I visited his 100,000+ acre Flying D ranch in Montana as his guests. We saw first hand that he has removed all the fence lines and allows his herd of buffalo (the American bison) to roam freely as of yore. We sat with Turner's ranch manager, Russell Miller, in his truck in the midst of 5,700 head of buffalo, the largest herd in the world, watching them graze, coming within 30 feet of us, the older bulls pawing the ground and then chasing the young ones away from their cows.

Neighboring ranchers do not like Ted's outspokenness about limiting the number of grazing animals to the carrying capacity of the land. Nor do they like his putting his land in trusts to protect it in perpetuity from development. Nevertheless, they invite Ted to speak at some of their meetings. He speaks his mind, and they appear to respect him for it.

In December 1994, Turner Broadcasting aired a two hour program on the first ten years of the *World of Audubon*. It was a great testimonial to what had been done. Excerpts from the forty hours of programming showed vividly the effective role that Audubon and Turner have played in bringing to millions of Americans a better understanding of serious threats to our environment and what is being done to combat them. These programs won sixty national and international awards. In 1994, Michael Eisner, CEO of the Disney channel, awarded Chris Palmer the top award of the Environmental Media Association for his work at Audubon. Clearly my early hunch about Chris was right on target. He has since left Audubon to become president and CEO of National Wildlife Productions, a subsidiary of the National Wildlife Federation, where he has created and is producing a huge multimedia program to increase understanding of the global environment and encourage people to stand up for the Earth.

31

The Better World Society

When, in the summer of 1984, I announced my decision to retire from Audubon, Ted Turner called to ask what I thought about his starting a new organization to be known as The Better World Society. It would use television to inform people "about our four issues:" population stabilization, prevention of nuclear war, protection of global environment, and reduction of world poverty. Although Turner has repeatedly given me credit publicly for getting him involved with this global agenda, it was Barbara Pyle and her assistant, J. J. Ebaugh, who developed the idea of creating The Better World Society.

When I told Ted his idea was great, he asked me to run it.

"Oh, no," I hastily responded. "I'm retiring from Audubon so I can get away from administrative work and fund raising and spend more of my time on writing and speaking on our issues." But we agreed I would help organize it.

Turner Broadcasting had already produced and aired a few of Barbara Pyle's documentaries on the global issues. In the process, they quickly learned that their salesmen could not sell advertising for documentaries. Ted said, "I want to continue these programs and expand them, but my pocket isn't deep enough to do it alone."

We invited approximately seventy-five heads of donor foundations to a luncheon to hear our plans and ask for their support. I asked Bob Allen, President of Kendall Foundation, who had good rapport with foundation executives, to join Ted and me in hosting the luncheon. Chris Palmer and Ted Turner's second in command, Bob Wussler, prepared the prospectus for the Better World Society. Turner Broadcasting produced a video showing excerpts from documentaries already aired by Turner and ideas for future programs. The luncheon was held on October 25, 1984 at the University Club in New York City with seventy foundation executives present.

Ted Turner's party for Jacques Cousteau's 75th birthday. Cousteau, Ben Vereen (clowning), Peterson, and Turner. Mount Vernon, June 9, 1985. Courtesy of the author.

That morning Carl Sagan and I met with Secretary General of the United Nations Pérez de Cuéllar to try to gain his support in informing the world about the threat of nuclear winter, because Dr. Sagan was the leading authority on the subject. Since prevention of nuclear war was one of the goals of the Better World Society, I asked Sagan to come with me and speak at our luncheon. He agreed.

At the University Club, we joined Ted Turner and a number of world authorities who were involved in protecting the global environment, including Jacques Cousteau, the world-famous undersea explorer, and Dr. Rafael Salas, head of the United Nations Fund for Population Activities.

I presided; Sagan, Cousteau and Salas spoke. Then Turner introduced the video his group had produced and expressed his strong commitment to the proposed Better World Society. He displayed his considerable knowledge of global issues and his deep, sincere commitment to doing something about them. The guests were clearly enthusiastic in their praise of his proposal. But time would show them to be much less generous with their contributions. Ted himself put up $500,000 to get us started.

I recruited Tom Belford, president of Vanguard Communications and Audubon's earlier TV consultant, as executive director. He and Victoria Markell did an excellent job over the next six years in managing the organization's global activities, with extensive help from Turner Broadcasting and advice from our board.

On February 6, 1985, Turner, Lester Brown, Jean-Michel Cousteau of France and I, the initial four members of the board, held an organizing meeting in the New York City headquarters of the National Audubon Society. Ted was elected chairman and I was chosen vice chairman and president.

On June 11, 1985, the Better World Society announced its formation at a press conference in the Warwick Hotel in New York City. The next day *The New York Times* reported that, "Mr. Turner said he decided last year to found the organization with Dr. Peterson because important global issues were not being addressed and people were not being informed about them."

That evening the board held its first annual meeting and dinner at the New York Yacht Club, where the America's Cup winner, Ted Turner, was welcomed enthusiastically. He beamed when he showed us the model of his winning boat, *Courageous.*

By this time our board was truly international. President Jimmy Carter; General Olusegun Obasanjo, former president of Nigeria; Rodrigo Corazo, former president of Costa Rica; Prince Sadruddin Aga Khan; Soviet leader Georgi Arbatov; Gro Harlem Brundtland, prime minister of Norway; Yasushi Akashi, undersecretary general of the United Nations; Dr. M. S. Swaminathan of India; Ambassador Zhou Boping, vice chairman of China's Family Planning Association; Lord Aubrey Buxton of Great Britain; and Dr. Julia Henderson, a former United Nations leader had joined us. Two years later we signed up Canadian Maurice Strong, first head of the United Nations Environment Program, as our president.

Meetings were organized with top government leaders in capitals around the world, including Prime Minister Margaret Thatcher at 10 Downing Street, Soviet leaders in the Kremlin, and Chinese leaders in the Great Hall of the People. Every place we went, the top leaders welcomed us with open arms. This was not because of the Better World Society, but because of Ted

Turner. All of them had TV sets tuned to CNN where they could get world news as it happened. They admired what Ted Turner had done and felt indebted to him.

We held spirited and helpful discussions about our programs on nuclear disarmament, reducing population growth and environmental protection. Everywhere we received strong support for our mission.

One night in Moscow at an elaborate dinner party hosted by Ted and attended by Soviet leaders including two members of the Politburo, he and I had our first and only clash. Near the end of the evening he announced that Better World Society was working toward total elimination of nuclear weapons.

Knowing that Ted had had much vodka, I should have kept quiet. But I injudiciously said, "Ted, that would be too dangerous. In such a case, any of the many nations that today have modest technical capability could secretly make a few nuclear weapons and hold us all hostage. I believe some of the current nuclear powers and/or the United Nations should retain a few such weapons so as to be able to protect the world from nuclear weapon blackmailers."

Ted exploded. "Damn it, you got me into this business, but there is not room for both of our views. One of us has to go."

At that point I was smart enough to keep quiet.

A long deadly silence descended on the meeting. Then some considerate soul changed the subject.

The next morning when I arrived at the curb to await a government limousine, I met Ted.

"Do you know what you said last night?" I asked. "You said there was not room for both of us in the Better World Society."

He put his arm around me and said, "Forget it. I had too much to drink."

Our disagreement never surfaced again. We both continued to push hard for nuclear disarmament. He probably concluded, as I did, that the world was so far from getting down to a few or no nuclear weapons that our disagreement was currently only of academic interest.

When our board convened in London, we officers were invited to meet with Prime Minister Margaret Thatcher at 10 Downing Street. She graciously received us, paying special tribute to Ted Turner. My negative attitude toward this strongly conservative leader gradually melted; this intelligent, witty former chemist positively charmed us. Because I had told Ted earlier that Mrs. Thatcher was cool toward the population movement, he asked me to tell her what we were doing toward stabilizing world population. She was interested, asked many pertinent questions, and seemed receptive to my argument that reducing world population growth was essential.

That noon we had lunch at the House of Lords. Mrs. Thatcher's chief of staff told me that the prime minister had been impressed with my statements on population. He said that she had kept several members of her staff with her for thirty minutes after we left to discuss our ideas. Then he asked for my business card, saying, "We may want to communicate with you." From that point on, the prime minister did become more receptive to funding family planning around the world. I like to think I had something to do with that.

The Better World Society held several annual gala black-tie dinners at the Waldorf Astoria in New York to present awards to people from around the world who had made major contributions to advancing one of our causes. However, its main mission was to produce TV documentaries on issues critical to mankind's survival, get them aired worldwide, and create a climate where other organizations would follow suit. This we accomplished.

In six years (1985–91) the Better World Society produced forty-three documentary films which were viewed by millions in sixty countries around the world. Over twenty-five awards were received for this work, including an Emmy and an Oscar.

When the Better World Society ceased operation in 1991, an array of issue-oriented organizations in the areas of environment, population, and global security were producing high quality television programming. That was a major change from 1985 when the use of television to alert people to critical controversial issues was embryonic. We believe Better World Society's groundbreaking work contributed to this change, and Tom Belford and Victoria Markell, who ran Better World Society, agree. In their words, "We did what we set out to do." They are justifiably proud of their contribution.

A major factor in the termination of the Better World Society was the organization's failure to accomplish its initial objective of gaining enough financial support from foundations to augment Ted Turner's earlier promising but limited production of issue-oriented documentaries. A few foundations provided modest support and some industrial corporations funded specific programs, but Ted was left to pick up the tab for most of the one-million dollar annual general operating costs.

During 1990–91 we in the Better World Society were able to witness the blossoming romance between Ted Turner and Jane Fonda. She became a strong partner in Ted's efforts to save the Earth, and in 1992 my wife Lillian and I were privileged to attend their wedding reception in Atlanta.

In 1997, Ted Turner again "put his money where his mouth is" in a big way. He gave the United Nations the largest contribution any individual has ever given to any institution—$1 billion. The money will establish The United Nations Foundation that will support United Nations efforts on critical global issues, including protecting the environment, stabilizing human population, and working toward a more environmentally benign energy future. The foundation will be headed by the uniquely qualified Timothy Wirth, a former U.S. senator who resigned as Undersecretary of State for Global Affairs to take the job.

Russ and Lillian Peterson at Jane Fonda and Ted Turner's wedding reception. Atlanta, 1992. Courtesy of the author.

In November 1997, June, my second wife, and I had the opportunity to have dinner at the United Nations in New York with Secretary General Kofi Annan and his wife, Ted Turner, Jane Fonda, and Undersecretary General for the Environment Elizabeth Dowdeswell. It was impressive to observe the warm rapport between the secretary general and Ted Turner. Clearly they are both dedicated world citizens deeply committed to the resolution of critical global issues. I predict we will see ever more direct effort by Ted Turner to support United Nations programs related to his interests.

That evening I was especially impressed by the secretary general who is deeply committed to alleviating the ills of the global community. He is a warm, articulate, highly knowledgeable leader. The United Nations made a good choice in selecting him as secretary general—the only person on Earth who can speak for all of us. Currently he is hamstrung by the United States' repeated failure to pay its past dues; we are $1.3 billion in arrears. Our legislators fail to appreciate how serious this negligence is to the future quality of life on Earth. We American citizens must change their minds.

32

Looking at the World as a Whole—Colleges of Integrated Studies

THE MORE ONE STUDIES THE ENVIRONMENT AND/OR SERVES IN broad leadership positions, the more one recognizes the need for more formal training across the disciplines. Over the years this conviction has led me to become increasingly concerned about the current practice of the world's universities to train people in ever narrower fields while the exploding knowledge of how everything in the real world is interconnected and interdependent calls for leadership by the best of generalists. This has led to my promoting the establishment by universities of separate colleges of integrated studies to provide bachelor's, master's, and doctor's degrees in integrated studies, that is to turn out professional generalists.

I do not mean that universities should forego training people who specialize in narrow fields. That approach has been of immense value and has continuously expanded the frontiers of knowledge. But what is needed now is an additional specialist— one trained to look at the world as a whole.

Although today's good liberal arts programs provide much of what is needed as an undergraduate foundation to support the more rigorous graduate work required for a professional generalist, much can be done to make such undergraduate programs more comprehensive and integrated.

Leadership today calls for the broadest training, not only so graduates are able to understand the complex world, but also so they are able to integrate the increasingly narrower slices of knowledge and make intelligent choices among alternative futures. The recently recognized need to integrate the many fields of knowledge has led to a proliferation of interdisciplinary research programs that pool the knowledge of specialists from several disciplines. They have been quite productive in spite of the difficulty specialists often have in leaving the prejudices of their own disciplines behind and operating effectively with other disciplines. The professional generalist, however, would be better able to operate effectively across the disciplines, benefit from symbiosis among them, and in the process make surprising discoveries. Self-trained generalists like Leonardo da Vinci and Thomas Jefferson displayed that ability.

After a lifetime of deep involvement in several careers, I conclude that it is more the rule than the exception that people enter the most influential positions in our society, ill-prepared for the breadth of their assignments. This includes presidents and other political leaders, captains of industry, university presidents and provosts, cabinet officers, judges, editors, ambassadors and heads of nonprofit organizations. Few institutions of higher learning provide formal training for such important posts.

As more people become aware of the global interconnectedness of all life and life support systems, as more faculty become disenchanted with their disciplines' lack of pertinence to the real world, and as more citizens recognize the ineptness of our specialists in coping with the complex issues of the day, the pressure on our educational system will build until discrete institutions of integrated studies are established within or without existing universities.

Today a minority of faculty on many, probably all, university campuses would strongly support the establishment of such institutions. I personally know dozens who would. They are struggling to make the college curriculum pertinent to the real world. A separate college of integrated studies would provide them with the environment and freedom needed to flourish. However, resistance to the idea of an integrated-studies discipline arises among members of the traditional disciplines who see the proposed metadisciplinary program as impinging on their territory, competing for funds, and clashing with the ideology that advanced training is best served by practicing it in ever narrower fields.

This was first illustrated for me at a dinner in Cambridge in 1978 when I was the director of the Congressional Office of Technology Assessment. Dr. Jerome Wiesner, then president of MIT, had invited me to meet with about thirty department heads and deans from MIT and Harvard. After dinner I suggested that these prestigious institutions set up a new graduate school specialty to produce professional generalists. I pointed out that my experience in industry and government had shown the great need for generalists and the very limited supply. At OTA we were assigned by statute to advise the Congress on the long-term, global impacts of technological applications on social, environmental, economic and political factors, truly an assignment for generalists.

My suggestion triggered a heated debate. About one-fourth of the group supported my suggestion and the remainder vigorously opposed it. A principal contention was that I would not be a generalist today—they called me a generalist—if I had not first studied for four years in graduate school the inhibition of air oxidation of vitamin C. This argument has been presented to me several times, but I continue to fail to see why anyone needs to become a Ph.D. specialist as a necessary stepping-stone to being a generalist. I have personally, however, encountered many Ph.D. specialists such as those at the Cambridge meeting who, through the narrowness of their training, are blinded to the need and opportunities for professional generalists.

The key jobs in our society call for people who understand the place of Homo sapiens in the biosphere; the interdependence of all people and nations; and how the world's economic, political, social, and management systems operate. Our leaders must be able to discern the possible long-term impacts of specific research and development projects. Their decisions should reflect a firm grasp of the historical record; the physical, chemical, and biological nature of things; and computerized techniques for assessing trends and appraising alternative futures.

Top leaders are not the only ones who could benefit from a good general education. We all need a broad understanding of the world around us at least as much as we need specialized skills and information. An American pediatrician who understands the implications of 30,000 children dying each day in developing countries would be more likely to seize an opportunity to work with the United Nations Children's Fund than someone less informed. A father might better understand his rebellious teenage daughter if he saw the relationships among the physical and psychological upheavals of adolescence, his formerly mild-mannered daughter's behavior, and the culture in which she is growing up. A young engineer working on petroleum exploration might decide to grab an opportunity to work on solar energy if he or she appreciated the uncertain future of fossil fuels. A mother concerned about her children's future and aware of the global interconnectedness of life might decide to lobby her senators to increase foreign aid for specific causes.

The discovery that all life, air, water, and land are interconnected and interdependent constitutes probably the most significant scientific finding of the past century, particularly since it has been coupled with the realization that human interventions in the natural world have long-term consequences. Rachel Carson's *Silent Spring,* Ado Leopold's *Sand County Almanac* and J. E. Lovelock's *GAIA* are examples of publications that have helped to foster this view. In light of its wide-ranging implications, I believe that anyone who fails to grasp this fundamental understanding of reality is inadequately educated.

Unfortunately, university administrators and department heads, with rare exception, have yet to catch up with the new holistic understanding. They continue to plan and manage their institutions from the reductionist and compartmentalized vantage point of the traditional disciplines. As the famous University of Wisconsin professor, Ado Leopold, stated in an essay published in *The River of the Mother of God,* "All the sciences and arts are taught as though they were separate. They are separate only in the classroom. Step out on the campus and they are immediately fused." Since Leopold's time, some faculty members throughout academe have broadened their own education, research, teaching, and outreach work well beyond the normal confines of their disciplines. Against much opposition, they have initiated and staffed the existing interdisciplinary programs.

Today there are fewer such programs than in the 1970s, with many existing in name only; in the 1980s interdisciplinary programs were seriously downgraded on university campuses across the United States primarily because of the opposition of faculty in the separate disciplines.

In 1986 I met with 100 leaders of environmental studies programs, truly interdisciplinary programs, from fifty-six universities. Every one of them agreed that they were treated as second-class citizens on their campuses. During lean financial years they received vastly disproportionate budget cuts and in most cases failed to gain approval for granting degrees or providing faculty tenure. Two key factors in this downgrading seem to be the increased competition for funding among the traditional disciplines and faculty members' concerns about intrusion into established academic territories. Furthermore, since interdisciplinary programs are comparatively new, they do not have the same type of institutional power base as the established disciplines. Meanwhile we continue to learn more about the way society, culture, and politics interact with the natural world. And polls show that people are increasingly concerned about protecting their global environment, a major interdisciplinary problem.

In 1983, Professor Lynton K. Caldwell of Indiana University expressed well the need for what he calls metadisciplinary knowledge. He wrote in *The Environmental Professional:* "the need to organize and focus complex bodies of knowledge is a consequence of human inability to wisely and effectively utilize that knowledge in disconnected specialized increments. Unless a better means of integrating and focusing our expanding knowledge is achieved, the advancement of all knowledge may be frustrated by the massive incoherence of increasing specialization."

Specialists often contend that breadth of knowledge means loss of depth. On the contrary, the knowledge required to cope with the problems our world now faces is of a high order. While specialists dig deeply to be sure, like digging an ever deeper well, generalists dig horizontally, like digging a tunnel, to come out on the other side and see a broad new horizon. Rather than requiring less rigor than training in one discipline, I believe training in a metadiscipline, to use Caldwell's term, calls for more rigor. Not understanding the interconnections, the specialist looks at a metadiscipline blindly.

Some educators ask who will hire graduates trained as generalists. My conviction is that once they are available, the market will grab them. Graduates from the rigorous program of integrated studies that I envision would have the flexibility and breadth of understanding, mental skills, and values to make them stand out in the competitive world of work. They would be strong contenders for leadership positions. They would be able to adjust readily to the frequent career changes that now characterize the work world.

The escalating rate of change in the world increases the need for interdisciplinary training and action, and for more attention to the future impacts of decisions. We no longer can muddle through, basing our decisions on fragments of specialized information or on this year's profit or next year's election if we wish to avoid unprecedented catastrophes. Just as we should no longer focus solely on the economic miracles that can be wrought by Adam Smith's "invisible hand," so we should also try to avoid being kicked by the "invisible foot" that has so clearly demonstrated its long-range destructiveness. For example, the development of nuclear energy in the 1960s was projected to provide electricity too cheap to meter; in 1985 one of the world's leading business magazines, *Forbes,* reported, "The failure of the United States' nuclear power program ranks as the largest managerial disaster in business history, a disaster on a monumental scale."

During these same years, the dumping of hazardous wastes has permitted the production of better things for better living at low cost, but now the Office of Technology Assessment of the U.S. Congress reports that it will take fifty years and hundreds of billions of dollars to clean up the resulting mess. The accompanying damage to human health and the environment goes unmeasured. It is hard to believe that these debacles would have occurred if enough professional generalists had been involved in government, industry, and finance.

While we in the affluent nations celebrate our success in providing an ever higher material standard of living for our people, the number of our species worldwide living in extreme poverty continues to grow. Population Action International's Human Suffering Index, based on ten quality of life parameters, rates seventy-four countries with two-thirds of all people on Earth as experiencing high to extreme human suffering. Our local successes can hardly justify our inattention to our species' failure to provide for its own kind. What is required to correct this multidimensional tragedy is a massive, sustained, interdisciplinary approach.

People in a number of educational institutions are becoming concerned about the inadequacy of the training they provide. For example, the faculty of the Massachusetts Institute of Technology voted to create a minor in the humanities, arts and social sciences. Samual Jay Keyser, associate provost for Education Policy and Programs at MIT was quoted as saying, "Among the engineers, there is a realization that the social and political implications of the technology are as important as the technology itself."

Many educators say that corporations are becoming interested in broadly educated employees rather than those who are well versed in a technology that may soon be obsolete. In April 1995, the National Research Council issued a study, "Reshaping the

Graduate Education of Scientists and Engineers," which advises that Ph.D. candidates should be discouraged from overspecialization, provided with opportunities to gain a variety of skills, and prepared for a world of work requiring changes in positions and even careers. The study reports that industrial employers claim that Ph.D.s are frequently "too specialized for the range of tasks that they will confront."

Universities must be more responsive to the need for more broadly educated graduates, and should take more seriously suggestions like mine that they establish separate colleges of integrated studies. I have spoken on many campuses about this. Invariably a few faculty members have come up to me after my talk to express strong support for the idea. Some professors have organized to push interdisciplinary training and have held conferences toward that end. I participated in one such conference and recognized that we participants were speaking to the converted. Not one of us had any significant authority to make our proposals happen. To establish a college of integrated studies, one or more leaders with the required authority to make it happen in a given institution would have to become convinced of the importance of the task and be willing to face up to those on the campus opposed to the idea.

While I was a visiting professor at Dartmouth in 1985 and at the University of Wisconsin-Madison in 1987, I tried to influence leaders to establish a separate college of integrated studies, making their institutions beachheads in academe. At Dartmouth the president, who had been chairman of the board of trustees, became strongly interested. He met with me and some faculty members on three occasions to consider how the new college might be established. I emphasized that it would be mark of leadership by Dartmouth, similar to its having established the first school of business in this country. Unfortunately the president, for some reason not related to the new college issue, was forced to resign. Our plan went nowhere.

Later at the University of Wisconsin I tried several schemes. As an alumnus who had received a B.S., a Ph.D., and an honorary Doctor of Laws, I was invited to write an article for the *Letters and Science* magazine. This publication received broad circulation throughout the university and was read regularly by the university's leadership. The topic I chose was, "Why Not a College of Integrated Studies?"

Dr. E. David Cronon, dean of the College of Letters and Science, in reviewing my article stated, "Although I am a strong supporter of interdisciplinary studies, I don't share Russell Peterson's enthusiasm for a new college or university of integrated studies, separate from or replacing the liberal arts college. I nevertheless welcome his opening up a discussion of this issue. For myself, I am enough of a traditionalist to retain a strong faith in the resiliency and adaptability of the various academic disciplines as they now exist and as some have been developing since classical times."

Dean Cronon did not get my message. I, too, think liberal arts colleges are very important. I am not suggesting that liberal arts and science colleges be changed or replaced. I am suggesting that a separate college of integrated studies be established—a pioneering step in academe—to provide students with another choice, a renaissance curriculum, for launching their careers.

The University of Wisconsin in its two-year integrated studies program already provides some outstanding students with such a curriculum. In this program each course is interdisciplinary, drawing on all major fields of study. The courses mesh and successive courses build on each another, developing deeper and deeper levels of understanding. The courses weave together classic ideas and contemporary problems. This program should be expanded to a rigorous full four-or five-year undergraduate program, then combined, in a separate college, with a graduate program tailored for the professional generalist.

When Dr. Donna Shalala came to the University of Wisconsin as chancellor, I wrote to her, encouraging her to consider a college of integrated studies. I knew her from the six years we had worked together on the Board of Visitors to the Kennedy School of Government at Harvard. She expressed an interest and sent copies of my letter for review by the same deans who had already turned down the proposal. Nothing came of this.

On another occasion I was hired by the university to participate on a panel considering the future of the university. Again I promoted the new college of integrated studies, a concept in tune with the future and with society's need for leadership better trained to choose among alternative futures. As in the past, a few members of the panel strongly supported the concept, but the leaders did not. My proposal was not included in the finished report of our panel.

Realizing that a major obstacle to establishing a new college was the concern that it would take funds from existing university budgets, I decided to investigate the possibility of the state governor and the board of trustees' taking the initiative to convince the state legislature to provide additional, separate funding for such a new college. I met with a former governor, who was a friend, and with the chairman of the board of trustees. They both liked the idea of the new college and agreed to talk to the new governor. After doing so their interest disappeared.

I believe a state governor who is convinced of the importance of a college of integrated studies could play the key role in obtaining the necessary funding. A governor could promote the concept as an opportunity for the state *and* state university to demonstrate how to train tomorrow's leaders to cope effectively with the interlocking global problems that threaten the quality of life of future generations. The next step would be to convince a few legislative leaders, the board of trustees which the governor appoints, and university leadership to go along. With such support I believe major foundations and corporations, who are already well aware of the need for more broadbased training for tomorrow's leaders, would contribute funds to match a large grant from the state legislature for a demonstration project. The students and faculty needed to build a college of integrated studies are already available, waiting on campuses for the necessary leadership and resources.

In September 1994, I was invited to meet with several leaders of the University of Wisconsin-Madison. We met in the office of the Dean of Letters and Science, Phil Certain. He explained that they now thought the time for a separate college of integrated studies had arrived—that I had been ahead of the time. They wanted me to know that they were going to start planning for such a new college and would appreciate any help I could provide. I cheered them on.

In October 1995, I was invited to meet with the chancellor of the university, David Ward. He expressed a strong interest in furthering interdisciplinary education but thought it was better, at least at that time, to do so by fostering programs that cut across the disciplines in each existing college.

Over the next two years, with the help of Provost John Wiley, he developed his approach into an exciting experimental program. Taking twelve of the 150 or so faculty positions available in 1997 as faculty retired, he invited departments throughout this large university to submit proposals of how they might employ four new professors in staffing new programs that crossed departmental and college lines. The twelve positions available would thus permit three so-called cluster hires. The chancellor's idea was received enthusiastically throughout the campus. Over ninety proposals were submitted by the end of 1997. Now the whole faculty was thinking about multidisciplinary training. Not only did the idea now have the open support of university leadership, but departments also had the incentive of acquiring four new professorships and the necessary funding.

Time will tell how far this approach will go. I think it will put the University of Wisconsin out front on the path to producing professional generalists and in finding solutions to the complex interdisciplinary problems confronting the real world. And it may finally lead to separate colleges of integrated studies.

33

Are We Going Forward or Backward?

Economic development that is environmentally sound and sustainable depends upon our devising an appropriate measure of economic progress that weighs environmental factors. The principal indicator used today by decision makers, both in government and in business, to rate progress—even quality of life—is the Gross Domestic Product (GDP). It is a faulty indicator, and its indiscriminate use has done much harm to the long term health of both our economy and our environment.

I have long advocated, as have several others, the need for something other than GDP to measure progress. Yet governments and the business world continue to use this absurd measurement, much to the detriment of our quality of life.

A country that uses the GDP as its sole indicator of progress could exhaust its mineral resources, cut down its forests, erode its soil, destroy its vistas, degrade its natural beauty, hunt its wildlife to extinction, pollute its air and aquifers, corrode its buildings and monuments, and damage the health of its citizenry, because it does not consider the costs and environmental impacts of these diminished resources.

This problem is particularly serious for countries whose economies strongly depend upon the exploitation of their natural resources, as is the case in many of the poorest countries. The problem, however, is also serious in the United States. We are the world's champion spender of the planet's natural capital, and our leaders and the news media contribute to this problem when they glorify growth in GDP as a measure of progress.

In recent years some economists, enlightened and driven by environmentalists, have been striving to develop a better indicator of economic progress. The International Society for Ecological Economics (ISEE) was formed in 1988 to build a bridge between the natural sciences and economics. ISEE's goal is to create an economy based on sustainability, not on excessive material growth. This group believes that to achieve sustainability, it is essential to slow both population growth and the production of goods and services.

In 1995, the United Nations Development Program, reporting on the injustice of GDP, pointed out that—in addition to its negative impact on the environment—it ignored the $11 trillion of women's work in the home and community, making most women virtual economic nonentities. Former World Bank President Barber Conable explained that GDP misleads people into thinking that it represents progress when it measures activities that are unsustainable.

Another 1995 report, "Redefining Progress," supported by nine major foundations and involving twenty-five economists and environmentalists, recommends the use of a new measure of progress, the Genuine Progress Indicator (GPI), to replace the GDP. The report estimated the economic value (positive and negative) of twenty social and environmental factors that the GDP ignores, including value of household work, cost of crime, cost of underemployment, cost of pollution, loss of farmland, and depletion of nonrenewable energy resources. This report also shows that on a per capita basis the GDP grew continuously, with an occasional dip, from $7900 in 1950 to $17,100 in 1994. The GPI per capita grew from $5700 in 1950, peaking in 1973 at $7300 and then falling off to $4100 in 1994. In other words, while the GDP per capita was doubling over the past 44 years, the GPI per capita shrank by 28 percent.

Although many of us knew that the GDP was seriously flawed as a measure of progress, and we could explain why we so believed, our society went on being steered by this faulty compass. But now we have a comprehensive, quantitative measure of progress, not perfect by any means, but much, much more sound than the GDP. Furthermore, it shows strikingly what many Americans have known: rather than improving over most of the past twenty years—as politicians, government leaders, mainstream economists and most business leaders would like us to believe—our economic health has been slipping. For this reason, I recommend appointment of a joint bipartisan presidential/congressional commission to develop a plan for defining a new indicator modeled after GPI.

My first awareness of an ecological indicator came in 1952 when I took my two young sons on an Audubon Society-sponsored trip into the Florida Everglades. The naturalist leading our group explained how birds were a good ecological indicator (yes, he used that term), how they traveled over wide areas sampling the air, water, insects, berries, fish, amphibians, rodents, and other birds. He told us that when something went wrong with the environment, the birds were among the first to indicate it. When their population fell off, it signalled a threat to other life, too, including human life.

In the intervening years on my many visits to the Everglades, I have seen that ecological indicator plummet—the egrets, herons, ibises, and other species are now present at a small fraction of their earlier wondrous abundance. Investigations have clearly shown that the ongoing destruction of the unique and irreplaceable Everglades habitat stems from the impact of millions of affluent people moving to Florida to enjoy its natural beauty, and from many more millions coming as tourists.

The Audubon Society was started over 100 years ago to stop the slaughter of the long-legged wading birds (egrets and herons) by plume hunters who sold the feathers to the millinery trade. The millinery trade then launched a major counterattack, using its own economic indicator—the loss of jobs—to oppose any ban on plume hunting. Audubon's first warden, Guy Bradley, was murdered by plume hunters in the Everglades. This led to intense lobbying of state and federal governments and the passage of laws to stop plume hunting. As a result the wading-bird population in the Everglades rebounded, reaching a peak in 1930 before ongoing habitat destruction lowered the population by 90 percent. Today the federal government, the state of Florida, and many environmental groups are engaged in a major multibillion dollar effort to reestablish the natural flow of water in southern Florida and thereby replenish the vital water supply to the Everglades. I hope my grandchildren will go there some day and see the glorious spectacle of wildlife I saw in 1952.

After Rachel Carson, a federal-government biologist, published *Silent Spring* in 1962, the world was alerted to the threat posed by chemical pesticides. When people learned that birds, the harbingers of spring and the renewal of life, were being wiped out by pesticides, they demanded action. The pesticide DDT was identified as the main culprit and despite the screams from its marketers, its manufacture and sale in the United States and many other countries were outlawed. Species such as the brown pelican, the osprey and the American bald eagle, which had been particularly hard hit, recovered over the next few decades and were removed from the endangered-species list. Today, when I watch the bald eagle, our American symbol, once again soaring over our open lands, I see it as a symbol of hope, of what can be done to save life on Earth, and as a challenge to get on with the job of protecting other species, including Homo sapiens, from the impacts of the growing human onslaught.

Over the years, as president of the National Audubon Society and as president of the International Council for Bird Preservation (ICBP), I have followed the bird population as an ecological indicator. Birds are the most extensively observed and studied form of wildlife. ICBP has compiled a global data base and has been using it to define priority areas for protecting biodiversity. It shows that where bird life is abundant, almost invariably other forms of life are also abundant. And where bird life is threatened, so is biodiversity.

Indonesia has the greatest number of threatened species (126), followed by Brazil (121), China (81), and Peru (71). Specific sites that have been targeted include those where deforestation and wetland destruction are the principal culprits. By focusing on these priority sites and stopping their degradation, we believe the world can not only save a large number of plant and animal species, an important part of our treasured heritage, but can demonstrate what might be done elsewhere to change the trends now threatening the extinction of ever more species.

As vice president of the International Union for the Conservation of Nature (IUCN) I became involved in the study of global biodiversity. I learned that experts agree that habitat destruction is driving species to extinction at a rate 1,000 to 10,000 times the rate of loss characteristic of the past 65 million years, an ecological indicator of the greatest moment. In the distant past, large-scale extinction occurred as the result of cataclysmic events such as a large meteor hitting the earth, but now it is humans who are making the cataclysmic decisions.

Harvard's renowned entomologist, Edward D. Wilson, advocates recognizing every species of life for the masterpiece that it is: "A creation assembled with extreme care by genius"—by the genius of natural selection through a vast number of steps over a long period of time. When one bird or mammal or fish or plant species is threatened with extinction, as many are today, he asks us to weigh that life with our hearts as well as our brains.

Longtime students of life on Earth believe, as I do, that we can still turn around the growing rush to extinction, but time to do so is running out.

VIII
Confronting the Main Causes of Environmental Degradation

34

Stabilizing Human Population Growth

Overcoming Entrenched Opposition to Family Planning

THOUGH DEFINITE WORLDWIDE PROGRESS IS BEING MADE TOWARD reducing many major negative impacts on the environment, every gain from these efforts will be wiped out unless human population growth can be stabilized at an acceptable level. Overpopulation threatens the quality of life everywhere. It stymies the efforts of the poorest nations to raise their standard of living, as programs to provide food, schools, houses and health care cannot keep up with the expanding number of humans to be served. It exacerbates hardships that lead to violence, wars and refugee camps. It creates ever more ghettos and slums. It brings millions of children into the world who die from hunger and neglect. It leads to millions of abortions every year by mothers seeking to avoid the burden of additional children.

World population reached two billion in 1930, the year I entered high school. It had taken over one century to add the second billion. In 1999, our population will reach six billion, having more than tripled in my lifetime. Fortunately about thirty years ago, some governments and nongovernmental organizations began to take the threat of exploding population seriously. Efforts in many countries to reduce birthrates grew progressively. The annual percentage growth in world population, after peaking at 2.1 percent in 1968, gradually fell to 1.35 percent in 1997. According to the U.S. Bureau of the Census, the absolute annual growth reached its highest level in history, eighty-seven million, in 1990. It then fell off, reaching eighty million in 1997. This is a remarkable turnaround.

Now it appears that if the world can sustain its currently strong commitment to reducing birth rates, world population might level off at ten billion or below by the year 2100. If world population had continued to grow at 2.1 percent per year, as it did thirty years ago, it would have grown to over sixty billion by 2100, almost certainly with catastrophic consequences.

The continuing revolution in reducing population growth has resulted from three major forces: the enlightenment of the people to the global, social, and environmental threat of an exploding population; development and application of the science of family planning; and increasing the education and empowerment of women.

Over the past thirty years, contraceptive use in developing countries has grown from 10 percent of couples to 55 percent. In developed countries it has reached 75 percent. The projection of world population stabilizing at ten billion or below is based on growing support of the three forces mentioned above leading to the two child family as a worldwide average.

Unfortunately, the projection of growing support has been shaken in the late 1990s by a hostile U.S. Congress that markedly cut the United States contribution for international population assistance. Previously the U.S. had been the leading donor in this area. Fortunately other nations have increased their commitments. Tiny Denmark now provides twice as much for the United Nations population program as does the U.S. It is my hope that the American people will convince Congress to once again support this moral mission.

Although limiting the world population to ten billion is a hopeful goal, we must recognize that adding another four billion to today's population of six billion will have a serious impact on the global environment.

The number of people living in absolute poverty worldwide is now over one billion and growing. More than 30,000 children die each day from malnutrition and diseases easily avoided in more affluent countries. As the poorest of the poor scramble for a living, they overgraze, overcrop, and overcut, destroying the resources on which their livelihood depends. During the past two decades, when 1.6 billion more people took up residence on our small and finite planet, deserts expanded by 300 million acres, 400 billion tons of topsoil were lost, and 500 million acres of tree cover were cleared. Clearly the world's natural resource base is shrinking rapidly as human population expands.

Lester Brown, president of the World Watch Institute, concerned about the failure of the world production of grain to keep up with population growth over the past decade concluded, "Achieving a humane balance between food and people now depends more on family planners than on farmers."

In 1992 the Union of Concerned Scientists warned, echoing the messages of scientific groups around the world, "A great change in our stewardship of the earth and the life on it is required, if vast human misery is to be avoided and our global home on this planet is not to be irretrievably mutilated." The United Nations Children's Fund (UNICEF) used to have reservations about family planning. No longer. Currently, they state, "The responsible planning of births is one of the most effective and least expensive ways of improving the quality of life on earth." Anyone with a decent respect for fellow human beings and anxiety about the immense human suffering now occurring must be concerned about the world's population growth.

I have had the opportunity to see this tragedy unfolding in the worst urban slums and poorest rural areas of many of the world's most impoverished countries. What an injustice to a child who is born into such an environment. What a contrast to the homes into which others of us are born.

As I traveled around the world, I was repeatedly amazed and thrilled by what can be learned by listening to the poorest of the poor. These people are not stupid. They can articulate, for example, the impact of population growth on their own families. While on a trip with the Overseas Development Council in southern Asia, I met a farmer and his wife on a farm in Sri Lanka where they had raised four sons and one daughter on 2.8 hectares of land, which is a little more than seven acres. They barely survived. Then the government undertook an irrigation project which permitted the farmer to raise two crops a year instead of one. Life was much better. The farmer wanted to divide his land among his sons, but they could not survive on only 0.7 hectare each. All four of them left home to look for a job in the capital, Colombo. The father did not know what happened to them, but hoped they were not in trouble.

I can still picture that man and woman, warm and friendly, inviting us into their one room home, offering us tea from their three cups. How proud they were of what they had accomplished. But tears ran down the wife's face as her husband explained that their sons had to leave. "People need to have fewer children," he said.

On another occasion in a horrible slum in Howrah, across the river from Calcutta, I watched a UNICEF aide pass out vitamin-fortified cookies to a crowd of young boys. Much to my initial consternation, a bigger and older boy forced his way through the crowd and came back with both hands full of cookies. He then passed them out, every one of them, to smaller children standing in the background. I asked my interpreter to help me speak to this young Samaritan. But it was not necessary. This fifteen-year-old boy could speak surprisingly good English. He had taught himself. When I commended him for helping the little ones, he said, "Nobody else helps them. We have way too many kids here." Then he told us an astonishing story. His mother had a job passing out birth-control pills to women while he helped her by delivering condoms to some of the men.

In the early 1960s my wife, Lillian, joined the board of Planned Parenthood of Delaware and worked as a volunteer in low-income neighborhoods on family planning issues. That is when I first became enlightened about the growing population problem. During this time I too worked as a volunteer in low-income neighborhoods on better quality of life issues. When we compared our experiences, we concluded that in addition to providing more job opportunities and better housing, we had to do more to discourage large families and to reduce population growth if we were going to help these people overcome their difficulties. Over the next thirty years I became increasingly involved locally, nationally, and internationally in helping to define this problem and find ways to cope with it.

As governor of Delaware (1969–73), I began to speak out about both the need to reduce population growth and the importance of family planning. In 1973, ten days before I became chairman of the President's Council on Environmental Quality I spoke on "Growth in the Quality of Life" at a symposium in Washington, D.C., sponsored by the National Science Foundation. I expressed my conviction that if the nations of the world were to improve quality of life for people everywhere, their leaders had to face the three interconnecting problems of population growth, resource depletion, and environmental degradation. I emphasized that the greatest threat to the future well-being of humanity was population growth. Among the problems of the world it clearly stood out.

My speech, which was prominently printed in the *Washington Post* and other newspapers, made readers realize that protecting the environment was an inclusive enterprise. It created a new group of influential friends and supporters for CEQ.

The *Washington Post* article triggered a call from General William Draper, who insisted on seeing me that very day. What a fortunate happenstance.

General Draper, then 79 years old, was world-renowned for his post World War II work in advising the United States military government in both Germany and Japan to forego reparations and establish governmental and financial structures that would permit the vanquished nations to rebuild into stable, democratic, and financially sound nations. Of course he was not alone in this effort. We know well the major leadership roles played by President Truman and General George Marshall; we know less about General Draper who also was honored by both the German and Japanese governments for his role in this effort.

At President Truman's request, General Draper studied the causes of humanitarian ills such as poverty in Latin America. He concluded the basic problem was population growth and decided to dedicate the remainder of his life to minimizing that problem worldwide. He played a key role in establishing the United Nations Fund for Population Activities and in raising major funding for it as well as for the International Family Planning Program. He convinced many heads of state to support family planning. As national chairman of the Population Crisis Committee, he led that highly effective group in lobbying the U.S. Congress to support family planning generously.

After his telephone call, General Draper came to my office, which was in an attractive town house on Lafayette Square across from the White House. I liked him immediately; he was dynamic, articulate, persuasive and friendly, and he wore his deep dedication to his cause on his sleeve. He shook my hand vigorously and said, "Thank God. We finally have someone connected with the White House who understands the population problem and isn't afraid to speak out about it publicly."

He asked me to become a member of the board of the Population Crisis Committee. Within a few months I was appointed vice chairman of the U.S. Delegation to the World Population Conference in Bucharest, August 1974. Bill Draper made that happen.

Secretary of Health, Education and Welfare Caspar Weinberger served as chairman of the U.S. Delegation. He came for only the first and last days, the ceremonial days, of the conference, so I served as acting chairman during the heart of the eleven-day conference. I was credited with playing an important role in that conference, thanks to Bill Draper's taking me under his wing and helping me to know the leaders of the conference and the heads of many delegations. We worked long hours overcoming opposition to the proposed Program of Action.

At the time of the Conference, there was great resistance to family planning among leaders of many developing countries. They accused the rich, wasteful industrialized countries who were promoting family planning of denying poorer countries the same freedom of action that the industrialized societies had enjoyed as they increased their wealth. China, later to become a champion of family planning, spent much of its time in Bucharest accusing the United States and the Soviet Union of seeking to dominate the affairs of underdeveloped countries. And the Vatican launched its religious crusade against family planning.

Despite the confrontational environment, most participants finally agreed on certain principles and remedies:

- Improvement in the status of women is critical to solving the population problem.
- Parents have the right to decide on the size of their families and the spacing of their children.
- Countries must provide their citizens with the knowledge and wherewithal to exercise the right to family planning.
- Population, resources, and environment are interdependent and must be considered as a whole.

I presented a paper on this last subject. It was well received and stirred up much discussion. It was drafted by my assistant, Dr. Paul F. Bente. Paul and I had become close friends when we worked together in graduate school. He, like I, worked in research for DuPont before becoming deeply involved in protecting the environment. Today he turns out an excellent annual report on the state of population, resources, and the environment for his friends and church.

The Bucharest conference drove home the need to solve our population growth problems and the conviction that we could do so. What was required was an unprecedented educational effort worldwide, as well as political will and money. National leaders, especially in the more affluent countries, had to put up some of the modest resources required. I resolved to do what I could toward that end.

Fifteen years had passed since Lillian had introduced me to the world-population problem. Now I was able to operate at the highest levels of government to help solve that problem nationally and internationally. When I returned home from Bucharest, I tried to get Secretary Weinberger to arrange a meeting with President Ford to gain his support for the conclusions of the conference. The secretary repeatedly put off making the appointment, so I arranged to meet with the president without the secretary. When I arrived at the Oval Office, however, there was Cap Weinberger. He made some insignificant remarks about the conference that led me to conclude he did not understand the seriousness of the population problem or the importance of the conference.

The president then said, "Russ, I understand you have some charts." At that, I went ahead with my ten-minute report. The president asked some pertinent questions and seemed receptive to my request that he tell the American people what his administration had agreed to in Bucharest.

Nothing happened in spite of several efforts on my part through his staff to get him to act. Finally, in 1976, he did send a telegram to every U.S. ambassador stating the United States population policy, a telegram I drafted. However, he never did convey this information to the American people. He was running for election and no doubt his staff thought it too controversial a subject. What a sad situation. A president of the United States gives priority to his desire to get elected over a policy in which he believes and which is of great import to the quality of life of people everywhere.

On the day before Thanksgiving in 1974, General Draper called me at Lillian's family's farm in Wisconsin where we were visiting. He told me he was flying out on Thanksgiving to see me. I told him we were returning to Washington on Thanksgiving Day so he met us at the airport in Washington and bluntly asked me to take over as national chairman of the Population Crisis Committee. He said, "I'm running out of steam and we need a young person like you." At that point, I was 59, and Bill Draper was 80. We had celebrated his birthday in Bucharest.

I told him I could not do as he asked. I thought I could do more for the population problem by continuing to try to get the president of the United States out front on the issue. We agreed, however, that if I did not succeed with the president by spring, I would consider heading the Population Crisis Committee. Four weeks later General Bill Draper was dead (December 26, 1974). I wondered if the urgency with which he approached me to succeed him was an indication he knew his remaining time was short. I was deeply moved by his funeral service and the impressive burial ceremony at Arlington National Cemetery.

Bill Drapers do not come around very often. He was a problem solver par excellence. And a great human being. How fortunate I was to have known him!

For twenty-four years I served on the board of Bill Draper's Population Crisis Committee, now called Population Action International (PAI). This committee plays an advocacy role at the highest levels of government around the world by promoting family planning and helping to formulate broad global funding strategies for such programs. Its credible education program is highly regarded by the news media which makes extensive use of PAI's information and provides worldwide coverage. Its board consists of people with many years of experience in top level federal government jobs, foreign service, and population activities.

As president of the National Audubon Society (1979–85), I made population stabilization one of the goals of our strategy for protecting the global environment. This led to confrontations with some influential members of Audubon's board of directors. They did not see why an organization whose mission was to protect bird life (their narrow definition) should get involved with human population growth. I explained that birds were threatened all over the globe because human populations were expanding into bird habitats. If this continued, as current trends indicated, there would soon be little bird habitat left and we would have to go to zoos to see most bird species. Furthermore, I emphasized, as had the great ornithologist Roger Tory Peterson, birds were good indicators of the quality of the environment for other species including humans. When birds were threatened, so were humans. The earlier practice of taking a canary into a mine to test for poison gas illustrated my point. This line of argument won them over. They accepted the fact that population growth is a critical environmental variable.

One day Donal O'Brien, chief counsel of many Rockefeller interests and chairman of Audubon's executive committee at the time, invited me to lunch in the Rainbow Room in Rockefeller Center. No doubt he had heard of the concerns of other members of Audubon's board. He brought with him Elizabeth McCormick, an influential adviser to many Rockefeller family foundations and donors, and George Zeidenstab, president of the Population Council founded by John D. Rockefeller III. They tried hard to talk me out of my plan to involve Audubon in population matters. I refused to go along with their request and explained why.

After lunch George and I walked down Fifth Avenue together. He was very unhappy with Don O'Brien for including him. He said he agreed with me, but could not buck the principal source of his funding. I told him I needed their funding, too. The next day Donal called me. He said that I had won him over during our luncheon meeting, and he became a strong supporter of our population program, as did Rockefeller family donors.

This experience illustrates well a lesson I have learned many times. The fact that others express disagreement with your ideas or proposals does not mean they do not agree with you or cannot be convinced to agree. Their initial response may be conditioned by the position of their employers, church, political party, club, or family. Articulate well what you believe, what you think is right. When you do that, you will be amazed at how many will join you, at least privately.

We in Audubon built the first significant staff in the environmental movement on the critical environmental variable of population growth and mobilized many of our 550,000 members to advocate support for population stabilization. In 1980 I organized a series of meetings of leaders of national environmental, population and natural resource organizations to discuss the global interdependence of population, resources, and the environment and their long term impact on the quality of human life. This led to a major Audubon-sponsored conference in January 1981 that called upon the president and Congress to declare a policy of coordinated planning toward the goal of population stabilization. At my suggestion the conference agreed to support the establishment of the Global Tomorrow Coalition which I chaired for its first six years. Through its members, publications, and Globescope conferences, it played an important role in advancing the concept of environmentally sustainable development. It eventually grew to 110 member organizations, including fifteen business corporations.

As vice president of the IUCN, I led the effort to get this worldwide organization, which represented fifty-six national governments and over 400 nongovernmental organizations, to face up to the population problem. When an IUCN committee submitted its final report, "Poverty in Africa," ignoring, apparently on religious grounds, the impact of Africa's exploding population, I objected vigorously at our governing council meeting. This was quite embarrassing to the council members, since the chairman of the committee that developed the report was a prominent and popular African who was sitting there with us.

Failing to block issuance of that report, I moved that a committee be formed to consider IUCN's position on the population problem. Our president, Dr. M. Swaminathan, a renowned botanist from India who brought the green revolution to Asia, strongly supported me. The committee was created, and I was appointed chairman. The heads of the United Nations Environment Program, United Nations Food and Agriculture Organization, UNESCO, United Nations Fund for Population Activities, the International Planned Parenthood Federation and the World Wildlife Fund agreed to assign top people to consult with the five of us from IUCN's council who formed the committee. We developed a report with which all of us agreed, including the consultants. It documented the major impact of population growth on environmental quality and nature conservation and called for IUCN to support efforts to stabilize population. We directed the staff person assigned to us to put the report in final shape for submittal to the next meeting of IUCN's council to be held in Ottawa, Canada, in June 1986.

Although I had been repeatedly assured the report would be ready in time for the meeting, I learned when I arrived in Ottawa that IUCN's senior program officer, notorious for his opposition to family planning, had reassigned our staff person and no one had been available to transcribe the conclusions of our last meeting and prepare a finished document. Worse yet, no staff person was free to help me in Ottawa. I took on the job myself. Staying up most of the night, I revised an interim report of our committee, bringing it in line with the decisions made at our last meeting. Early the next morning Lillian took it to a local secretarial service that promptly produced a finished document. The members of my committee, all of whom were present in Ottawa, signed the final report. The next day I presented it to the council that, after much discussion, approved it.

Now IUCN was officially on record as supporting a worldwide effort to stabilize population growth. But IUCN had no staff to carry out this all-important mission. The director general told me he had no funds to hire anyone. Again, taking matters into my own hands, I raised $100,000 in the United States and with the director general's blessing, recruited Dr. Perdita Huston as our population program officer. She had worked in many developing countries and had written extensively on women and village life in those countries. Furthermore, she was tough and able to stand up to her male colleagues who disagreed with her assignment. She and I worked together closely. Soon IUCN was actively involved in the population movement. Dr. Huston launched an important magazine which is now entitled *People and the Planet.* It is a highly authoritative publication attested to by the fact that three other major international organizations have now joined IUCN in sponsoring it: the United Nations Population Fund, The International Planned Parenthood Federation and the World Wide Fund for Nature (WWF).

At an earlier date IUCN, working with conservationists worldwide, produced the "World Conservation Strategy." It was released with great fanfare around the world. Unfortunately, it ignored the basic problem, the threat of population growth to the environment. This came as a surprise and frustration to many who had participated in its development.

IUCN was a principal force in the omission of the critical population variable. Upon IUCN's subsequent official enlightenment on the population problem and aggressive action by several of us at international meetings, the "World Conservation Strategy" was revised, making the reduction of population growth a major goal.

This is another example of the need for vigilance and diligence in problem solving. Even when the facts clearly support a line of action and the people overwhelmingly support it, as is the case with the population problem, a few opponents, can stymie any

action. On the other hand, there are times when a few proponents, or sometimes only one, can overcome the opposition.

I have encountered many frustrations in my life, but usually I
have been able to persist or change my approach to overcome
them. And, as mentioned earlier, I have been asked on a number
of occasions, "Peterson, how come you keep going when you encounter so many frustrating obstacles?"

If I am unusually persistent, it is probably due to my training
and experience as a scientist. A scientist constantly works with
unknowns, pursues theories that prove to be wrong, and then
regroups and tries another approach. So it goes in the social
arena. You just cannot give up.

Looking Toward the Future

Today much of the resistance to family planning has been overcome. More and more of the world community is working to stop
population growth. And the population movement is increasingly
optimistic that this can and will be done.

All the industrialized countries have lowered their birthrates
below the replacement level of 2.1 per mother except the United
States, which in recent years increased its average births per
mother from 1.7 to 2.1. Thirty countries have already stabilized
their populations. About 55 percent of couples in developing
countries now use contraceptives. In 1965 only 10 percent did so.
As a result, the number of children per mother in these countries
declined from 6 to 3.5, a remarkable accomplishment in a single
generation. This trend allows us to hope that we can stabilize
world population in another generation.

Education and advocacy have been the keys. Pioneers in the
population movement created organizations to educate, lobby, and
raise funds. These organizations grew and spawned others. The
United States government, responding to pressure from citizen
groups, and with bipartisan leadership from Congress, led the
way internationally in funding family planning, including the cost
of contraceptives. European nations, Japan, Canada, and Austra-
lia have also been important contributors.

With increased funding, the International Planned Parenthood
Federation became a greater and greater force. The United Nations Fund for Population Activities was formed, catalyzing more

extensive involvement of national governments. Most of these international efforts were aided substantially by the advocacy role of Population Action International where I was involved for twenty-four years.

Recognition that population growth, degradation of the environment, resource depletion, poverty, and economic development were interconnected brought more allies to the population movement. This was especially true of environmental groups such as National Audubon and National Wildlife Federation who brought their large, activist organizations into the population battle. Population growth became identified as a fundamental environmental variable.

The United Nations World Conferences on Population in 1974 and 1984 helped to focus worldwide effort on the problem. Over the past 25 years, heads of developing nations moved from almost unanimous indifference or opposition to family planning to almost unanimous support, budgeting substantial funds and working more and more effectively with donors. Today East Asia provides an outstanding example of the effectiveness of family planning in developing countries. China, Taiwan, South Korea, Hong Kong, and Singapore all have lowered their level of fertility below the replacement level of 2.1 children per mother.

With 1.2 billion people crowded together, and its population sky rocketing, China had been headed for disaster. By rejuvenating its family planning late in 1978 after the Cultural Revolution, that nation has worked a miracle. China has been criticized, however, for coercive practices in its ambitious family-planning program that calls for limiting parents to having one child. The program has been implemented effectively in cities where families now average 1.3 children, but in rural areas where parents have been allowed more leniency, families are averaging two to three children. Parents are given a small grant and promised special educational opportunities for the first child. But such favorable treatment is reduced or eliminated when a second child is born. This is harsh when judged by Western standards. But how will it be judged in the long course of history? China was heading for disaster, but by making what seemed a sacrifice to limit family size, the country has avoided an overpopulation disaster. Today China is able to focus its resources on a more limited population, and in so doing is rapidly improving the country's standard of living.

China's family planning program has also been criticized for furthering female infanticide. Historically Chinese culture has favored male babies, leading to such infanticide. Ambassador Zhou, vice chairman of China's Family Planning Association, doubts that the problem is worse than before. He believes steps to raise the status of women and to limit family size will eventually wipe out that ancient scourge.

Ambassador Zhou and I served together for several years on the board of the Better World Society and became good friends. One day, after he explained to me the difficulty his government experienced in administering its family planning program, I asked him how he responded to the criticism that the Chinese government was forcing people to have small families. He replied, "I might best answer your question this way: when I recently visited Los Angeles, I noted on television and in the newspapers many reports of murders, rapes, muggings and robberies. That must be your government's policy."

"Touché," I said.

India, the second most populous nation with over 930 million people, has not done as well as China. India's population is destined to pass that of China's early next century. But five of India's states (Maharashtra, Punjab, Gujarat, Kerala and Tamil Nadu), each with a population larger than the majority of the countries of the world, have achieved relatively high levels of contraceptive use and significantly smaller family size.

Kerala has done an especially good job. *World Watch* in its May/June 1998 issue described Kerala's exceptional system leading to a 100 percent literacy rating by the United Nations. It has virtually no population growth and an infant mortality rate of less than two percent, compared to an average of 9 percent for the developing world as a whole. In spite of a diverse society that includes Hindus, Muslims and Christians crowded into a narrow strip of land, ethnic strife is almost unknown.

Thailand, with sixty million people, is another success story. From 6.2 children per woman in 1970, Thailand has now reached the replacement level of 2.1, with 75 percent of couples using contraceptives. This was achieved on a strictly voluntary basis and with cooperation between government and the private sector.

Starting in 1973, when Mexico's government abandoned its pro-natalist policies and started to promote family planning, its fertility level dropped from six children per mother to 2.8 in

1995. Indonesia, the fourth largest country in the world with 195 million people in 1996, is considered by population experts a major success story. This primarily Muslim country with a low per capita income of just $600 per year has raised its contraceptive use to about 55 percent of reproductive-age couples. The average fertility level is 2.9, but it has reached the replacement level in some large provinces and is only 1.9 in the capital, Jakarta. Knowledge of family planning is almost universal and most young couples want only two children.

No nation in Africa has reached the replacement level of fertility. Tunisia and Morocco have cut their fertility in half over the past thirty years to about 3.3 children per mother. With the major effort they now have under way to advance women's education and rights, they expect further improvement. Although Kenya, Zimbabwe, and Botswana made essentially no headway in the 1960s and 1970s, they have, over the past fifteen years, markedly increased the use of contraceptives and fostered girls' education. Their programs are promising, but as recently as 1995, their fertility levels were still high.

An important improvement in the developing world occurred in 1994 when ten countries (Bangladesh, Colombia, Egypt, Indonesia, Kenya, Mexico, Morocco, Thailand, Tunisia, and Zimbabwe) formed Partners in Population and Development (PPD). Each had imaginative family planning programs. Together they set out to create a means to facilitate developing countries' sharing their experiences in family planning. In contrast, over the past twenty years the Vatican has become more and more vocal in its opposition to family planning. Its obstructionist efforts crested at the 1994 United Nations International Conference on Population and Development (ICPD) in Cairo. Just before that conference in a meeting in the Vatican with Dr. Nafis Sadik, secretary general of that conference, Pope John Paul II delivered a scathing attack on U.N. attempts to limit family size. The Pope reiterated his belief that contraception was immoral. Families, he said, should be able to decide on their own, "free from all social or legal coercion, the number of children they will have and the spacing of their births." As proof of waning Vatican influence, two Catholic countries in the developed world, Spain and Italy, have the lowest birth rates anywhere at 1.2 children per woman.

Antiabortion groups around the world, and especially in the United States, have no doubt reduced support for family planning. Why they target family planning is a mystery to me. The best way to reduce abortions is to prevent unwanted pregnancies. About fifty million abortions are performed each year worldwide, and an estimated 100,000 women die after submitting to dangerous procedures or not receiving proper follow-up treatment. With an aggressive educational effort on behalf of family planning and a program to supply contraceptives, the number of unwanted pregnancies could be markedly reduced, and there would be tens of millions fewer abortions and tens of thousands fewer women dying. Antiabortion groups should be engineering the campaign for family planning, not trying to derail it.

ICPD, which involved 190 nations and 3,000 nongovernmental groups, brought a sense of hopefulness about stabilizing population growth. Conferees emphasized the importance of the education, reproductive health, and empowerment of women to the success of any global effort to stabilize human population. It set a goal of universal access to family planning by 2015. And, as stated before, women played a major leadership role, as exemplified by Pakistan's Dr. Nafis Sadik who chaired the ICPD. *People And The Planet*, Vol. 2, 1993, reported that another participant, Dr. Attiya Inayatullah of the Family Planning Association of Pakistan said, "As an advocate for Third World and Muslim women, I believe that history was made at Cairo with the acknowledgment that the practice of family planning is the cheapest and most accessible solution in making motherhood the gift of life and not the threat of death." She went on to say that this was "the first conference to begin undoing the cruel and unjust gender apartheid in the Third World."

The world is now on its way toward stabilizing population and, in the process, doing the single most important thing to protect the global environment and reduce poverty.

35

Restraining Growth in the Consumption of Resources

W HILE POPULATION TRIPLED IN THE TWENTIETH CENTURY, THE consumption of resources as measured by the Gross World Product (GWP) increased twentyfold. Each person who increases his standard of living also increases his ability to impact the environment. People in affluent nations use many times more resources than people in the poorest countries. Average Americans use more energy, produce more waste, consume more trees, and create more greenhouse gasses than their counterparts in any other country. To compound matters, America's population is growing faster than that of any other industrialized country. We are now the third most populated country in the world.

Fortunately efforts are underway to use energy more efficiently, move from fossil and nuclear fuels to renewable sources of energy, recover and recycle materials, reduce production of waste and pollutants, farm with fewer chemicals, and renovate rather than bulldoze.

Nevertheless we need to practice environmentally sustainable development rather than the environmentally destructive development that has characterized much of our past. The World Commission on Environment and Development, then headed by Prime Minister Gro Harlem Brundtland of Norway, first popularized the term "sustainable development." In its 1987 report, *Our Common Future*, it defined this term as development meeting the basic needs of all the world's people today without compromising the ability of future generations to meet their needs. In contrast, those who think our current rates of consumption can go on forever believe there are no limits to such growth. They define sustainable development as continuing current development. However, I believe the term *environmentally sustainable development*, coined by Worldwatch Institute President Lester Brown is preferable. It means replacing the practice of providing ever more resources for ever more people with the goal of maximizing growth in the quality of life for a limited population—that is, providing adequate food, shelter, health care, better education, greater safety, less injustice, and better communication and transportation for everyone. Reaching this goal will require limiting our consumption of resources. Toward this end, the revolution now occurring in communication technology may well teach people, especially those who are already rich in material things, that there is much greater wealth in accumulating and using knowledge.

Many of the world's leading industrialists now take seriously the need for environmentally sustainable development. Proponents include leaders of several hundred major companies, the United Nations Environment Programme, the U.S. Environmental Protection Agency and the World Resources Institute. Most significant was the dialogue of powerful business leaders with 114 heads of state at the 1992 United Nations Earth Summit in Rio de Janeiro. There they discussed how to continue economic development on an environmentally sound, sustainable basis.

The Soft-Energy Path—A Win-Win Situation

A good area to practice sustainable development, as emphasized in Rio, is in the production and use of energy. The huge increase in the world's economic growth has been a principal cause of environmental degradation, including urban smog, acid rain, oil spills, the greenhouse gas carbon dioxide, and radioactive waste. But now we know we can provide for growth in the services we need, such as transportation, heating, cooling, cooking, and lighting, without the traditional devastating impact on the environment by using energy more efficiently and by moving to environmentally benign and abundant solar energy and wind energy. This so-called soft energy path would lead to reduced pollution and lower energy costs, while simultaneously making industry more competitive, reducing oil imports, and minimizing the use of nuclear power with its dangerous waste and possibility of weapons proliferation.

I have been involved with promoting the soft-energy path since 1973. While chairman of the Council on Environmental Quality,

I led the 1974 development of our Half and Half Energy Plan which encouraged America to get half of its new energy needs by using energy more efficiently. Although it received much publicity, the Half and Half plan had little impact on President Ford's administration. It did, however, help influence Ford's successor, President Carter. His administration launched a major and highly promising effort to use energy more efficiently. It also led to my serving for seventeen years as a founding board member of the Alliance to Save Energy, a group founded by Illinois Senator Charles Percy that played an important role in involving federal and state governments, industry, and public interest organizations in this cause.

As president of the National Audubon Society I initiated and promoted The Audubon Energy Plan, showing the nation how to use energy more efficiently, develop solar and other renewable forms of energy, and phase out nuclear energy. In 1979 I became chairman of the board of advisors to the U.S. Department of Energy's Solar Energy Research Institute, resigning that post in 1981 when I decided to oppose publicly President Reagan's dismantling of the government's soft energy programs. Since 1978 I also have been a member of the advisory board of the Center for Environmental Legal Studies of Pace University's School of Law. The Center has been working with New York, Florida, and Michigan on laws to advance energy conservation and reform electric utilities. These experiences allowed me to participate in the energy revolution and to witness the dawning of the soft energy era.

The 1970s were an especially effective period in advancing the more efficient use of energy. This occurred as a result of the sevenfold increase in the price of oil, financial incentives legislated by the U.S. federal government and some states, and strong leadership by President Carter. Between 1972 and 1985, national energy consumption grew by only three percent, while the real size of the economy grew by 39 percent. If the earlier trend had continued, the U.S. would have consumed 33 percent more energy in 1985 than it actually did. The energy saved equaled the output of either 350 coal-fired or nuclear-fired 1000 megawatt power plants.

In the 1980s the Reagan and Bush Administrations essentially abandoned federal programs to stimulate the development of energy efficiency—a major disservice to America. This, combined with oil priced at its lowest level in forty years, led to resumption of rapid growth in energy consumption. However, some states, especially California, New York, and the New England states, continued working with industry on renewable sources of energy and its more efficient use.

The utility industry's own research arm, the Electric Power Research Institute, now estimates that by using new technology already available, our national electricity consumption could be reduced by 44 percent within ten years. Amory and Hunter Lovins's Rocky Mountain Institute, a pioneer in advancing the soft energy path, estimates that 75 percent of *total* U.S. energy demand could be avoided by cost-effective investments in more energy-efficient vehicles, appliances, buildings, lighting, and motors.

Many national and international organizations and many national governments are now promoting more efficient use of energy as the cheapest, quickest, and most effective route to reducing a plethora of environmental problems and advancing economic competitiveness.

Our federal government, after a long hiatus, should resume the strong support for energy efficiency it initiated in the 1970s. This is the single best route to coping with the threat of global warming. This conclusion is not based on conjecture, but on confidence stemming from the successful, nationwide experiment run in the 1970s. Let me give an example of what can be gained by using energy more efficiently. By replacing a conventional 75-watt incandescent lightbulb, which costs $1.07, with a new fluorescent bulb that costs $19.00, but lasts 13 times as long, one can gain a 50 percent tax-free and inflation-free return per year on the investment over the six-year lifetime of the fluorescent bulb, since this bulb will use only 24 percent as much electricity as the incandescent bulb. If the electricity comes from a coal-fired plant, for example, the new bulb will also save 500 pounds of coal, avoid the release of one ton of the greenhouse gas, carbon dioxide, and 21 pounds of the acid rain precursor, sulfur dioxide. The Electric Power Research Institute estimates that half of the electricity now used for lighting could be saved by adopting fluorescent lighting.

A champion practitioner of the soft-energy path is David Freeman, former head of the Tennessee Valley Authority and leader of the Ford Foundation's energy program in the 1970s. Over the years Freeman has made headlines by canceling orders for nuclear power plants in the Tennessee Valley, Sacramento, and New York. He has fulfilled energy needs by launching innovative energy saving programs. His conservation program for the Sacramento Municipal Utility District, for example, included the planting of 50,000 shade trees for homes, offices, and public buildings as well as financial inducements to install home insulation and replace wasteful old refrigerators and other appliances. The program reduced electricity demand enough to allow cancellation of the planned Rancho Seco nuclear plant.

California's largest utilities, Southern California Edison and Pacific Gas and Electric Company, aided by strong financial help from state government, have led the way during the last twenty years through major soft-energy incentive programs.

Amory Lovins points out that between 1979 and 1994, the United States received seven times more new energy via the soft-energy path (efficiency plus renewables) than from new plants using fossil or nuclear fuels. As an adviser to developing countries, especially China, he continues to promote strategy based on efficiency and pollution prevention. He points out, for example, that by spending $7.5 million to build a plant to manufacture compact fluorescent lamps, a country could save enough electricity to avoid building a one-billion dollar power plant. A $10 million factory that makes super insulating windows could save $2 billion worth of power plants and also avoid the plants' pollution.

It is in the whole world's interest to help developing countries vault into an industrial future based on the energy efficient, more pollution-free industries now being pioneered in advanced countries. Multinational businesses are currently contributing by incorporating their most efficient technology into the new plants they build in developing countries. This brings hope that the billions of poor in the world may be able to climb the economic ladder without causing the devastating per capita impact on the environment that has characterized the history of industrialization to date.

Lester Brown and Christopher Flavin of World Watch Institute have recently pointed out how China, with its economy growing 10 to 14 percent per year, emerged by the mid 1990s as an economic superpower; its economy is now second to that of the United States. This carries with it the need to recognize how important it is for China to choose from its options for development those alternatives that are environmentally sustainable.

In 1995 China consumed twice as much grain and red meat, 40 percent more fertilizer and slightly more steel than the United

States while becoming the world's second largest grain importer. By powering its huge growth with energy from coal, China is already paying a high penalty in increased numbers of respiratory ailments and lower crop yields stemming from extreme air pollution. If China's massive population continues to move in this direction, following the consumption pattern practiced in the United States, the world will see that such a pattern is unsustainable when practiced by a major fraction of the world's population.

Our choice must not be to sit back and observe while we count stock dividends, but to join China and others in investing ourselves and our resources in the world's environmentally sustainable development.

To sustain an adequate life-supporting environment the world will need to develop a mode of transportation much more fuel-efficient than the current automobile. Much could be done near term by governments mandating higher efficiency. As a result of legislation passed by Congress in the 1970s, auto companies were required to raise the average fuel efficiency of their new car fleets to 27.5 mpg. This approximately doubled the average fuel efficiency and thereby cut in half the oil imports that otherwise would have been required. Americans would now be paying $40 billion more per year at the gas pump if the auto companies had not been forced to take this step.

By increasing the new fleet standard to 40 mpg, for example, U.S. oil consumption could be reduced by 2.8 million barrels per day, more than we have ever imported per day from all the Mideast countries combined. It would also reduce by 40 percent the amount of the greenhouse gas carbon dioxide emitted by the new cars.

Attempts to pass such legislation have been blocked by the auto companies' supporters in Congress and the White House. While the Big Three did agree with the Clinton Administration in 1993 to proceed with the design and testing of a markedly more efficient automobile in a program called "A Partnership for a New Generation of Vehicles," so far no progress is obvious. The auto companies contend that legislation to force more efficiency would lead to smaller autos and decreased auto safety. But the Energy Conservation Coalition points out, "Since 1974, as fuel economy for cars doubled, 86 percent of the improvement came from new technology, and only 2 percent occurred as a result of shifting to smaller cars. Over that period the death rate from auto accidents fell by 40 percent."

Of special concern today is the auto companies' success in moving almost half of American families away from smaller, more fuel-efficient cars to more profitable minivans and sport utility vehicles. These larger, heavier vehicles, in addition to being markedly less fuel efficient, emit more pollutants and more greenhouse gas, are more hazardous on the highway, and add to America's already exorbitant use of resources. In spite of their primary use as passenger cars, they are classified as light trucks, thereby allowing their manufacturers to avoid the federal fuel efficiency and pollution emission standards, as well as the gas guzzler taxes that apply to cars.

At the same time, the Detroit Big Three continue the fight against any meaningful participation by the United States in a world treaty to minimize the threat of global warming—a stance they have taken on every new environmental regulation proposed during the past twenty-five years.

American owners of the so-called light trucks need to be better informed of the consequences of what they are driving. Auto companies need to be required to design and build all passenger vehicles (cars and light trucks) to meet higher fuel efficiency standards (minimum forty miles per gallon) and to meet the same tough emission standards currently required in California.

In addition to using energy more efficiently, we need a major effort to develop environmentally benign and renewable solar energy. Under solar energy I include not only the direct radiation from the sun, but also wind and photosynthesis, which are powered by the sun. The sun is the only safe nuclear reactor. It is properly sited and keeps its wastes in space. It has already provided life on Earth with nearly all of its energy needs. The challenge is to develop technology that uses a small fraction of the huge amount of energy the sun beams to the Earth to fulfill those needs now satisfied by fossil and nuclear fuels. Especially attractive is the development of photovoltaic devices which convert sunlight directly to electricity and which promise to be economically competitive with nuclear energy by about 2006.

Imagine this scenario: as our oil-producing states deplete their rapidly diminishing oil reserves, our sunbelt states build a new industry, producing electricity directly from infinitely renewable sunlight and using it to electrolyze water to produce hydrogen, which could then be transported all over the country through pipelines and in tank cars. Hydrogen could be used as a fuel in automobiles and homes, and the only by-product of this super power source would be water. What a contrast to nuclear energy and coal. Some worry about the safety of hydrogen. In my judgment it is no more unsafe than today's fuels—gasoline, propane, and natural gas.

Another promising development is wind energy. After some difficult years it now appears to be taking off. Some sources estimate that 40 percent of the U.S. demand for electricity could be met by wind. Thirty-seven states have adequate wind resources. Wind farms in California, which now produce as much electricity as is used by San Francisco, have demonstrated that wind energy can be cost effective, (5.4 cents per kilowatt hour), clean, and reliable. The Pacific Gas and Electric Company has concluded that wind energy will become the most economic new baseload source by 2002, even without any more technical breakthroughs.

Although growth in wind energy has stalled in California—temporarily, I believe, since government incentives were withdrawn—it is skyrocketing in Europe, where it tripled between 1992 and 1995. Germany leads the way.

Some people are still promoting the idea of rejuvenating the nuclear power industry. The sooner that chapter in world history is behind us, the better off all life on Earth will be. The worldwide experiment with nuclear power has clearly failed economically, technically, environmentally, socially, and politically. Every major country using nuclear energy, including France, has slowed or stopped its nuclear program. Sweden, Denmark, Italy, Austria, and Switzerland have all voted to reject it. For twenty-four years in the United States, no new nuclear power reactor has been ordered without being subsequently canceled. By 1997, ninety-two reactors around the world had been permanently shut down after an average service life of less than eighteen years. The cost of disposing of them has been projected to be higher than the original amount spent to build them.

Now that the former Soviet Union has been opened to inspection, citizen action, and free speech, we know that the 1986 Chernobyl nuclear accident was a much greater disaster than claimed earlier. At least 5,000 of the 25,000 young people who were assigned to help clean up the site have died from exposure to radiation. Millions of acres were contaminated and are now not usable for food production. Entire villages have been bulldozed and buried. Several hundred thousand people have been permanently evacuated from their homes. In 1990 the Soviet government reported that the accident's total cost was $358 billion and that the Soviet economy would be better off if nuclear reactors had never been built.

The cost of trying to make nuclear energy plants safe has driven the cost of electricity from such plants in the U.S. to twice that of electricity generated from fossil fuels and to five to ten times the cost of saving an equivalent amount of energy through improved efficiency.

Much has been made of late of the development by nuclear reactor manufacturers of designs for fail-safe reactors. Even in the unlikely event a design 100 percent accident free and economically attractive could be developed, it would not eliminate nuclear energy's two terminal ailments, the production of deadly radioactive waste and the creation of an even greater supply of plutonium with its potential for use in nuclear weapons.

The nuclear industry produces the world's most hazardous waste. Even after forty years of high priority attention, no satisfactory disposal method has been developed, and the citizenry's objection to proposals for storing the waste continues to mount. Meanwhile, at each of our nuclear power plants, one-third of the reactor tubes with their spent fuel, a witch's brew of super-hazardous radioactive elements, is removed from the reactors each year and stored on the reactor site awaiting some decision on what to do with them.

What is required throughout our government is more concern for future generations. It will take several decades to make the transition to a soft energy future. Doing so will provide, next to stabilizing population, the second best path to resolving the global predicament.

Waste Reduction, Recycling, Re-use

Other major routes to reducing the consumption of resources include minimizing waste, and recycling and reusing materials, renovating old buildings instead of bulldozing them, and saving open land by building on old sites instead of new ones.

Production of solid waste in the U.S. grew four to five percent per year during the 1960s and 1970s. The easiest way to get rid of it was to dump it in any convenient place or send it to a landfill. Sprouting everywhere, landfills covered more and more square miles, leaking their poisonous juices into adjoining streams and farmlands and downgrading neighboring lands with their foul odors. By the early 1970s, there were over 20,000 official landfills operating in the U.S., along with countless unauthorized dumps. Litter plagued our highways and pathways. Starting about the time of the first Earth Day in 1970, Americans began to take this problem more seriously. We in Delaware joined in, at the time I was governor, and sparked a number of cleanup activities. One specific project made an impression on me.

Near our house in Rehoboth, along an undeveloped stretch of ocean front, was Whiskey Beach, a very beautiful and popular place where several thousand sophisticated young people, primarily from Washington, D.C., spent their summer weekends, swimming, riding the surf, playing beach volleyball, sunbathing, flirting, relaxing, conversing, eating, and drinking. Their beer cans, papers, plastic cups, food wrappings, and garbage were strewn everywhere, reaching from the water's edge to the sand dunes. My wife, Lillian, and I decided to do something about this. Arriving at the beach one Sunday afternoon in our swimsuits, we started to pick up trash and put it in the almost-empty waste drums. Stopping beside groups assembled on the sand, I would say, "I'm the governor of Delaware. I'd like to know how many of you have heard of Earth Day." About half raised a hand. "My wife, Lillian, and I have decided to help clean up our Earth," I said. "How about you folks joining us right here?" The message spread across the beach. Within fifteen minutes the waste drums were filled to overflowing.

The next day I arranged to have more drums installed, each painted, "Every Day is Earth Day." When I arrived three weeks later, several young men and women ran over to me. "How does it look, Governor?" they asked. I was amazed. I could see no sign of litter. And they kept their beach—our beach—clean the rest of the summer. This demonstrated well how each of us can make a difference. An infinitesimal effort by each member resulted in the group as a whole converting a common problem into an asset. So it goes with the big problems of the world. If each of us does a little, we can solve them.

Since the early 1970s much headway has been made in reducing litter, thanks to improved lifestyles and to the volunteer efforts of millions of people in cleaning up our highways, byways and waterfronts. There are now fewer than 4,500 landfills in the U.S., down 80 percent in the past fifteen years, and they are designed with appropriate liners and controls, thanks to new governmental regulations. However, designing better ways to dispose of our waste is not the solution to the waste problem. We must stop creating it and we must recover and recycle used materials.

Certainly we must put an end to designing, producing, and marketing products without also thinking about how or where we will eventually dispose of them. We must also consider the costs to the community and the environment of their disposal. Manufacturers can design products which lend themselves to easy repair and recycling, which use less material and which are more durable. Governments can establish regulations and provide incentives to further recycling.

Germany, followed by the Netherlands, Sweden, and Austria, has been showing the way by applying "the polluter pays" principle to the manufacture and marketing of packaging materials by mandating that manufacturers, wholesalers, and retailers must pay for the disposing of or recycling their products' packaging. This beginning-to-end responsibility has provided a potent incentive for businesses to reshape their strategies. Germany's Environmental Ministry is pushing legislation that would extend this approach to manufacturers of cars and appliances, mandating that they be responsible for recovering and recycling their used products.

I promoted this idea twenty-two years ago, albeit without success, while chairman of CEQ. The Senate Environment and Public Works Committee proposed (but could not get passed) legislation requiring manufacturers to take responsibility for the life cycle of a product, from its creation to its ultimate disposal. Now the U.S. Resource Conservation and Recovery Act (RCRA) needs to be amended to include that requirement.

Industry has made a major commitment to reduce waste. For example, a number of corporations have set individual goals of reducing such waste to zero by 2000. The National Recycling Coalition gives an annual award for outstanding corporate leadership. In 1996 Chrysler Corporation was so honored. At one of its many plants, Chrysler reused much of what had previously been discarded, earned $212,000 from the sale of recycled material, and saved $350,000 in landfill fees and waste-hauling costs.

The first of many source-reduction programs at the consumer level started in Seattle in 1981 and has markedly reduced the amount of material discarded by the average household. At the heart of all these programs is a "pay-as-you-throw" strategy that involves charging the consumer for each bag or each pound of trash. These programs have met with favorable citizen response and a marked decrease in the amount of discarded household trash.

Where trash collection and disposal are paid by property taxes (a common practice), householders have no financial incentive to discard less. But when required to pay by the bag or pound for the full cost of collecting and disposing, they have clear incentives to modify their purchases, recycle, and compost. Programs are also under way to charge to the entities that created the waste the costs of collecting and disposing of it, as well as the costs inflicted on the environment by the waste. This will give manufacturers a powerful financial incentive to re-design their products to reduce waste and be recyclable.

The state of California estimated that it would have to charge manufacturers disposal fees totaling $5.1 billion annually in order to cover the full disposal cost of everything sold in that state. The state estimated disposal fees carefully tailored for each product— for instance, five cents on a gallon of juice, one cent on a lunch at McDonalds, three cents on the daily newspaper and eight to ten dollars for a gallon of oil-based paint. Although the current antitax mood in America makes the future of this economically and environmentally sound approach to paying for waste management uncertain, I believe we citizens should push to make it happen.

Incineration is a highly controversial method of disposing of municipal solid waste. Although some waste managers see it as convenient, many environmentalists and private citizens are strongly opposed. Under some conditions incinerators emit hazardous materials. Moreover, because they seem an easy way out, incinerators distract the community from pursuing source reduction, recycling, and composting.

The recycling of municipal solid waste has grown dramatically in the United States, tripling between 1989 and 1995. Twenty percent of our municipal solid waste is recycled, with Minnesota,

New Jersey, and Washington leading the way at twice the national average. The growth of such recycling has continued despite the fact that the supply of recyclable products far exceeds the capacity of industry to process them and the readiness of the market to accept recycled products. Major efforts are underway to correct this. For example, the paper industry is making a substantial investment in providing additional facilities for de-inking and processing used paper; some publishers are voluntarily purchasing recycled paper; and mandates by government that they do so promise to bring the supply of and demand for used paper into balance. Until a material is actually being reused, however, it is misleading to report it as recycled. Recycling calls for a variety of incentives and dis-incentives and a broad-based, nationwide effort involving government at all levels. It also requires that a significant number of manufacturing and marketing companies cooperate in the effort.

To help create markets for recycled materials, all fifty states and many municipalities have established procurement programs that specify minimum percentages of recycled material in certain products they purchase. Environmentalists and local governments favor federal and state involvement in bringing the supply of and demand for recycled products into balance. Typically, much of the pertinent industry is opposed.

Take the recycled paper problem, where a glut of sorted, used paper threatens to quash enthusiasm for recycling. The American Paper Institute and the American Newspaper Publishers Association are opposing strengthening the Resource Conservation and Recovery Act just as the beverage makers previously defeated a federal bottle deposit bill. Both groups claim the proposed regulations would be too costly for their businesses. But it is not just the manufacturers' costs; it is the current and future costs of present practices to the whole society that must be weighed.

The public's enthusiasm for recycling was stimulated when environmentalists convinced twenty-five state governments and many local governments to mandate the collection of recyclable materials from households. This led to remarkably successful curbside recycling, with more than 100 million people now being served.

Recycling not only reduces the waste flow to landfills and saves resources, it also saves energy and creates jobs. Consider aluminum as one example. It takes twenty times as much energy to make a beverage can from aluminum ore as it does from recycled aluminum cans. The Aluminum Company of America reported that aluminum recycling employed 30,000 people in 1991—twice the number working in aluminum manufacturing. By following trends already established and getting the federal government to play a greater role in requiring that manufacturers take responsibility for the final disposition of their products, the United States could bring its solid waste problem under fairly close control by early in the next century.

36

Containing Harmful Fallout from New Technology

WHEN WE LIST THE IMMENSE CONTRIBUTIONS OF RESEARCH AND development—greater life expectancy, lower infant-mortality rates, less human suffering from diseases like smallpox that once destroyed whole populations, improved transportation, global communication on the information superhighway, and increased agricultural productivity—it is easy to see how we have benefitted from research and development. Thus it may appear heretical for someone who has spent much of his life in research and development, and who looks forward to research and development's solving some of our current problems, to accuse research and development of also being a source of our current environmental predicament.

We must recognize, however, that in addition to the many benefits, research and development have also given us nuclear weapons, hazardous chemicals, a depleted ozone layer, damaged health, acid rain, contaminated water, urban smog, massive oil spills, pesticides, mountains of waste, including nuclear waste, and the loss of forests, grasslands, free-flowing rivers, wildlife, and scenic vistas.

Nuclear energy is a prime example of negative fallout from research and development. Civilization would be far better off without it. In 1999 the single greatest threat to life on earth is still the nuclear bomb. Despite all our efforts to reduce the world's massive arsenals of nuclear weapons and all our treaties to control them, such weapons will remain a major threat for the foreseeable future. Years ago nuclear energy was projected to give us electricity at a price too low to meter. That never happened. Think of what was buried in the ground and released into the air at Hanford, Washington, and a dozen other nuclear-weapons manufacturing sites. Or think of Chernobyl. Or Three Mile Island. Think of those places, and you will better know the price of nuclear energy.

The challenge now before us is to analyze thoroughly the long-term impact of new technology, weighing its potential benefits against its negative effects before we put it to use. In short, we must support the work of those professionals involved in technology assessment, many of whom work at universities, environmental organizations, and various think tanks around the world. Their job is to discover the potential fallout from new technology, harmful as well as helpful.

This is not a new idea. In the mid 1970s the U.S. Congress established an Office of Technology Assessment (OTA) that became a highly credible institution in the eyes of the scientific community. I had the privilege of being director of OTA from 1978 to 1979. Unfortunately, a regressive Congress abolished it in 1995. Former employees are now seeking to establish a similar institution in the private sector. I believe that the American people should force Congress to reestablish OTA so we will again have competent, in-house sentinels to inform and advise members early of the likely impacts, positive and negative, of new technology.

Moreover, for the past twenty-five years many Americans have been pushing to have Congress establish a well-funded National Institute for the Environment, an independent, multidisciplinary institution like the National Institutes of Health. The concept has broad support from both scientists and environmental organizations and some bipartisan sponsorship in Congress.

As chairman of CEQ, I tried unsuccessfully for three years—the last year with the help of Vice President Nelson Rockefeller—to convince the president and the Office of Management and Budget to fund an office that would provide government with an ongoing, comprehensive analysis of global trends and give advice on dealing with the many economic, technical, environmental, and social factors pertinent to making choices among alternative futures.

When President Carter came into office, he authorized CEQ to carry out such a study, a one-shot effort. It appeared in 1980, at the end of his term, as *The Global 2000 Report To The President.* In addition to pointing out how poorly equipped our government was to perform such a comprehensive study, it emphasized that if current global policies continued, the growing population, natural-resource, and environmental stresses threatened "global problems of alarming proportions by the year 2000." Although President Reagan belittled the study and ignored the proposed solutions advanced by CEQ, *The Global 2000 Report* led to similar studies in Europe and Japan.

In 1981 I was instrumental in helping form The Global Tomorrow Coalition, which I chaired for its first six years. It brought together 115 environmental, population, and business organizations dedicated to educating its more than ten million constituent members about global population, resources, environment and development issues, and motivating them to act today to assure a more equitable, sustainable global community tomorrow. One of our objectives was to get the U.S. government to establish a Foresight Office in the Office of the President. Legislation toward this end was introduced in Congress, but received only token support.

The Clinton administration moved in this direction by establishing an Under Secretary for Global Issues in the Department of State. Former Senator Tim Wirth headed this operation and brought his long-standing commitment to foresight capability and his knowledge of global issues to bear at world conferences on population, environment, development, and technology. He has now moved on to head the United Nations Foundation, funded by Ted Turner's billion-dollar contribution.

The international banning of CFCs, an event of major historical significance, showed how an increasingly enlightened world community can assess technology and protect citizens in spite of business opposition. It is a clear signal of our developing ability to choose wisely among alternative futures. It also demonstrates how, through technology, we can replace harmful products with safer alternatives.

Technology assessment also led to our studying the long-term impact of the so-called greenhouse gasses, especially carbon dioxide. A century ago, in 1896, the Swedish chemist Svante Arrhenius theorized that the emission of carbon dioxide from the burning of coal would, over time, cause global warming. Little was done about it, however, until the environmental movement, technology assessment, and modern computers brought this issue to the forefront of environmental concerns during the 1980s. Global warming's potential impact on temperature, rainfall, storms, and sea-level rise could be devastating to agriculture, biological diversity, and human coastal settlements. The complexity of research and slow rate of change have made it difficult to show climate change with scientific certainty, leading some political leaders, advised by a few naysaying scientists, to stall in implementing international agreements to reduce greenhouse gas emissions.

By 1992 at the Rio Earth Summit, global warming had become a priority. Conference participants signed a Framework Convention on Climate Change that called for nations to prepare strategies for reducing greenhouse gas emissions by a given amount by target dates. Industrial countries *voluntarily* committed themselves, reducing growth in such emissions so they would be no higher in 2000 than they were in 1990. Germany, Denmark, and The Netherlands promptly set tougher goals and are well on the way to meeting them. (In contrast, the United States did little and its greenhouse gas emissions continue to grow rapidly.) Thirty-six small island states, whose existence would be threatened by the projected rising seas, formed an alliance to lobby for programs to reduce global warming.

At the first Conference of the Parties to the Climate Convention in Berlin, April 1995, the Berlin Mandate was adopted. It commits treaty members from industrial countries to adopt a protocol "setting quantified limitations and reduction objectives within specified time frames." The date of December 1997 was set for a world conference in Kyoto, Japan, to agree on such protocol. The Berlin Mandate provided some optimism that the industrial countries were taking the threat of global warming seriously. This triggered a high-powered publicity campaign in the United States to discredit global warming, primarily by the Global Climate Coalition, sponsored by coal, oil, electric utility, auto and chemical companies.

With ever more scientists researching the problem, evidence to support the theory of global warming kept mounting. In December 1995, the United Nations Intergovernmental Panel on Climate Change (IPCC), made up of 2,500 scientists, reported that "a pattern of climate response to human activities is identifiable in the climatological record." This was the first time climate science experts expressed confidence that global climate change was actually occurring and that, at least in part, it was caused by human action.

IPCC projected a rise of 1.8 to 6.3 degrees Fahrenheit over the next 100 years. Such a rise could have disastrous impacts. The

6.3-degree rise would cause, among other things, major changes in plant growth, super-violent weather, and melting of glaciers and Antarctic and Arctic ice leading to a catastrophic rise in sea level.

The Global Warming Theory is based on three indisputable facts, each directly measurable: more and more greenhouse gasses are being emitted, the amount in the atmosphere is increasing, and each such gas reflects energy radiating from the Earth back to the Earth, just as a greenhouse captures and holds energy from the sun.

Uncertainties arise when scientists consider the magnitude and timing of the impact of the projected global warming on the earth's climate, as well as on plant and animal life. To cope with this complex problem, they use sophisticated computer modelling that markedly expands their ability to work with such multivariable issues. This technique has evolved into an amazingly dependable scientific tool since I used it forty years ago in the DuPont Company in the much simpler assignment of appraising the potential of promising new business ventures.

The Kyoto Conference, held December 1–12, 1997, was attended by representatives from 160 countries, essentially the whole world community. It produced the Kyoto Protocol. Upon ratification, it requires that developed countries lower their greenhouse-gas emissions 5.2 percent (on the average) below 1990 levels by the year 2010. The United States, the world's single most serious offender, would be required to lower its emissions to 7 percent below the 1990 level, the European Union by 8 percent, and Japan by 6 percent.

This was a remarkable milestone in the history of the environmental movement and in the use of technology assessment. It capped the five-year effort since the Rio Earth Summit to inform, educate, and involve governmental leaders everywhere in the critical issue of global warming. The conference, and its many preparatory meetings, alerted the news media, which in turn informed many millions around the globe of the huge stake our children and future generations have in resolving the threat of global warming. It also committed world leaders to action.

Unfortunately, the Kyoto Conference failed to convince developing countries to adopt quantitative goals for limiting their greenhouse-gas emissions. These countries currently emit only a small fraction of the total, so it is understandable they want to be shown that the huge emitters are truly going to do something, rather than just talk, about cutting their own emissions.

At the same time, we need to realize that the highly populated, developing nations such as China, India, and Indonesia, will become superemitters of greenhouse gases if they follow the fossil fuel path that the current, highly industrialized nations have followed. I do not believe this will happen, however. I have faith that the current big emitters will demonstrate their commitment to the Kyoto Protocol and will help provide developing nations with the technology and capital investments to follow the soft energy path. After all, as I pointed out earlier, the soft energy path is a win-win route even without the incentive of global warming.

President Clinton, and especially Vice President Gore, have become outstanding champions of the effort to mitigate global warming. They understand the issue, can forcibly articulate it, and are using the powerful pulpits of their offices to inform and motivate millions of people to action. Vice President Gore's presence and leadership greatly influenced the successful outcome of the Kyoto Conference. For the first time since President Carter was in office, the American environmental movement has strong supporters in the White House.

However, the Kyoto Treaty triggered the outrage of defenders of the status quo. In the United States, the well-financed fossil-fuel purveyors and users' Global Climate Coalition vowed to launch a major publicity campaign to block the treaty's ratification in the senate. Republican leaders in Congress also vowed to block the treaty, openly stating that they saw this as an opportunity to humiliate Clinton and Gore and thereby advance the Republicans' chances of winning the presidency in the year 2000. Clearly these two groups believed their short-term interests were more important than the quality of their children and grandchildren's lives.

Business interests, such as the Big Three auto manufacturers, once again resorted to blackmail. They contended that the treaty would cause the loss of hundreds of thousands of jobs, maybe even millions, and drive the economy into depression. If they had data to support this outrageous, irresponsible contention, where was it? Did they use computer modeling to analyze the effects of the Kyoto Treaty on the economy as scientists did when they analyzed the global climate, a much more complex problem? If they had done this, I believe they would have found how wrong they were in predicting that huge job losses would result from the treaty.

Several nonbusiness groups *have made* in-depth studies. Their results indicate that programs to reduce global warming through more efficient use of energy and renewable energy will improve the economy, not hurt it. But there are still people willing to gamble the Earth to maintain today's market for fossil fuels and gas-guzzling automobiles or to win an election. *The New York Times* reported on April 26, 1998, that the Global Climate Coalition, under the leadership of the American Petroleum Institute, was busily planning to recruit a few dissident scientists and train them in public relations so they could lead a major effort to teach the American public that the global warming theory was based on faulty science.

Some business leaders with vision, however, see opportunity where others see calamity. John Browne, CEO of British Petroleum, has been at the forefront of multinationals willing to combat global warming. He believes business should accept scientists' conviction, "an effective consensus," that global warming is real. He calls for business to invest in energy efficiency and solar energy, and his company is the leading energy company in the development of solar energy, with a goal of reaching $1 billion of such business early in the twenty-first century. No wonder he praised the outcome of the Kyoto Conference.

On May 9, 1998, H. Josef Hebert of the Associated Press reported that twelve large industrial corporations joined British Petroleum as members of the Pew Center on Global Climate Change, committed to advancing programs to reduce global warming. Participants whose total worldwide revenue exceeds $340 billion include Boeing, Lockheed Martin, 3M, Enron, Sun Oil, United Technologies, Toyota, American Electric Power Company, Whirlpool Corporation, and Maytag. Their joint press release stated, "Climate change is one of our generation's greatest challenges. . . . We accept the views of most scientists that enough is known about the science and environmental impacts of climate change for us to take action to address its consequences."

As of November 1998, this group has grown to twenty members, including my former employer, the DuPont Company. For some time DuPont has been working in its own plants worldwide to demonstrate by example how to help solve the problem of global warming by reducing emissions of greenhouse gasses and using energy more efficiently. DuPont president and CEO John Krol, in a speech in Norway at the Environment Northern Seas Conference, on August 26, 1997, presented one of the most comprehensive and enlightened views I have read of what corporations can and should do through the development and use of new technology to advance sustainability and in the process reduce the global warming threat. He sees industry's role as responding to human needs by providing products and service with radically reduced consumption of energy and raw materials and little or no waste either in production or after the useful life of the product. He cites examples of how DuPont is doing this on a major scale in its own plants and also bringing its newest technology to bear to help developing countries acquire some of the most resource-efficient and lowest polluting plants in the world. He states, "Large multinational corporations have a moral and social obligation to help develop sustainable growth practices in developing economies." One example he uses is the importance of helping China avoid powering its growing economy with coal. Instead he believes China should be encouraged to use natural gas and renewable energy sources and to adopt the most energy-efficient technology available today.

Shell Oil Company is also concerned about global warming and, like British Petroleum, is working hard to be a leader in the solar-energy revolution. On the other hand, Exxon Corporation, a leader of solar-energy development in the early 1980s, is now under new management and is waiting for scientists to prove that global warming is not real. Eventually Exxon will be dragged kicking and screaming into the future, making money as she goes. And the oil well drillers and coal miners who lose their dirty, dangerous jobs will find new jobs making solar panels, windmills, or more energy-efficient motors and appliances.

My hope is that those politicians who work to scuttle the Kyoto agreement, giving priority to winning reelection, instead will be thrown out of office by their more enlightened constituents who give priority to the quality of life of future generations.

The threat to the global environment from technology's harmful fallout has been well illustrated by the three major examples I have discussed: nuclear energy, chlorofluorocarbons, and global warming. They also show how the world community has become increasingly sensitive to potential fallout and has developed techniques for dealing with it, such as environmental impact assessment and technology assessment. These examples demonstrate how the United Nations can now bring the interests of all the world's people to bear on these issues and can recruit worldwide resources to deal with the harmful fallout.

It is important to recognize, however, that enthusiasm for the positive results of new technology can cloud the search for negative impacts. One new field of research, where we need to be especially vigilant is biotechnology. Biotechnological research is growing explosively, promising great accomplishments such as a cure for the scourge of cancer. Biochemists at the frontier of this work quite naturally play up its potential positives and minimize its potential negatives, just as nuclear physicists and engineers did earlier for nuclear energy. And the industry that wishes to capitalize on their work will typically belittle the naysaying of regulatory bureaucrats. But society needs watchdogs who will save it from the blindness of the developers. In fact, society has a responsibility to control and regulate its products and processes—new and old—and the more threatening they are the greater the responsibility. Especially threatening are those products that can do damage on a planetary scale.

Let me emphasize again that there are many good reasons for supporting science. But just as we cannot forego the search for new knowledge, so we should not presume new technology to be innocent until proven guilty.

Science brings something even more important than the specific discoveries that it makes. It brings the scientific method—a rational means for solving problems, for searching for the truth not only in the technical arena, but in the social arena as well. It is an antidote for witchcraft and pseudo-science and myths. It involves developing a theory about what is going on in a given area and then devising and carrying out experiments to check the hypothesis. Successful experimentation brings conviction of what needs to be done. Failure calls for changing the theory and then testing the revised theory by experiment.

The world greatly needs more leaders—more decision makers and problem solvers—who are proficient in using the scientific method. The quality of future life on Earth depends upon it.

IX
A Call to Action

37

Together We Can Save the Earth

THE GREATEST THREAT TO LIFE ON EARTH IS THE GROWING IMPACT of environmental degradation stemming from uncontrolled population growth, overconsumption of resources, and harmful fallout from new technology. The three are interrelated and constitute what might be called the global predicament. Just as we have caused the global predicament, so we have the potential for solving it. To do so, we must first see ourselves as an integral part of nature, one of many species of life, all dependent on each other as well as on the air, water, land, and sun. There is evidence that we have already begun to do so.

Over the past twenty-five years there has been a growing movement that promises to avert the threatened tragedy and provide the global community with the opportunity to create a decent quality of life that will be sustainable through successive generations. This hopeful movement is the result of an escalating, worldwide enlightenment about the nature and seriousness of the global predicament.

Certainly resolving the global predicament is a worthy cause. What could be better than working to provide humanity, including one's own descendants, with a sustainable livelihood? What better vocation is there than striving to save life on Earth? The opportunity for job satisfaction is high, as millions of people have already discovered. And the risk is minor: being belittled by those who do not believe the predicament exists, those for whom the predicament is a means of making money or getting elected, and those who champion the status quo because they live only for the present.

It is true that the task is huge and the problems are still growing. The world will have eighty million more people next year. Resource consumption continues to escalate in both affluent and developing countries. Too little attention is being given to assessing

375

the potential negative impacts of new technology. Millions of people, including many world leaders, do not want to reduce population growth, constrain resource consumption or question new technology. Nevertheless, I am optimistic that if we build on the many positive trends that have been established over the past twenty-five years, we will be able to solve the global predicament, not near term, but during the lifetime of my recently born great grandchildren. This optimism stems in part from my experiences over the past twenty-five years as I traveled all over the world, meeting and working with hundreds of well informed leaders who are dedicated to resolving critical global issues and who share my positive outlook.

The Coming Together of the World Community

To resolve the global predicament, the world needs leaders who understand it, are aware of the information now available for coping with it, and can persuade others to help solve it. But leaders cannot resolve the predicament alone. A ground-up approach is required, involving millions of individual advocates around the world, along with their organizations, businesses, and governments. Over the past twenty-five years such collaboration has grown markedly, accelerating in the 1990s. Nongovernment volunteer organizations, especially environmental and population groups, have grown to tens of millions of members, become much more sophisticated, and learned to network effectively around the globe, using modern communication tools. Many business leaders have switched from fighting environmentalists to joining them. Underlying these advances has been a tremendous growth in what we know about the natural world and the forces which threaten it.

The United Nations has participated in this process by sponsoring world conferences on the environment, population, development, human settlements, women, global warming and social issues. They demonstrated the tremendous progress that has been made in understanding the nature of the global predicament and how to cope with it. Each conference was preceded by a series of preparatory meetings in which government and nongovernment participants diligently reviewed and thrashed out what must be done, then queried their respective governments on their willingness to contribute resources. During each conference a forum

Peterson with Olaf Palmé, prime minister of Sweden, at Kennedy School of Government, Harvard University, April 3, 1984. Peterson asked Palmé to take leadership with other heads of non-nuclear states to inform the world about the biological consequences of nuclear war. Palmé agreed. Courtesy of the author.

Peterson with Prince Philip of Britain and Prince Bernhard of The Netherlands at fundraising dinner for wildlife conservation. St. Johns College, Cambridge University, England, January 13, 1988. Courtesy of the author.

Russ Peterson with Her Imperial Majesty the Shahbanou of Iran and Robert Anderson, Chairman of Aspen Institute and of ARCO. Aspen Institute, Aspen, Colorado, July 1977. Courtesy of the author.

Reviewing French American Undersea Study of Mid-Atlantic Rift—the Azores, July 1974. Robert White, head of National Oceanographic and Atmospheric Administration, and Russ Peterson. Courtesy of NOAA.

Board members of Better World Society (left to right) Rodrigo Corazo, former President of Costa Rica, Julia Henderson, Peterson, President Arias, Ted Turner, Jean Michel Cousteau, Ambassador Zhou, General Obasanjo, former president of Nigeria. San José, Costa Rica, Home of President Arias, February 12, 1988. Courtesy of the author.

Lillian and Russ Peterson in Antartica with Gentoo penguins. January 1987. Courtesy of the author.

Meeting of leaders of Global Atmospheric Research Program's Atlantic Tropical Experiment with President Leopold Senghor (center), with Robert White, head of NOAA on his right and Guy Stever, head of National Science Foundation on his left at the President's Office, Dakar, Senegal, July 1974. Courtesy of NOAA.

Prince Bernhard pinning Order of the Golden Ark on Russ Peterson. Soestdijk Palace, The Netherlands, October 5, 1985. Courtesy of the author.

Peterson with Prince Sadruddin Aga Khan and his wife. Soestdijk Palace, the Netherlands, October 5, 1985. Courtesy of the author.

separate from the proceedings of the official delegations also took place, involving thousands of knowledgeable, dedicated nongovernment participants. The forum permitted activists from many countries to meet and learn from each other, plan together, influence their official delegations, and agree to return home to advocate more action by their respective governments.

In the previous chapter on population I described in some detail my first rewarding exposure to a UN conference, the one on population in Bucharest in 1974 where I served as vice chairman of the U.S. Delegation. In 1976 I served in the same capacity at the UN Conference in Vancouver on Human Settlements. By then I was getting to know many of the exciting people who participated regularly in international conferences on environmental issues.

One of these was Barbara Ward who had been knighted Lady Jackson by the British Crown. She and René Dubos had co-authored the book, *Only One Earth,* as background for the 1972 Conference on the Environment. Lady Jackson and I had gotten to know each other over dinner at an earlier meeting in San Francisco, and I thought her a brilliant, compassionate, warm person. Now she was to give the keynote speech at Vancouver. When we met, she insisted I spend some time with Nobel Prize-winning Mother Teresa who was to speak at the forum. She knew that I was a free-thinking Unitarian, so I could not help wondering if she were trying to save me; she herself had left the Church of England to become a devout Roman Catholic.

Mother Teresa and I met privately for one whole hour. This diminutive woman in her simple white habit initiated our conversation by saying, with a twinkle in her eyes, "Lady Jackson said you were a do-gooder like she and I are." What a compliment, coming from one of the greatest humanitarians of all time.

Not long before, I had visited the Calcutta slums where Mother Teresa launched her world-famous Sisters of Charity to help the poorest of the poor, so I asked her to tell me about her work among them. It is difficult to relate her enthusiasm for what she was doing. She emphasized the strength of these people—how with modest help they could make important strides in improving their lives, how they helped each other, how much they still needed our help. Then she asked me about my role in protecting the environment and displayed a profound knowledge of the subject and a love of all life. What a moving experience our hour together was.

Peterson with two untouchables, India. 1978. Courtesy of the author.

She encouraged me to join her on the dais that afternoon when she spoke at the forum. Just three of us were on the dais—Mother Teresa, a young Kenyan, Dr. Julia Ojiambo, who introduced Mother Teresa, and me. The small dais was in the center of a large circular arena with thousands seated around it. As I listened to Mother Teresa's message, tears came to my eyes. It was not hard to feel love for this woman who absolutely radiated her own love of humanity. Even later, when I congratulated her on her speech, her selflessness was apparent. Instead of thanking me she said, "Don't forget the poor."

In September 1997, this 86-year-old nun died in Calcutta. Those she served poured out their sorrow, love, and thanks. Hundreds of thousands passed by her bier. Most nations of the world sent representatives to her funeral; millions who admired her watched the service on television. It is believed that someday the Roman Catholic Church will make her a saint. In my view, she already is.

✳   ✳   ✳

Mother Teresa speaking at the United Nations World Conference on Human Settlements in Vancouver with Dr. Julia Ojiambo from Kenya and Peterson on dais. June 1976. Courtesy of the author.

I have followed closely the proceedings of all the UN world conferences since 1972. The growth in the number of participants, in their sophistication and commitment, and in the harmony and resolution of the meetings has been impressive. The 1972 Conference on the Environment in Stockholm gave the world its first clear picture of the escalating threat to the global environment and called for establishing the United Nations Environment Programme (UNEP). In the intervening years UNEP has played a key role in involving the family of nations in confronting environmental problems. One of UNEP's particularly significant accomplishments was its success, through the Montreal Protocol and other agreements, at getting countries to work together to establish goals for stopping the production of chlorofluorocarbons that are destroying the earth's protective ozone layer. I served on the governing board of UNEP in 1974 and have been active with it ever since, including helping UNEP plan the 1992 Conference on the Environment and Development in Rio de Janeiro.

Among the contributions of the 1992 conference was the establishment of Agenda 21, a worldwide effort to improve our environment in the twenty-first century. The agenda set national goals and timetables for reducing the emissions of greenhouse gasses. It also sparked establishment of the United Nations Council on Sustainable Development to assist nations and businesses in facing up to the need to use resources in ways that do not shortchange future generations.

The Rio conference became known as the Earth Summit which was a direct result of a 1991 meeting in New York. Two former U.S. cabinet officers, Edmund Muskie and Elliot Richardson, UN Secretary General Perez de Cuellar, Jeffrey Laurenti of the United Nations, and I met to discuss the forthcoming conference. Prior to going to de Cuellar's office, the two former secretaries and I met in the International Hotel. When I told them I planned to encourage the secretary general to make the Rio conference a summit meeting and invite all heads of state, Elliot Richardson objected. He felt that heads of state would not attend a conference solely on the environment. I argued that protecting the global environment was of major importance and the fact that few heads of state paid any attention to it was all the more reason to call a summit meeting. Before attending they would have to study environmental issues and stake out some positions, thereby getting themselves and their countries more involved.

When we met with the secretary general I presented my suggestion and the rationale behind it. Secretary Muskie, whose view carried great weight in UN circles, strongly supported me. As we talked, Secretary General de Cuellar became increasingly interested and called in some of his top aides to discuss specifics. They, too, were interested and agreed to pursue the idea. Secretary Muskie and I subsequently met with leaders of the U.S. Congress to gain their support in encouraging President Bush to attend. No doubt we played a role in getting the conference named the Earth Summit and bringing together the largest group of heads of state ever assembled, with 110 attending, including President Bush. The Earth Summit, as well as the 1994 Cairo Conference on Population and Development, became, in essence, conferences on the global predicament. Both gatherings recognized the essential need for considering the interconnecting problems of population growth, environmental degradation, human development, resource consumption, and poverty.

The deep involvement of women in the Cairo conference and the official recognition of the important and necessary role of women in resolving the global predicament added an important dimension. The Program of Action called for a major effort to empower, educate and improve the reproductive health of women. The UN conference on women held in Beijing in 1995 impressively expanded on the importance of this effort. Their empowerment is now growing rapidly and will add immeasurably to the worldwide collaboration that is needed to resolve the global predicament.

The United States has played a prime role in all these conferences and has, with bipartisan political support, given major financial support to the United Nations and to international programs in family planning, humanitarian aid, and environmental protection. However, it has lagged seriously in recent years, falling well behind other industrialized nations relative to their Gross Domestic Products. The UN itself is being starved by the failure of some of the largest countries to pay their dues in full. The United States is the U.N.'s biggest deadbeat. As of January 1998, we owed the United Nations $1.3 billion, seriously hamstringing its operations.

In November 1997, I had dinner in New York with UN Secretary General Kofi Annan and Ted Turner. The secretary general described the UN's serious financial predicament. He had, for example, temporarily borrowed money from the UN Peacekeeping Fund to meet the monthly payroll. He pointed out that in the following week, the U.S. House of Representatives would be voting on whether to pay the United States' past dues. Ted Turner offered to contact his congressman, Newt Gingrich, the next day. But Newt did not produce.

The next week the House adjourned for six weeks without acting, having failed to muster the votes necessary to block an outrageous antiabortion amendment that Representative Chris Smith of New Jersey perennially attempts to attach to important legislation. This congressman wants to force his religious convictions on everyone. He is the antithesis of what the United States and the United Nations stand for—religious tolerance, brotherhood, and pluralism.

This downturn in U.S. support for solving the global predicament, toward saving the Earth, or if you prefer, toward saving God's creation, has paralleled the growth of the conservative, head-in-the-sand political movement. It reached its nadir in 1994–96 when Republicans under Senator Dole and Speaker Gingrich took control of Congress and assigned long term antienvironment, antifamily planning, antihumanitarian aid, anti-United Nations members of Congress to head those congressional committees that dealt with global issues. They chopped programs that had been built up by bipartisan action over the years, going so far as to slash funds for international family planning available in fiscal 1996 by 85 percent, thereby causing tens of millions of unwanted pregnancies and millions of abortions. Fortunately, their most threatening attacks were blocked by President Clinton's vetoes and threats of veto, as well as by the votes of moderate members of Congress, including some Republicans.

The true philosophy of the national Republican party in 1996 was spelled out in the party's platform developed by delegates from all areas of the country and unanimously endorsed at its national convention. It was so extreme that even the party's conservative candidate for president, Bob Dole, could not stomach it, hiding behind his contention that he had not bothered to read it.

From Elephant to Donkey

For fifty years I was a moderate to liberal Republican. When I was governor, we Delaware Republicans were the liberals and the Democrats the conservatives. Next, I cherished a year's work with moderate Republican Governor Nelson Rockefeller before going to work in the White House for conservative Republicans Nixon and Ford. At this point I started to become a rebel within the party, trying to change its positions. I had some successes and some failures.

During the Ford Administration I tried unsuccessfully, despite help from Vice President Nelson Rockefeller, to persuade the president to approve funding for the Council on Environmental Quality to study long-range global issues. When Jimmy Carter became president, he approved such a program and at the end of his term he issued his respected *Global 2000* study, our government's first comprehensive look at the global predicament. Although we came from different parties, Jimmy Carter and I had become good friends when we were governors. I was in the White House with him or his aides about once a month during the four years of his administration, and I fulfilled several assignments at his request.

Ronald Reagan and I had also served simultaneously as governors. Although from the same party, we had frequent collisions at governors' conferences. On becoming president, Reagan denigrated Carter's *Global 2000* and launched his own crusade to undo environmental protection and family planning. Through his Secretary of the Interior James Watt and his Administrator of EPA Anne Gorsuch, he sought to undermine the nation's environmental regulations and institutions. But strong bipartisan sentiment in Congress blocked most of his attack on environmental laws. During this time I was president of the National Audubon Society, lobbying Congress and opposing the president. I also worked with other national environmental leaders to rally our troops nationwide. Not surprisingly, President Reagan ignored my requests to discuss environmental, population, and nuclear energy issues during his eight years in the White House. I had a similar experience with Republican President George Bush.

During this time I got to know many members of Congress, mainly Democrats, with whom I shared a similar view of the world. Democratic Senators Al Gore, Tim Wirth, and George Mitchell, and Republican Senator John Chafee of Rhode Island, another former colleague as governor, greatly impressed me.

In 1992 when I was asked by the Clinton-Gore Campaign for the presidency to cochair Environmentalists for Clinton-Gore, and in 1996 to cochair Republicans for Clinton-Gore, I was pleased to do so. I travelled around the country campaigning for them. As a former Republican governor, I received much attention from the news media.

I was especially pleased after the Clinton-Gore victory when President Clinton made Vice President Gore his right arm and located him in the White House and also made Tim Wirth his undersecretary of state for global issues. These two men are among the best informed and most dedicated leaders in the world when it comes to the problems related to population, environment, and resource use. They became leaders at UN conferences on the global predicament and helped to regain America's leadership in this cause. Others in key positions on the Clinton team who share a similar commitment are my long-time friend, former Governor Bruce Babbitt, who is secretary of the interior; Jack Gibbons, who succeeded me as director of the Office of Technol-

Al Gore, candidate for the vice presidency; Tom Carper, candidate for governor of Delaware; and Peterson, who introduced Gore. Clinton-Gore rally, New Castle, Delaware. *The News Journal,* **Fred Comegys, September 30, 1992. Courtesy of** *The News Journal.*

ogy Assessment and is now science advisor to the president; and Caroline Browner, administrator of the Environmental Protection Agency. Secretary of State Madeleine Albright (our former ambassador to the United Nations) can be counted on to help strengthen the UN's role in resolving the global predicament. At a recent meeting in Wilmington, Delaware, she expressed at length her dedication to this cause.

On several occasions in recent years I seriously considered switching my registration to the Democratic party. But my Republican friends, who tend to be moderate Republicans, always talked me out of it. I should remain in the party, they told me, so I could help move the party back to the center. However, after the disastrous actions of the Republican-led Congress in 1994–96, and after an extremist party platform was adopted in 1996, it was obvious the party was moving farther and farther to the right. I concluded I could do little in my remaining lifetime to help turn that around. I also knew time was running out on our facing up

Jack Jurden, *The News Journal.* **October 1996. Courtesy of** *The News Journal.*

to the global predicament. The world needed American leadership. So did my children and grandchildren and future generations everywhere. My best bet, I concluded, was to get behind the
Clinton-Gore team and help them where I could, while simultaneously encouraging the national environmental and population
groups to lobby Congress.

So, on October 8, 1996, I became a Democrat.

Two days later I spoke at a large rally for Vice President Al
Gore at the University of Delaware. When I was introduced by the
chairman of the Delaware Democratic Party, I received a standing
ovation. I was also warmly welcomed into the party by the other
speakers, all friends of mine, Governor Tom Carper, U.S. Senator
Joe Biden and Vice President Al Gore. The Governor told the
crowd that I had been quoted in a newspaper as wondering
whether the Democratic Party would welcome me. He asked, "Do
you welcome him?" He repeated this three times, receiving an
ever louder, "Yes" each time. And when the vice president spoke,
his message was music to my ears. After years of feeling abandoned by the Republican Party, I had found a home.

The news media and many friends, including those who are still Republicans, treated my switch kindly. I received only three hate letters, each with a religious twist. One anonymous Republican wrote to the "Dishonorable Governor Peterson," calling me a traitor and telling me I would get my comeuppance when I met my Maker and He sends me to Hell. The writer apparently thought that God is a Republican.

Time to Invest in Saving Our Earth

The time is ripe for the U.S. to regain its leadership in tackling our global problems and to invest generously in the effort. No other investment offers as high a long-term return. The question is, "Where will the money come from?

One good source would be from what the Center for Defense Information calls the "sacred military cow," that is, the Pentagon. Pushed by the world's most potent lobby, the military-industrial complex and its huge retinue of hangers-on who make their money and/or reputations supporting it, the United States government continues to pour tens of billions of dollars per year into military programs not needed for our military security. The Center for Defense Information, led by distinguished former military officers, convincingly makes the case that the U.S. could safely reduce its annual military spending from the current level of $270 billion to about $200 billion. That would free $70 billion for other purposes. It appears to me that any portion of that $70 billion invested in solving the global predicament would buy much more security for Americans and other people of the world than the same amount spent on our military.

Although diverting some excess military money to this global predicament project is logical and reasonable, there are other sources, as well. For example, the opportunity for investing wisely and profitably in such a project is so compelling that if our leaders were to articulate that opportunity forcefully and ask for more taxes to realize it, I believe the American people would agree. But political leaders do not often ask their constituents to contribute tax dollars to a sacred cause. They are too busy trying to buy their constituents' votes by promising a reduction in their taxes. The truth is that it would cost each citizen of the U.S. only $4 per year for this nation to provide a billion dollars toward solving the global predicament. Or $40 a year for a $10 billion program.

It is outrageous and shameful that so many politicians continue to harp on reducing taxes as if tax reduction, by itself, were a sacred cause. What is even more disturbing is how so many of us get conned by such messages. Instead we should be asking about the true cost of such shortsighted, antisocial pandering. What obligation must our society renege on as a result of cutting taxes? At what cost to our children's future, to the disadvantaged, to the environment? How much better it would be if we asked how we could invest a few more tax dollars in building a better society and a better world.

Particularly ridiculous is the politicians' fear of raising gasoline taxes. This is sheer folly, considering the good that could be accomplished if only we had the sense to submit to an additional tax of, say, fifty cents per gallon. For every penny per gallon of gasoline tax, the nation collects one billion dollars. Every other industrialized country taxes two to three dollars per gallon of gasoline and uses that money to build and maintain roads and bridges and support public transportation. For us as well, this would be a fair and reasonable user fee to cover the horrendous cost of our love affair with the automobile. Yet a recently passed tax of only four cents per gallon to help balance the budget triggered a major uproar in the 1996 presidential election. In addition, if auto manufacturers would stop fighting legislation to raise the fuel economy standards and get on with doubling the miles per gallon as they surely can, then we could markedly increase the gasoline tax without also increasing our personal budgets for fuel.

Vehicle customers, often unknowingly, are contributing to the problem when they buy ever more pick-up trucks and vans instead of conventional cars. Since pick-ups and vans are exempt from fuel efficiency standards enacted in the 1970s, many old cars going to the junkyards have higher fuel efficiency on the average than some new passenger vehicles. Moreover, the consumption of gasoline has been skyrocketing. Its price in constant dollars is the lowest in history. But since we now import over half of what we use, our energy security is at a much lower level than when we were in the energy crisis of the 1970s. At that time we were importing only 30 percent of the oil we consumed.

A day of reckoning is coming. Early next century world oil production will peak and start a long decline toward zero. This is what happened in 1970 in our lower forty-eight states when oil production there peaked, then started its continuous decline.

The Promising Collaborative Approach

Governments and international governmental organizations are no longer the sole actors. The private sector, in the form of individuals and a huge number of non-governmental organizations (NGOs), is now playing an important role in shaping global strategies. All the players are now benefitting from the computer and communication revolutions that markedly facilitate the collaborative process.

As a follow-up to the 1992 Conference on Environment and Development, President Clinton appointed the President's Council on Sustainable Development to chart a course for the U.S. to achieve long-term economic growth while preserving the nation's natural resources. The council also functioned as a network of business executives, heads of national environmental organizations, members of the president's cabinet, and leaders of labor and civil rights groups. Jonathan Lash, president of the World Resources Institute, and David T. Buzzelli, vice president of Dow Chemical Company, cochaired the group. After nearly three years of work the council reached consensus: the twin goals of environmental protection and economic development are mutually supportable, so there should be partnership between them instead of conflict.

The Global Tomorrow Coalition (GTC) of environmental, population, business, labor, and other civic groups also clearly demonstrated, through its Globescope Conferences around the country, the power of citizen groups who come together to discuss the critical global issues. It was exciting to participate in some of those regional meetings where leaders from many different communities gathered for several days in serious workshops to learn from each other and to develop local plans of action for facing up to the global issues. Those conferences built a significant ongoing commitment to resolve the global predicament by "thinking globally and acting locally."

Nongovernment environmental organizations, now networking with many other groups, have become a formidable force for educating and motivating citizens to fight for all the interconnecting global issues. They reach tens of millions of citizens with their publications and calls to action. I believe this is the main reason why polls now repeatedly show that Americans overwhelmingly (60 to 80 percent) support environmental protection, international family planning, foreign humanitarian aid, and the United Nations. Certainly this enlightenment has not—until recently—come from the podiums of our elected officials.

In contrast, politicians who give priority to getting reelected fail at what we have elected them to accomplish. We need ways to get such people *un*-elected and to replace them with responsible leaders who will work on the community's problems, and be willing to risk losing an election in pursuit of what is right. Term limits will help.

It is surprising that so few candidates for office make protecting our global environment the prime plank in their platform. Were they to do so, they would find that a potent constituency already exists and is just waiting to be led. If we could elect a majority in Congress who would deal with the critical global issues and capitalize on citizen support for these issues, Congress could put the United States where it belongs: as the world leader in resolving the global predicament. It is essential to the well-being of our grandchildren and all future generations that we make this happen.

Nongovernment organizations have also done a good job of collaborating in drafting legislation, getting it passed and seeing that it is enforced in the courts. The Natural Resources Defense Council, the Environmental Defense Fund, the Sierra Club Legal Defense Fund and the Environmental Law Institute have contributed much in this area. All of them were created about the same time, only twenty-five years ago.

Foundations and wealthy individuals also have played a significant role, not only in funding existing nongovernment organizations, but also in creating new institutions to support specific high priority objectives. Without them the environmental movement would not have gotten very far. Robert Allen, formerly executive director of the Kendall Foundation, was particularly adept at orchestrating support for multi-NGO efforts. For example, he and I founded the Group of Ten—the CEOs of the ten largest national environmental organizations. He stimulated us to pool our efforts to attack major problems and found the donors to back us. One project involved the joint participation of all ten CEOs in writing the 1985 book, *An Environmental Agenda For The Future*. This exercise helped us point our agendas toward the most important issues.

The Threat of Nuclear War

One of the Group of Ten's top priority issues was to face up to the threat of nuclear war. Toward this end Bob Allen joined with Robert Scrivner of the Rockefeller Brothers Fund to define the need for and raise the money to analyze nuclear war's devastating consequences to the entire world, not just to the nations who might be involved in an exchange of bombs. They invited me to chair such an effort. We assembled more than 100 world-renowned scientists, about half physicists and half biologists. Carl Sagan led the physicists and Paul Ehrlich the biologists. They focused on a newly completed study by Carl Sagan and others. That 1982 study described potential climatic changes from a nuclear exchange. It indicated that a series of nuclear detonations would create dust storms that would block sunlight, causing a few degrees temperature loss worldwide for many months, leading to the death by starvation of a billion people around the world—in addition to the billion people killed outright by the blasts, heat, and radiation. We organized a major conference of scientists and public leaders in Washington in 1983. The conference culminated in a discussion among United States and Soviet experts assembled in Washington and a group of Soviet National Academy of Science leaders assembled in Moscow, in the first-ever satellite television link of its kind. This collaborative effort occurred almost a decade before Glasnost.

The televised discussion and much of the conference were carried live throughout the Soviet Union, but no U.S. network picked up the Soviet-U.S. nuclear winter dialogue, not even for one minute on the evening news. However, Ted Turner's superstation televised a delayed broadcast of the ninety-minute trans-Atlantic discussion. The conference and the extensive publicity it received in the Soviet Union may have been factors in reducing the nuclear "trigger finger" mentality prevailing in some quarters there at that time and in starting a movement to end the cold war.

Some Soviet Scientists Think So

Scientists have always had a higher status in the Soviet Union than in most countries and have had close ties to Soviet leadership. This was particularly true when Mikhail Gorbachev became chairman. Academician Velikov, the head of the Soviet Academy of Sciences who chaired the Soviet group in the TV dialogue on nuclear war, actually travelled with Gorbachev to international conferences. He claimed that it became broadly accepted among Soviet leaders that a nuclear exchange would destroy their country, and thus any strategy to use such weapons would be foolhardy. Most American scientists shared this view but a few, especially Edward Teller, the father of the hydrogen bomb, convinced President Reagan to spend billions of dollars on the wishful goal of exempting the U.S. from such mutually assured destruction by building a "star wars" shield over America. In later years when President Reagan took credit for winning the Cold War, a top aide to Gorbachev said, "That's like the rooster taking credit for the dawn." Soviet scientists like to quote this analogy.

Shortly after this joint U.S.-Soviet presentation I wrote, as chairman of the Committee on the Consequences of Nuclear War (CCNW), to President Reagan, asking for an appointment. Several of us wanted to meet with him to express our concern about the long term atmospheric and biological consequences of nuclear war. This led to a meeting on June 12, 1984 at the U.S. Arms Control and Disarmament Agency (ACDA) with its director, Kenneth L. Adelman, and forty-one others from the Departments of Defense and State, the White House, the Central Intelligence Agency and ACDA. Carl Sagan, Chaplin Tyler, our executive director, and I represented CCNW. The key people who planned our country's nuclear weapon strategy, including those who actually selected the targets at which our missiles were pointed were there. The president's chief arms control and disarmament negotiators with the Soviets were also there: Ambassador Edward L. Rowny and Ambassador Paul Nitze.

After my introduction, Carl Sagan gave a brilliant chart talk using the technical and in-house lingo of the nuclear warriors to describe how they held the world's fate in their hands. A lengthy, serious discussion ensued but the conclusion of the meeting was encapsulated in Paul Nitze's statement, "So what? All we need to do is to retarget our missiles to avoid burning large cities, thereby lofting less soot into the atmosphere."

We concluded that we had not changed any minds. But one month later Kenneth Adelman told me that the meeting had an important impact: it lead to much discussion and concern in the upper echelons of the Reagan Administration about the long-term biological impact of a nuclear exchange. The Department of Defense subsequently launched a study of the significance of nuclear winter to the department's strategic planning for nuclear warfare and civil defense.

Carl Sagan and Paul Ehrlich, the U.S. principals in the Soviet-U.S. TV dialogue on nuclear war, are recognized as highly accomplished scientists and professors who have excelled at bringing the world of science alive in the average home. Sagan's TV series, *Cosmos,* reached 400 million people and made him a worldwide celebrity—likely the greatest popularizer of science of all time. Ehrlich's book, *The Population Bomb,* was a best-seller that alerted millions to the long-term threat of world population growth. Both were early advocates for facing up to the global predicament. Both helped members of the world's major religions in their recent efforts to come together to save the Earth.

As a result of their celebrity status and deep involvement as public advocates, they were looked down upon by many pure scientists who traditionally stay confined in their laboratories, publish only in important technical journals incomprehensible to the average citizen, and resent colleagues who venture into the public arena. Yet, thanks to scientists like Sagan and Ehrlich, the public better understands the importance of science and more easily supports federal funding of research by university-bound scientists. Eventually both were elected to the National Academy of Science but, as some members have reported, only after some of their less prestigious colleagues decided not to block their election.

One day in New York City I walked down the street with Carl Sagan to the United Nations building where we were to meet with Secretary General de Cuellar. It was amazing how many people, young and old, paused to say, "Hello, Mr. Sagan" or "Hi, Dr. Sagan" or "Thanks, Carl."

Our goal that day was to encourage the secretary general to speak out on the threat of nuclear war to all life on Earth. We emphasized that since he was the only person who could speak for all the world's people, it was his duty to articulate the nuclear threat. He agreed to do so, but pointed out that few in the news media paid any attention to him. "*The New York Times* puts my words on a back page, if they publish them at all," he said. We promised to help him with his message and to encourage the U.S. news media to cover it.

He produced a strong message. But he was right. The news media paid little attention. Even *The New York Times* buried it.

Not long afterward, I called my friends Marian Heiskell and John Oakes, influential members of the Sulzberger family who own and run *The New York Times,* to see about meeting with the editorial board to explain the biological consequences of a nuclear war. On several occasions in the past, starting when I was governor, I had met with their editorial board for lunch when publisher Arthur Ochs Sulzberger, Jr. and his key lieutenants were present. Now I was informed that I would have that opportunity again on June 10, 1985.

I called Carl Sagan to see if he would be free. He was, and I notified the *Times* that Sagan, Jacob Scherr, our executive director, and I would be there. I also telephoned Karl Meyer, who arranged editorial-board meetings, to explain what we wished to discuss. When we arrived we were ushered into a small meeting room, not the publisher's dining room. Karl Meyer and three other members of the editorial staff joined us. We were disillusioned when Meyer asked, "Now what are you here for?" After our presentation and response to a few perfunctory questions Meyer terminated the meeting. No one took any notes. And there was no lunch!

So Carl and I enjoyed a hot dog on a street corner, wondering what happened.

A careful survey of *The New York Times* in subsequent days indicated we had no impact. No editorial appeared. And so we had failed. Months later I was told confidentially that the *Times'* principal science advisor did not agree with our message and did not like either Carl or me.

Carl Sagan died at the young age of 62 on December 20, 1996. He had made a major contribution to the world. *The New York Times* put his picture on the front page and ran a long and laudatory obituary, including a reference to his work on nuclear winter.

I miss Carl. In 1989 he invited me to be one of the five members on the board of his Institute on Extraterrestrial Intelligence. As

I was completely overextended at the time, I reluctantly turned him down. Now I wish I had joined his institute's search for life elsewhere, crying out so to speak, "Are you there? Is anyone listening?"

Someday, Carl, the answer will come back, "Yes, we are!"

Religion and Business Join In

An especially heartening change that gives much hope for the future is the mobilizing of religious groups to save the Earth. Many now take the biblical admonition for man to take dominion over the Earth to mean that humans have the God-given responsibility to serve as good stewards of the Earth.

Reverend Douglas Hunt, who coordinated the coalition of environmental, population and women's groups at the 1994 Cairo Conference, believes that the most effective way to organize people is with a sense of hope and empowerment, which is the language of the church. He points out how the ecumenical movement to save the Earth has been building over the past 25 years. An early crusader for this was the Reverend James Parks Morton, Dean of the Cathedral of St. John the Divine in New York City, one of the largest religious congregations in the world. At first he had difficulty getting other clerics to forego their belief that man is the center of the cosmos. But over the years, with the help of scientists, including Carl Sagan and Paul Ehrlich, he gradually won over clerics from several religious faiths. In 1990, the Joint Appeal on Religion and Science for the Environment, an outcome of Morton's work, was launched to convince top-level religious leadership to take action on the global environmental crisis. This led to the establishment in 1993 of the National Faith Partnership for the Environment, consisting of the U.S. Catholic Conference, the National Council of Churches, the Coalition on the Environment and Jewish Life, and the Evangelical Environmental Network. This consortium is now enlisting churches and synagogues across the continent to become advocates for the environment.

As an outcome of a 1986 Worldwide Fund for Nature conference in Assisi, Italy, an alliance was forged between conservationists and five of the world's great religions—Islam, Christianity, Hinduism, Buddhism, and Judaism. Out of this has grown increased communication among the groups and joint efforts to advance understanding and commitment to protecting the Earth. I believe this growing spiritual force can help bring the world community together to resolve the global predicament.

Also encouraging is the growing cooperation between business and environmental leaders. For too long the gospel according to Wall Street has decreed that environmental regulations cost jobs and hurt business. But now many chief executives have learned from their own experience that environmental regulations can actually benefit the bottom line—that they create jobs and business opportunities.

Most of them now agree, as does the conservative economist and Nobel Laureate Milton Friedman, that the forces of the free marketplace do not insure the freedom to breathe clean air, drink safe water, save endangered species, or protect the ozone layer. These freedoms require government regulation.

This enlightened view by business is very important. Without it, the nations of the world cannot develop an environmentally sustainable economy. Because business is responsible for much of the past and present damage to the environment, it must now be the locus for correcting many of the problems. Business has the necessary capital, technical competence and management know-how to develop the environmentally benign products and processes that will be required. Many multinational corporations have more resources and much more power to make things happen on the global scene than most nation states.

I believe that a revolution is now taking place. Enlightened corporate leaders are beginning to see business as a positive force in integrating economic growth with many environmental objectives. Not only do they agree with the concept of environmentally sustainable development, but also they see industry as a principal actor in promulgating this concept. As they build new manufacturing plants in developing countries, they are installing technology that provides low, if not zero, emissions. In so doing they are giving these poorer countries a jump start toward sound economic development.

A world leader in this enlightened approach is Edgar S. Woolard, former CEO and chairman of the board of The DuPont Company. Almost immediately upon becoming CEO in 1989, he told a meeting of the International Chamber of Commerce in London that industry had a duty and responsibility to be a leader in environmental protection. He soon became known as the environmental president of DuPont.

An example of his leadership was pointing DuPont, a giant operator of pollution-prone chemical, oil, coal and pharmaceutical industries, toward the twin goals of zero pollution and zero waste. DuPont is making good progress toward those goals in its plants all over the world. In the U.S. it has reduced emissions of airborne carcinogens by 70 percent since 1987, and expects a 90 percent reduction by 2000. At its plants in Canada and in the Asia Pacific region, DuPont has reduced such emissions by 75 percent since 1990, and plans to cut greenhouse gas emissions substantially by the end of this decade. A recently started-up plant in Indonesia has been designed for zero waste and emissions. Similar progress is occurring in many large multinational companies, including CIBA-Geigy, ICI, 3M, BMW, Dow, BASF and Cannon.

The Second Annual World Congress on Zero Emissions, sponsored by the United Nations University in 1996, challenged business to achieve zero emissions and good economic growth at the same time. Woolard told the conference that if society is to achieve its goal of sustainable development, only industry has the required resources to make it happen.

Recognizing that attaining zero emissions is only one step toward protecting the global environment, Woolard identified land use as another pressing issue. He pointed out that in many countries, greenfields (productive open spaces) continue to be used for industrial development while abandoned areas, so-called brownfields, are not used. He called for a goal of zero development of greenfields the world over.

For industry to work toward such a goal goes well beyond using brownfields. It spotlights the need to preserve open spaces—to avoid building on prime farmland, wetlands, and other critical natural areas. It encourages increased production per acre at existing plant sites rather than expanding to new sites.

Woolard of DuPont, Buzzelli of Dow Chemical, John Browne of British Petroleum, Keizo Yamaji of Canon, Curt Nicolin of Asea Brown Boveri and other world industrialists are clearly pioneers who share an enlightened view of the role of industry in protecting the global environment. It would be naive to conclude, however, the whole business community will easily develop such a far-sighted approach. The powerful forces that impel business and government to push for endless growth, for ever more economic development, will be hard to restrain. But they can and must be restrained.

The CEO of Dow Chemical Company, William S. Stavropoulos, announced recently that Dow would invest one-billion dollars over the ensuing ten years to improve its environmental, health, and safety performance. It has already budgeted $100 million, expecting a 30 to 40 percent return on that investment. Stavropoulos points out that industry's long-term concern about the bottom line should foster environmental progress, not hinder it. Poor environmental performance wastes a company's precious resources—its raw materials, capital, people, and the support of their communities. The key requirement is foresight. Exhibiting this quality in abundance, Dow's CEO claimed that industry will lead the next wave of environmentalism, shifting from protest to prevention, from regulation to responsibility.

At the 1996 World Chemical Industry Forum in Paris, executives of major auto companies, electric utilities, and consulting firms joined chemical company leaders in discussing how to reduce pollution and use resources, especially energy, more efficiently. They agreed that industry had an opportunity and responsibility to protect the environment and, in the process, improve its own bottom line.

This conference served the important function of exposing many top executives to the examples provided by out-front companies in advancing environmental protection. Thus it helped to strengthen their newfound commitment to environmentally sustainable development. Environmental protection has now become one of the fastest growing sectors of the global economy, aided by a persistent flow of environmental regulations.

In 1996 the Environmental Protection Agency concluded that between 1970 and 1990 the U.S. spent $436 billion to clean the air, but produced $6.8 trillion in benefits to human health. That is a $16 return on each dollar expended. And this study did not include such benefits as reducing air pollution damage to crops and forests and reducing cancer from airborne toxic chemicals.

The Importance of Education

Another hopeful sign is the burgeoning interest in the natural world and the threats to it. More students graduating with degrees in some aspect of environmental science or environmental law go on to influential positions in business, government and public interest organizations, thereby educating others. A 1997 survey by the National Environmental Education and Training Foundation showed that 95 percent of the American public strongly supports environmental education in the schools.

Universities have recognized that solving critical global problems requires more comprehensive education than is traditionally offered via the separate discipline approach. As a result, some have established interdisciplinary educational and research programs and are offering courses that cut across the disciplines. However, universities need still more commitment to expanding multidisciplinary training, as I have already explained.

Another influential group who could help is the network broadcasters who do far too little to inform their huge audiences about the major issues that impact so greatly on our future. Walter Cronkite once told me that of all the things he covered in his many years as anchorman for *CBS Evening News,* he was most proud of what he and other anchormen had done in helping to launch the "environmental revolution." We need more Cronkites now.

The Need for Leadership

The major progress I have described in advancing collaboration from the grass roots up brings hope for resolving the global predicament. This work needs to be augmented by committed world leaders who will not dictate, but rather will coordinate, facilitate, and inspire. Of special importance is the effective leadership of both the United Nations and the United States. I believe the new secretary general of the United Nations, Kofi Annan, clearly understands the global predicament and will increase the commitment exhibited by his able predecessor, Boutros Boutros Ghali. He has strong support from the developing countries whose participation in resolving the global predicament is particularly important. He is ably backed by Gus Speth, the head of the United Nations Development Programme, who helps coordinate UN agencies most involved with the population, resources, environment and development issues. (Gus is a good friend from the United States who helped found the Natural Resources Defense

Walter Cronkite and Russ Peterson on Cronkite's boat *Wyntje.* **Martha's Vineyard, September 6, 1984. Courtesy of the author.**

Council, was chairman of the Council on Environmental Quality, and founded the World Resources Institute.)

Most countries look up to United States for leadership in this area. The Clinton Administration has the potential to fill that role well, if it gets more backing by Congress. The president is extremely well served in this area by Vice President Al Gore and Secretary of State Madeleine Albright. They have put environmental issues in the mainstream of America's foreign policy.

The Final Word

To those who argue that our global family is careening toward disaster by pursuing a way of life that is unsustainable, I reply that we know how to avoid it. We know how to change the current trends. If we work together we *can* change them.

We can stabilize the world population and then lower it. We can use resources more efficiently and reduce wasteful consumption.

We can stop using the Gross Domestic Product (GDP) as a measure of progress and replace it with the Genuine Progress Indicator (GPI). We can prevent most pollution at its source. We can forgo development that threatens our natural life support systems. We can, through early assessment of new technology, capitalize on its beneficial impacts while avoiding its harmful effects. We can save plant and animal species from the current tidal wave of extinction. We can further the revolution that has been occurring in environmental education and in the involvement of women and of business, religious, non-governmental, and governmental institutions in these causes. These are not pipe dreams. As this book shows, the world is already making them happen.

I say to the armchair strategists who belittle my optimism, "Stand up and help change the threatening trends of today. Even if you try and fail, how much better than not having tried at all." Each of us can make a difference. It is our moral duty to recognize the wondrous uniqueness of life on Earth and to dedicate ourselves to passing it on in good health to future generations.

We need not wait for others. Each of us has within us the high authority to act. Our individual actions, added together, will give us the power to save the Earth, the only known home of any life anywhere.

Epilogue

On may 9, 1998, i went back to the rocks on the christina River in Wilmington, Delaware, where the Swedes landed in 1638. This time it was to participate in the commissioning of an authentic replica of the *Kalmar Nyckel,* the 139 foot, three-masted warship that brought the Swedes, the first Europeans, to the Delaware Valley.

This was a festive day—the culmination of a decade-long struggle to build the replica. As an honorary trustee of this group I had reviewed closely the struggle of these persistent volunteers to overcome community resistance and find the necessary funding. When we members of the Governor's Task Force on the Future of the Brandywine and Christina Rivers developed our vision for rejuvenating the Wilmington riverfront, we included the desire to build *Kalmar Nyckel II* and to make the historic seventeenth-century Swedish settlement a major tourist destination. We saw the building of the *Kalmar Nyckel II* as symbolic of what we could do to bring new life to the entire Wilmington riverfront.

When the Delaware Riverfront Development Corporation (RDC) was established by the state Legislature and Governor Thomas Carper to carry out the vision for the waterfront, we granted $200,000 to the Kalmar Nyckel Foundation and loaned them $2.5 million. This assured that the ship would be built.

Now our elegant tall ship rode there in the river, flying the flags of Sweden, Finland, The Netherlands, America, and Delaware. Her three masts supported 6,800 square feet of sail furled on the yards, and on deck, ten cannon stood ready in their ports. A fierce lion—a symbol of power—was sculpted on her bow.

Then, while Governor Thomas Carper; Mayor James Sills; representatives from Sweden, Finland, and The Netherlands; Masterbuilder Alan Rawl; and leaders of the Kalmar Nyckel Foundation, Hugh Miller, Hunter Lott, and Peggy Tigue cheered, the ship's Captain David Hiott called on his crew to "bring the ship to life." Men climbed the rigging and unfurled sails; the

406

ship's cannon roared. At last *Kalmar Nyckel II* was ready to ply the seas as Delaware's goodwill ambassador and to help bring to life the dream of a rejuvenated Wilmington waterfront.

The year 1998 witnessed the first blossoming of that dream. Several RDC-sponsored ventures came to life, including the Riverfront Park, the first sections of a several mile riverfront walkway, a showpiece art center exhibiting Nicholas and Alexandra's treasures on loan from the Hermitage Museum in St. Petersburg, Russia, and Amtrak's National Operations Center. Other major developments are underway, including a unique retail outlet center for prestigious catalog companies and a 285 acre urban wildlife refuge. A civic arena, a movie theater and a marina are planned. Enthusiasm about the bright future of our riverfront is mounting.

Not far away, one stretch of Wilmington's nineteenth-century industrialized waterfront was reclaimed over one century ago to create Brandywine Park. This treasured site owes its existence to the foresight and dedication of citizen volunteers led by mill owner William P. Bancroft. They set a good example for us today.

Brandywine Park has special meaning for me. It is where my wife, Lillian, and I walked many times over the years, enjoying that waterfront and comparing it to other natural areas we had visited around the world. Today there is a monument to Lillian there, contributed by her associates in the National Audubon Society and Delaware friends. It consists of a large native rock beside the stream, surrounded by flowering shrubs and towering trees and an attractive bench. A plaque on the rock is inscribed with this message I wrote:

> The world's my home, as is this site
> Beside the stream, beneath the trees,
> Amidst the birds and butterflies.
> Come sit with me; romanticize.

When my wife, June, and I visit this site, we usually find another couple on the bench holding hands, presumably romanticizing.

Only a few yards away is a large rock on which June and I were seated when I proposed to her in 1995. She had lost her husband of 44 years, Bill Jenkins, a Ph.D. chemist and DuPont Company research director, as I had been. I had lost Lillian, my wife of 57 years.

Kalmar Nyckel II. May 1998. Courtesy of Chris Queeney.

Russ proposes to June Jenkins here. May 11, 1995. Brandywine Park, Wilmington, Delaware. Courtesy of the author.

Both June and I were miserable, greatly shaken by the loss of our beloved partners. But we found each other, strangers until then, and fell in love. When I proposed on the rock, she said, "Yes." We were married three years ago and are sharing a wonderful, highly active life. We enjoy many common, lifelong interests—protecting the environment, helping children and the disadvantaged, fighting injustice, savoring music and the arts.

We believe the future will be bright. The Wilmington waterfront will become a jewel. Like Sweden and America, markedly changed for the better since 1638, the world community will work together to face its problems, save the Earth, and alleviate much of the suffering and injustice that still plague humanity.

We must push the naysayers aside and get on with the job.

Index